THE MUSIC
OF CENTRAL AFRICA

An Ethnomusicological Study

FORMER FRENCH EQUATORIAL AFRICA
THE FORMER BELGIAN CONGO, RUANDA-URUNDI
UGANDA, TANGANYIKA

by

ROSE BRANDEL

MARTINUS NIJHOFF / THE HAGUE

Photomechanical Reprint, 1973

ISBN 90 247 0634 3

PRINTED IN THE NETHERLANDS

PREFACE

Under the inspiring guidance of my mentor, Curt Sachs, this work was conceived, planned, and executed. It gained in dimension under the acute and patient perusal of Gustave Reese to whose brilliant propensity for clarity of thought and of style I owe a huge debt.

Furthermore, the helpful suggestions made by Martin Bernstein and by Jan LaRue are gratefully acknowledged.

If Jaap Kunst had not kindly gone to the trouble of ordering, supervising the construction of, and mailing to me from Amsterdam his personally designed monochord, an important section of this work could not have taken form.

This preface is not complete, of course, without final thanks to my husband, Harvey B. Natanson, for his sustained interest and encouragement.

R.B.

Note

As the present work goes to press, the political map of Africa is flowing into a new mold. Several countries have obtained independence, and new names and data should be considered: French Equatorial Africa has become (November 28–December 1, 1958) four independent countries – Republic of the Congo: Brazzaville (formerly Middle Congo), Gabon Republic (formerly Gabon), Central African Republic (formerly Ubangi-Shari), and Republic of Chad (formerly Chad). The Belgian Congo has become (June 30, 1960) the Republic of the Congo: Léopoldville. The tribes listed in the present work under French Equatorial Africa are from the new Republic of the Congo: Brazzaville, and those listed under Belgian Congo are from the new Republic of the Congo: Léopold-ville. (The city- after the country-name is at present appended by the United Nations delegations from Central Africa for distinction between the two Congos.)

Second Note, 1973

In 1962, Ruanda-Urundi became two independent countries, Rwanda and Burundi. Tanganyika and Zanzibar became Tanzania in 1964. In 1971, the Republic of the Congo: Kinshasa (Léopoldville) was renamed Zaire.

Photomechanical Reprint, 1973

CONTENTS

Preface   V

Note   VII

PART ONE

  I. Introduction: Geographical, cultural, and language areas outlined   3

 II. The Music and Some Preliminary Considerations   8

    Terminology defined: "primitive," "simple," "complex," "high civilization"   8

    Harmony: parallel thirds as precursors of functional harmony; comparison with protoharmony of European *gymel* and European folk music; chronology of intervals of third, fourth, fifth   13

    Rhythm: misconceptions concerning African rhythm; the African hemiola style and its relationship to the traditional European hemiola; relationship to additive rhythms of Orient; Western offbeat syncopation versus the African hemiola style   14

    Scale Make-up and Terminology: "diatonic" as indicating a scale comprising only tones and semitones; "chasmatonic" as indicating a scale comprising one or more intervals greater than a tone; "pentatonic" as a special species of chasmatonic, within the octave span   17

    Antiphonal and Responsorial Singing: clarification of terminology   18

    Names of Instruments: the significance of similar names in different areas   18

III. Musical Ethnology of Central Africa   20

    Music for the Ceremonial: healing; initiation (puberty circumcision, secret society, royal); birth; marriage; hunting; new year and new moon   20

    The Work Song   32

    Music for Entertainment: group participation; professionalism   35

    Music for Litigation: vocal music as a vehicle for criticism and airing of grievances   39

    The Dance: realistic, entrovert versus abstract, introvert   40

    Speech Melody and the "Talking" Drum   47

IV. The Music—Analysis and Discussion   51

Melody Types (diatonic, chasmatonic, short-lined, long-lined): one- or two-step nucleus; descending tetrachord; rising pentachord fanfare; hexachord; minor seventh with tritone effect; octave (descending and ascending; zig-zag thirds); supra-octave ladder of thirds; non-tempered intervals   51

Rhythm: the African hemiola style; horizontal hemiola (close-paced; sectional); vertical hemiola (instrumental, vocal, vocal-instrumental); tempo (rapid gamut)   72

Polyphony and Form: parallelism (thirds, fourths, fifths); overlapping antiphonal and responsorial singing (canon at fifth and at unison; elongated cadence); ostinato and drone-ostinato; contrapuntal movement (dual- or triple-melody type; interjection-variation type); "hanging chords"; combination of polyphonic devices; raised "leading-tone"; litany form; rondo form; sequence or lai form; development in melody or in overall form   83

V. Singing Style   93

Problem of Identifying Factors Comprising a Vocal Style: structure of music; voice-production components   93

Physio-Acoustical Terms Defined: registration (use of the two groups of muscles, arytenoid and thyroid, controlling the vocal cords); upper register (timbre resulting from the functioning of the arytenoid group of muscles); lower register (timbre resulting from the functioning of the thyroid group of muscles); isolated register (timbre resulting from the functioning of one group of laryngeal muscles without the other); resonance (amplification of sound in a tuned cavity, notably the pharynx)   94

African Female Singing: combined registration with lower register predominating; high intensities; lower pitch range; result equals typical stridency of low register at maximum   95

African Male Singing: combined registration with upper register predominating; high intensities; upper pitch range; result equals typical hoarse-guttural "tenor" quality of upper register at maximum   96

Gutturalness: especially in men's voices; resulting from upper register at high intensity, from pressure of neck constrictor-muscles on larynx, and from tongue hyoid-muscle pressed towards rear of oral pharynx   96

Resonance: non-pharyngeal; mouth resonance (in both men and women)   97

Absence of Vibrato: occasional tremolo   98

Emphatic, Outdoor, Group Style: shouting and screaming; dynamic and timbre accents (points of excessive breathiness, gutturalness, nasality)   98

Ornaments: not common except in Arab-style singing; different-pitched and same-pitched grace note before the beat; "Scotch-snap"; mordent; double-mordent; note-clusters between two tones; double grace-notes before beat   99

Special Effects: yodelling; humming; *Sprechstimme;* hocket; glissando; whistling; drum duplication of vocal melody   99

Syllabic, Non-melismatic Style   99

VI. Conclusion 100

Possibility of "Musical Map": common, widespread style elements; sporadic elements 100

Symmetry and Asymmetry in Central African Art Forms 101

PART TWO

Preface to Transcriptions 107
Transcriptions
    1. Mangbetu choral song 111
    2. Babira choral song 119
    3. Babira choral song 120
    4. Babira circumcision drums 121
    5. Babira circumcision dance 122
    6. Babira circumcision dance 123
    7. Bapere circumcision dance 125
    8. Bapere circumcision bird 127
    9. Bapere circumcision flagellation 129
    10. Bapere horns (Cent-Frequency Chart 1) 131
    11. Bapere xylophone (Cent-Frequency Chart 2) 133
    12. Mambuti Pygmies elephant feast 135
    13. Mambuti Pygmies dance; flutes and drum (Cent-Frequency Chart 3) 140
    14. Mambuti Pygmies hunting song 142
    15. Batwa Pygmies dance 145
    16. Batwa Pygmies dance 148
    17. Bahutu dance 150
    18. Watutsi royal drums 152
    19. Watutsi royal drums 157
    20. Watutsi epic song of war 162
    21. Watutsi epic song of war 163
    22. Babunda new year song 164
    23. Bambala drum telegraphy 166
    24. Baya dance 167
    25. Mboko mouth bow (Cent-Frequency Chart 4) 169
    26. Mboko riddle song; zither (Cent-Frequency Chart 5) 171
    27. Pomo perambulating song 174
    28. N'Gundi humorous love song; sanza (Cent-Frequency Chart 6) 176
    29. N'Gundi song 180
    30. Babinga Pygmies elephant-hunt ritual 182
    31. Babinga Pygmies social dance 184
    32. Yaswa xylophones (Cent-Frequency Chart 7) 187
    33. Kukuya ivory horns (Cent-Frequency Chart 8) 191
    34. Kuyu shaman's alligator-song; horn (Cent-Frequency Chart 9) 193

35. Kuyu birth-of-twins dance   197
36. Bongili banana work song   199
37. Baduma paddlers' song   200
38. Baduma paddlers' song; sanza (Cent-Frequency Chart 10)   202
39. Okandi women's dance   206
40. Banyoro xylophone (Cent-Frequency Chart 11)   208
41. Banyoro royal horns (Cent-Frequency Chart 12)   211
42. Batoro dance   213
43. Bamba flutes (Cent-Frequency Chart 13)   216
44. Baganda historic song; harp (Cent-Frequency Chart 14)   218
45. Baganda historic song   220
46. Baganda royal xylophones (Cent-Frequency Chart 15)   221
47. Wasukuma wedding song   225
48. Wanyamwezi chief installation   229
49. Wanyamwezi wedding tune on sanza (Cent-Frequency Chart 16)   235
50. Wachaga chief-praise song   238
51. Wameru spell-breaking party song   241
52. Wahehe elephant hunting song   243

Melody Type Chart   247

Cent-Frequency Charts   249

     1. Bapere horns   249
     2. Bapere xylophone   249
     3. Mambuti flutes   250
     4. Mboko mouth bow   250
     5. Mboko zither   251
     6. N'Gundi sanza   251
     7. Yaswa xylophones   252
     8. Kukuya horns   252
     9. Kuyu horn   253
    10. Baduma sanza   253
    11. Banyoro xylophone   253
    12. Banyoro royal horns   254
    13. Bamba flutes   254
    14. Baganda harp   255
    15. Baganda royal xylophones   255
    16. Wanyamwezi sanza   256

Numerical-Territorial Index of Transcriptions   257
Tribal Index   260
Bibliography   261
Index-Glossary   267
Illustrations   following 104

PART ONE

CHAPTER ONE

INTRODUCTION

THE DRAMATIC cultural upheavals taking place in Africa today will be historical data to our space-ship successors. Since the rate of acceleration of these changes is so rapid that it appears to increase from week to week, it is somewhat questionable whether the historical-minded of the future will have available to them all the necessary pre-acculturative material vital to the reconstruction of a living image of traditional Africa.

It is, therefore, with a sense of the press of onrushing history that the present author has prepared a work on an important dimension of Central African culture – its music. "Musics" would probably be a more fitting designation, since diversity of style is evident, but it is the eventual goal of all scholarly probing to arrive at some broad unifying stratum common to an apparent diversity. Whether such a stratum can at present be rigidly defined is highly problematic – the body of data projected upon the analytic screen is being constantly enlarged – but movement in the direction of synthesis as well as in the converse direction of analysis is the dual aim of the present study.

The geographical area under consideration is a broad belt cutting latitudinally across Central Africa but not reaching the coasts. A rough map of this area might be drawn up with the following measurements: c. 5° north latitude, c. 9° south latitude, c. 37° east longitude, and c. 14° east longitude. It is clear from these rough boundary marks that political territories involved are French Equatorial Africa, the Belgian Congo and Ruanda-Urundi, Uganda, and Tanganyika. The musical transcriptions appended to the present work are, in fact, examples from these territories.

The culture areas along this equatorial belt are basically two: The cattle area in the eastern portion and the agricultural area in the remainder (to the west of the central lakes). These two culture areas, as outlined by various anthropologists, notably Melville J. Herskovits,[1] are identified not merely by economic structure but by numerous other culture components – folklore, religion, social organization, etc. – each of which is generally homogeneous for the given area. Thus, the cattle complex is, on the whole, characterized by herding and dairying activities, round huts, patrilineal organization, polygamy, male age-grouping, lack of strong interest in secret cults, flexible monotheism, and some ancestor worship. The agricultural complex is broadly characterized by farming and marketing activities, rectangular huts, communal land ownership,

---

[1] Melville J. Herskovits, "A Preliminary Consideration of the Culture Areas of Africa," *American Anthropologist*, XXVI (1924), pp. 50–63. Also see Ralph Linton, *The Tree of Culture* (New York, 1957), pp. 431 ff.

matrilineal and some superimposed patrilineal organization, polygamy, secret cults, ceremonial masks and wood carvings, and ancestor worship with prominent fetishistic components.

The Pygmies of Central Africa may, in a sense, be considered as occupying a third culture area, a broken one geographically, the portions of which are interspersed among the other two. Such an "area," however, is not easily pinpointed, owing to the nomadic nature of Pygmy life. In essence, rather than geography, this culture area differs sufficiently from the others to warrant special classificatory consideration.[2] Basically, the Pygmy culture is one of the simplest, mirroring Paleolithic elements such as hunting, nomadism, loose tribal organization, monogamy, and monotheism. A paucity of religious ceremonial as well as of the graphic and plastic arts is also evident. Unlike their South African counterparts – the Bushmen – the Central African Pygmies live in a vassal-like arrangement with the surrounding large Negroes. The arrangement – almost symbiotic, were it not for distinct Negro domination – involves exchange of agricultural and metal products for hunting and scouting services. In addition, the large Negroes extend a kind of "patronage" to the Pygmies attached to their villages. In recent years, however, this relationship appears to be dissolving owing to changing social conditions, notably the end of intertribal war. Their scouting services no longer as much in demand, the Pygmies are today probably being forced back again upon their own resources for food and tools,[3] except where their services are of such a specialized nature as to forestall a cleavage.[4]

The Pygmies, considered to be the aborigines of tropical Africa, inhabit the deep forests and marshlands into which they have been driven by the large Negroes and are found scattered through several such areas in Central Africa. Among the racially purest Pygmies (averaging in height *c.* 4′11″[5]) are the Mambuti, the Efé, and the Aka of the Ituri Forest in the northeast Belgian Congo. In French Equatorial Africa, in the area of the Sanga and Ubangi Rivers, are found the Babinga Pygmies. Further west, near the Ogowé River in the Gabon section of French Equatorial Africa, lives another cluster of Pygmies, taking their names from surrounding Negro groups (e.g., the Bongos, Bekus, and Koas[6]). These three main groups – of the Ituri Forest, the Sanga-Ubangi, and Gabon areas – are the true Pygmies,[7] although Pygmoid people are also found in Central Africa. Among these people, who average slightly greater heights than the true Pygmies, are the Tshwa and Fôtes of the Belgian Congo, in the inner circle of the Congo River, and the Batwa of Ruanda. Other Pygmoid groups are found in the Belgian

[2] Cf. Paul Schebesta, *Among Congo Pygmies* (London, 1933); Ralph Linton, *Tree*, pp. 156 ff; Melville J. Herskovits, "Peoples and Cultures. Belgian Congo," in J. A. Goris, *Belgium*, U.N. Series (1945), pp. 353–365, also H. Baumann and D. Westermann, *Les Peuples et les civilisations de l'Afrique* (Paris, 1948), pp. 90 f, 193 ff, 451 ff.

[3] Ralph Linton, *Tree*, pp. 156–157.

[4] Note the royal musical bands of Batwa Pygmies in Ruanda. Cf. below, Chapter III, "The Dance."

[5] Louis R. Sullivan, "Pygmy Races of Man," *Natural History*, XIX (1919), pp. 687–695.

[6] H. Baumann and D. Westermann, *Peuples de l'Afrique*, p. 193.

[7] The Ituri and Gabon area Pygmies, however, are considered by H. Baumann to be racially more pure than the Pygmies of the Sanga-Ubangi area. See *Peuples de l'Afrique*, p. 193.

Congo among the Bashongo Negroes (between the Sankuru and Lualaba Rivers) and in the area of the Baluba-Hemba Negroes (directly to the west of Lake Tanganyika).[8]

Language groupings of Central Africa do not readily fit in with the culture areas defined above, but give rise to a "language map" that is more or less independent of such areas. The most important language group of Central Africa is the Bantu, extending downward from c. 4° above the Equator and including, in fact, all of South Africa (with the exception of the Hottentots and Bushmen). Towards the east, in the Kenya-Tanganyika area, the uppermost boundary of the Bantu map dips jaggedly to about 4° south of the Equator.[9] A second group, the Sudanic language family, extends from the Sahara Desert to the northern Bantu line, with some overlapping. In the Nile region to the east of Lake Albert are found the Nilotic (related to the Sudanic), the Nilo-Hamitic, and the Hamitic groups. Thus, it may be seen that a fair portion of French Equatorial Africa, most of the Belgian Congo, at least half of Uganda, and most of Tanganyika come under the Bantu classification. Most of the musical transcriptions in the present work are, in fact, drawn from Bantu-speaking tribes. Only two examples are taken from Sudanic people, the Mangbetu of the north Belgian Congo and the Baya of French Equatorial Africa.[10]

The Pygmies at one time may have had their own language, but this seems to have vanished together with the once greater concentration of Pygmies in Central Africa. Today, Pygmies adopt the languages of neighboring Negro tribes. In the Belgian Congo, the Mambuti of the south Ituri Forest speak a Bantu language, Kibira (language of the Babira-Bakumu tribes with whom they were formerly allied[11]); the Efé Pygmies of the east Ituri Forest speak Efé, a Sudanese language (of the Mamvu-Walese tribes); while the Aka Pygmies of the northwest Ituri Forest speak a Sudanic dialect.[12] In French Equatorial Africa, the two sub-groups of the Babinga Pygmies, the Babenzele and the Bangombe, speak the Bantu languages of their overlords, the Pomo and the N'Gundi, respectively.[13]

The Bantu speech family, while divided into some 150 languages, is distinguished as a whole by several unifying characteristics, for example, polysyllabism (with a nasal and sonorous consonant in the second syllable), class prefixes, the genitive after the governing noun, and, of most importance from an ethnomusicological point of view, pitch levels. The Sudanic languages are characterized by monosyllabism, absence of

[8] The musical transcriptions in the present work contain examples from the Mambuti (Belgian Congo), Batwa (Ruanda), and Babinga Pygmies (French Equatorial Africa). The term "Pygmies" will henceforth, in the present work, be used for both the true Pygmies and the Pygmoid groups.

[9] Cf. maps in H. Baumann, *Peuples de l'Afrique*, pp. 203–204, and in G. W. B. Huntingford and C. R. V. Bell, *East African Background* (London, 1950), map appendix.

[10] The Mangbetu and Baya languages actually belong to one of the Sudanic sub-groups, the Nigritique. This sub-group has some common vocabulary with the Bantu languages. Cf. D. Westermann in H. Baumann, *Peuples de l'Afrique*, pp. 449 ff.

[11] Later patrons of the Mambuti were the Bakongo. See Paul Schebesta, *Congo Pygmies*, pp. 27 f.

[12] Cf. H. Baumann and D. Westermann, *Peuples de l'Afrique*, pp. 193 f, 451 f; also Paul Schebesta, *Congo Pygmies*, pp. 27 f. According to Schebesta, Efé may have been the original Pygmy language.

[13] Gilbert Rouget, "Note sur les travaux d'ethnographie musicale de la mission Ogooué-Congo," *Conferência Internacional dos Africanistas Ocidentais*, 2, Bissau, *Actas*, V (1947), Parte 2, pp. 199 f.

gender, genitive before the governing noun, as well as pitch levels. The function of the pitch levels is different for the two groups: In the Sudanic languages, tonetic variation affects semantic structure, while in the Bantu it affects grammatic as well as semantic structure.[14] The average Bantu language has two or three tone levels, but a few languages run as high as nine levels.[15]

The historic derivation of the Bantu language family has, by at least one philologist, been traced to ancient Sumerian.[16] This idea is strengthened by evidence of the early diffusion of the Southwest Asian complex to Africa.[17] Another early migration – the Malayo-Polynesian to Madagascar and to the East African coast [18] – as well as invasions of ancient Egypt below the Sudan,[19] South Indian contacts, [20] and later Moslem entries [21] without doubt all served to infuse linguistic and other culture components in varying proportions into Central Africa.

The indigenous races of the central belt outlined above are essentially three: the Negro, the Pygmy,[22] and the Hamite. (The term "Hamite" refers, therefore, both to a race and to a language family; "Bantu" simply refers to a language family.) Most of the tribes under discussion in the present work are of the Negro or Negroid class; the one example of Hamitic (actually an admixture of Negro and Hamitic) type is the Watutsi group of Ruanda, which originally derived from the conquering Galla of the

---

[14] Cf. D. Westermann in H. Baumann, *Peuples de l'Afrique*, pp. 449 ff; also, Clement M. Doke, *Bantu. Modern Grammatical, Phonetical, and Lexicographical Studies since 1860* (London, 1945), 119 pp; also, Joseph H. Greenberg, "The Classification of African Languages," *American Anthropologist*, L (1948), pp. 24 ff. The function of Bantu prefixes is illustrated by the following: Buganda (country), Baganda (people of Buganda), Luganda (language of the Baganda people), Muganda (one person of the Baganda people).

[15] Cf. "Speech Melody and the Talking Drum" section in Chapter III, below.

[16] The tracing has been based on grammatical as well as vocabulary similarities, e.g., Sumerian *banda* (little) and Bantu (Zulu) *isi-banda*; Sumerian *buru* (ear) and Bantu *buru*; or Sumerian *u-lili* (wailing) and Bantu (Zulu) *lila*. See B.W. Wanger, "Gemeinschaftliches Sprachgut in Sumer und Ntu (Bantu)," *P. Wilhelm Schmidt Festschrift*, 1928, pp. 157–164; also "Linguistics and Dogma," *Bibliotheca Ethnologica-Linguistica Africana*, IV, 2 (1930–31), pp. 54–66.

[17] Ralph Linton, *Tree*, pp. 395 f.

[18] Iron-work, yams, and bananas seem to have been introduced into Negro Africa by the Indonesians. The Indonesian migrations began *c.* 2000 B.C. and continued until *c.* 500 A.D. The exact date with reference to earliest settlement in Africa is unknown. See Ralph Linton, *Tree*, pp. 110, 177, 181–182. Also note African xylophone-tuning correlations with Indonesian *pelog* and *salendro* scales. Cf. Chapter IV, end of "Melody Types" section, below.

[19] An ancient Osiris statuette has been excavated as far south as the Lualaba River near Kubalo (southeast Belgian Congo). See R. Grawet, "An Egyptian Statuette in Katanga," synopsis in *The Belgian Congo Today*, XIV (1955), pp. 69–70. Also see discussion of the Uganda arched harp and its similarity to ancient Egyptian harps, in Chapter III, "Music for Entertainment," below.

[20] South Indian trading ships were in direct contact with the East African coast during the second or third century B.C. Cf. Ralph Linton, *Tree*, p. 487.

[21] Moslems spread into Africa after 622 A.D., the year of the Flight of Mohammed. See G. W. B. Huntingford, *Background*, p. 5.

[22] The Pygmies, according to a theory of c. 1910, notably that of P. W. Schmidt, came from one race which spread to scattered areas throughout the world. Modern views emphasize the development of various independent groups, and the African Pygmy is actually considered to be an "exaggerated Negroid type," a vestige of an early proto-Negro. See Wilfrid D. Hambly, *Source Book for African Anthropology*, Parts 1 and 2, Chicago: Field Museum of Natural History, Publications, Anthropological Series, No. 26 (1937), p. 204; also Ralph Linton, *Tree*, p. 156; M. J. Herskovits, "Belgian Congo," pp. 353 f.

East Horn [23] and possibly from Ancient Egypt.[24] The Hamites are of Caucasoid stem, and distinct Caucasoid elements may be noted in Watutsi physiognomy. The great physical height, *c.* 7 feet, of the Watutsi allies them with several other tall people, notably the Bahima of Uganda (who are also Galla descendents).

Culture area, language, and race may be seen to form independent analytic categories especially with regard to the Watutsi. These people belong to the cattle complex (pastoral activities are their most significant "means of livelihood"[25]), their language is Bantu,[26] and racially they are of the Hamitic type. Similarly, the Mangbetu of the north Belgian Congo are an agricultural people, speak a Sudanic language, and belong to the Negro type. The categorical "maps" thus seem to overlap, while retaining independent identities, and this circumstance directs our attention to the possible shape and size of a musical "map" (i.e., musical-style map) and the kind of alignment it would have with the maps of culture area, language, and race. It is hoped that the present study will contribute to the drawing up of such a map – a map that can only be fully completed when every tribal culture within its confines has been musically explored.

[23] Cf. J. Czekanowski, *Wissenschaftliche Ergebnisse der deutschen Zentral-Afrika-Expedition,* 1907–1908, VI, 1 (Leipzig, 1917), Chapter 6; also G. W. B. Huntingford, *Background,* p. 110.

[24] Watutsi legends and ceremonial incantations make mention of the connection with Ancient Egypt. Furthermore, certain ceremonies involving sacred bulls (cf. Chapter III, "Initiation Ceremonies," below), the highly elaborate care given the sacred drums, the ritualistic "feeding" of these drums, as well as structural similarities between the *lilis* or goblet-shaped drum of Sumer and the footed goblet drum of the entire East African region, would seem to fortify the idea of the existence of ethnic threads between the Watutsi and ancient Mesopotamian cultures. Cf. Curt Sachs, *The History of Musical Instruments* (New York, 1940), pp. 77–78.

[25] The Watutsi and Bahima overlords actually do no menial work of any kind. Their serfs – the Negro Bahutu and Batwa Pygmies, with regard to the Watutsi; the Negro Bairu, with regard to the Bahima – attend to all maintenance activities (cf. Chapter III, "Music for Entertainment," below). Cattle ownership, incidentally, is a sign of wealth, and only the overlords own cattle. The Bahutu and Bairu are basically agricultural Bantu who were conquered by the Hamites.

[26] The Watutsi speak the Ruanda language, which differs from the neighboring Rundi language only in dialect. Cf. Amaat Burssens, *Introduction à l'étude des langues bantoues du Congo Belge* (Antwerp, 1954), p. 25; also Clement H. Doke, *Bantu,* p. 13.

CHAPTER TWO

THE MUSIC AND SOME
PRELIMINARY CONSIDERATIONS

EVERY OBJECT has a name, or some identifiable label by which we may recognize that it is the object in question we are referring to and not to something else. This labeling is, of course, one of the functions of language, a function that is basic. No one could call both a book and a pen by the label "book" and expect to make himself intelligible. Of necessity, each label must possess the quality of exclusiveness, that is, it must belong to a particular object and preferably to none other. Thus, when we use the label "book" we know the object to which it refers. Our knowledge, furthermore, is not simply a nominative one, but also an analytic one. The label not only denotes the object, book, but simultaneously tells us that a book has pages and a cover. In a subtle, gradual process of language development, labeling terms have been set up definitionally. Each object-name that we use is an implicit definition, an unconscious analytic assertion.

Few will question the definitions that live behind the linguistic scenes, in the case of simple, visual objects. But it is when we begin to deal with the more complex or abstract phenomena that we find an accumulation of disagreement, contradiction, and confusion arising. The disorder is often twofold: It may be a disorder of unconscious usage, a matter of "taking-for-granted" the loose, vague, and divergent meanings of a term which people carelessly employ, or it may be a disorder inadvertently caused by the experts, those who have bravely made the attempt to pin down elusive subject-matter.

Several such terms have been spot-lighted recently, owing to the emergence of the discipline previously known as comparative musicology, and now called ethnomusicology. Since this writer's present study falls directly within the province of this discipline, and since these terms, notably, "primitive," "simple," "complex," "high civilization," will be constantly employed throughout the study, it is necessary that some examination of the terms be made in order to avoid the pitfalls of ambiguity, equivocation, and false application.

It is obvious that these terms are connected and are part of the same problem, and that to identify one of them would in effect be to clarify all of them. At first glance, the terms "primitive" and "simple" seem to form one group, while "complex" and "high civilization" seem to form another group. At second glance, difficulties arise: Doesn't simple music exist in so-called high civilization, and isn't some primitive music complex? Also, how primeval is music that comes from a society that is called primitive? Is primitive music the earliest or source music, or is primitive music the simplest music, or both?

"Primitive," etymologically, derives from the Latin *primus*, meaning "first," "source," or "beginning." Hence, one very clear connotation involves the idea of time or chronology – in this case, the earliest time. However, "primitive" has also attached to it a structural meaning, involving the concept of development. In accordance with this, to be primitive is to be simple, diffuse, undifferentiated.

It is the second interpretation of "primitive" that involves us in difficulties, for the implication has thus far been that the two meanings are *necessarily* concomitant. Historically and logically this is not so. The development of a written language, for example, has followed a path of constant simplification, beginning with quite intricate forms.[1] In fact, the early complexities of writing were such as to prohibit the spread of literacy and invite the development of a special class of scribes. Ralph Linton even underlines the possibility that as "Against the advantages of greater simplification and wider distribution of literacy within the society, scribes weighed the possibilities of technological unemployment and were content with the status quo."[2]

For musical purposes, the term "primitive," in its structural reference, is also open to discussion. Many of the elements of the music of advanced civilization appear to be present in early societies, and in some cases these elements far exceed in complexity their "civilized" neighbors. Certainly, it can be stated that rhythmically, for example, African music is far more complex than Western music, or that many of the sophisticated devices of Western polyphony, such as canon, may be found in several archaic-culture areas.[3]

In effect, it would seem wise to limit the term "primitive" to its chronological meaning, and avoid possible faulty identification of "early" and "simple." (Actually, the present writer began to use the term "origin-al" in an attempt to overcome the ambiguities of the term "primitive," since "origin-al" seems to be more clearly associated with chronology: Obviously, a source or origin is first in time.[4] However, "origin-al" is, in the present work, being replaced with "primeval," which also clearly indicates early time.)

The problem, however, is not so easily resolved, it appears, when we realize that most primitive societies existing today are not so early, historically. There are few paleolithic cultures in existence today, and in Central Africa the Pygmies are the only survivors of this most ancient stratum. Of what importance, then, is it to say that the music of

---

[1] The early pictograph and ideograph systems involved a tremendous number of pictures, signs, and symbols; the next system, that of the syllabary, was more concise, but the most simple and contained of all is the present or alphabet stage.

[2] Ralph Linton, *The Tree of Culture* (New York, 1957), p. 112.

[3] Two examples of canon from Malacca and Flores are given in Curt Sachs, *The Rise of Music in the Ancient World, East and West* (New York, 1943), p. 51. Also see Marius Schneider, *Geschichte der Mehrstimmigkeit*, I (Berlin, 1934), music examples 6, 8, 9, and 14, from Malacca. The present writer has two examples containing canon from French Equatorial Africa, found among the Babinga Pygmies and among the Bongili (cf. Transcr. 30 and 36).

[4] Cf. Rose Brandel, "Music of the Giants and the Pygmies of the Belgian Congo," *Journal of the American Musicological Society*, V (1952), pp. 16–28.

the Watutsi of Ruanda, for example, is primitive, when we do not mean that the music is simple, and we do not mean that this is the earliest style of music. All we can mean, in using the term, "primitive," is that the music is relatively early, as compared to the music of Western civilization. But this would be to say nothing, for there would be no means of distinguishing the Watutsi music from any music that is "earlier than" something else. Certainly, Far Eastern music is prior to Western music and yet quite different from Watutsi music.

Obviously, for the term "primitive" to be currently meaningful even in its chronological sense, some important dividing line must be identified with respect to history. Since pre-history or paleolithic time is hardly represented today among the cultures of the world, we need some later cultural phenomenon to guide us. The clue to this might lie in the concept of "high civilization." If the meaning of this term could be clarified, then it would be of significance to call a music "primitive," since we would at least know that the music belongs to a particular type of culture importantly different from high civilization.

In attempting some clarification of "high civilization," we would be doing two things: 1) Although it is already understood that relative earliness is not sufficient in classifying a music as "primitive," yet a definite statement as to the nature of "high" as opposed to "primitive" civilization would actually be giving us a temporal dividing line, since it is generally accepted that high civilization began some 6000 years ago. Thus, the chronological aspect of the term "primitive" would still be important. 2) Any juxtaposition of "high" and "primitive" would also involve some structural and developmental considerations, culturally speaking, and in this case the term "primitive music" might seemingly be again caught up in a hierarchy of "simple" and "complex." However, this may be avoided by remembering that the phrase "primitive music" would be used to inform us of the cultural setting and not of the music itself, in this particular plan of procedure.

Most ethnologists actually shy away from defining "high" or advanced civilization, while at the same time employing the term freely. Ralph Linton, however, has attempted some tentative characterization of the term in stating that "They [processes of cultural evolution] can be regarded as evolutionary only insofar as the changes which have gone on in culture show some definite, fairly consistent direction. In the evolution of cultures ... the change processes have been, in general, directed toward a better adjustment of the social organism to its environment." [5] He then goes on to define what he means by adjustment, namely, technological improvement, leading to greater control of the natural environment. All further adjustments rest essentially upon the primary adjustment – the technological one. It is evident, therefore, that a civilization is more advanced, for Linton, if it is technologically more developed. This line of thinking appears to be of small aid to us in our search for some demarcation between "primitive" and "high" civilization. Is the most technologically developed culture to be considered "high" and all the others "primitive"? If so, then the Far Eastern civili-

---

[5] Ralph Linton, *Tree*, p. 50.

zations would have to be called "primitive," at least for the time preceding the twentieth century.

Arnold Toynbee, in his *A Study of History*, admits the great difficulty in distinguishing "primitive" from "high" society. Discarding the question of the presence or absence of institutions, for all societies have institutions, and discarding the idea that the division of labor is characteristic of "high" civilizations only, Toynbee goes on to investigate the static-dynamic position of the two kinds of societies. Approaching the problem with a unique reference to social mimesis or imitation, he points up the apparently basic difference between the two cultures through the following mode of reasoning: Since imitation in a primitive group is directed backwards in time, i.e., towards its ancestors, "custom rules and society remains static." [6] However, in high civilization "mimesis is directed towards creative personalities who command a following because they are pioneers. In such societies, 'the cake of custom'. . . is broken and society is in dynamic motion along a course of change and growth." [7] Hence, it can be said that, basically, the primitive culture is static, while the higher culture is dynamic. At the point where the former culture "mutates" into the latter culture, can be found "a transition from a static condition to a dynamic activity." [8]

Toynbee is quick to qualify, by adding that the cultural difference is not a permanent and fundamental one, since it is obvious that primitive cultures, as we know them today, must at one time have been in a dynamic state, in their earliest development from the barest kind of social organization.

Unfortunately, it seems that Toynbee's qualification applies to high civilizations as well. If we consider that the Orient has been in a rather static condition for hundreds of years, that its music, for example, has remained unchanged for centuries, the value of the static-dynamic distinction seems to disappear entirely. Few would venture to call Oriental cultures "primitive."

Thus, if historical movement does exhibit a contrast of periods of greater and lesser change, or dynamic and static conditions, it would appear that such conditions exist in all types of cultures, both primitive and advanced. All that can be said, in effect, is that the primitive cultures in evidence today do appear to be arrested or static (before acculturation has set in); but the converse, i.e., that all static cultures are primitive, does not hold. We can, thus, partially make use of the static-dynamic concept in discussing "primitive music," but always remembering that we are utilizing a one-way implication and not an equivalence. Thus, if the Mambuti Pygmies of the Belgian Congo are considered a "primitive" group (meaning twofoldly that they are in a culturally static condition, and that their technology, etc., are at a very early stage), we could apparently assume that their music is traditionally static, undergoing little change historically. (This assumes, of course, that the art of a society reflects the pace of the culture as a whole.) The converse, that given the historically static music of the Mambuti we could deduce a primitive culture, would be fallacious.

---

[6] Arnold Toynbee, *A Study of History*, Abridgement of Volumes I–VI (New York, 1947), p. 49.

[7] *Ibid.*, p. 49.

[8] *Ibid.*, p. 50.

The cultural setting, however, needs more exclusive identification if the term "primitive" is to be applied judiciously. The state of technology and the static or dynamic character of a society are limited if not fallacious means of determining the "primitiveness" or "advancement" of that society, as pointed out previously. Some more binding or necessary factor is required, for definitional purposes.

In this respect, the development of a written language ought to be considered. This would provide a neat dividing line, since, without exception, the so-called "high" civilizations possess written languages and the "primitive" cultures do not. Furthermore, the distinction would not be as superficial as might at first seem, since the presence of a written language implies a wealth of other developments, such as science, mathematics, philosophy, etc., none of which could possibly develop without the tool of writing. This is clear enough, for these disciplines automatically presuppose not only the human ability to form generalized concepts on a large and systematic scale, but the recording of these concepts as well.

Of specific interest is the fact that writing, with its concomitant scientific restlessness, appears in a musical as well as a literary form, in the "high" cultures. Conversely, none of the "primitive" cultures – certainly none of those investigated to date – have been found to possess musical scripts. This fact has prompted Curt Sachs to make use of the excellent phrase, "non-literate music," in referring to the music of these societies. The phrase, of course, is a replacement of the debatable "primitive music" which we have been analyzing thus far, and not only aims at characterizing the music (viz., lack of script), but also assumes the cultural division based on the presence or absence of a written language to be a valid one.

It is apparent that, in the attempt to clarify, adjust, or modify some older terminology, new phrases come to the fore, some tentative, some probably permanent. The success of these replacements depends to some extent on the degree to which they relate or break with the older terminology. Usage is a difficult barrier to overcome. In addition, many terms, because of the nature of their subject matter, become fluid as time passes on and lose their earlier compactness. The replacements may eventually suffer the fate of the discarded terminology. However, this process is an inevitable part of language development and does not deter the analyst from seeking order when the language tools become ambiguous.

The present writer proposes the following terms and meanings for use throughout this entire work and will deviate only upon preparing the reader:

Primitive culture: A culture without a written language (and therefore without the developments that possession of a written language implies). It should be pointed out that there are transitional cultural stages.

Primitive music: The music belonging to a primitive culture.

Primeval music: The earliest type of music (not having any *necessary* connection with "primitive music" as defined above). "Source music" may also be used here.

Non-literate music: The music of a non-literate culture (primitive culture, as defined above); also, music that exists without a musical script. (The term will be used interchangeably with "primitive music.")

Simple music: Music that is uncomplicated, composed of the smallest number of musical factors, from the point of view of number of notes, steps, rhythms, etc., as well as overall structure. (No necessary connection with "primitive music.") "Primal music" may be used interchangeably with "simple music."

High civilization: A culture possessing a written language plus many of the concomitant developments of a written language.

SOME PRELIMINARY REMARKS concerning harmony, rhythm, and scale, as found in Central Africa, ought to be made at this point.

Although the European harmonic complex with its broad theoretical base appears to be unique in history, some preharmonic elements may be discovered in various other places of the world, and Africa may be counted among these places. The role such elements play in the historical movement towards harmony can only be tentatively posited, since pertinent musical archeology is far from complete.[9] Nevertheless, some broad links can be observed, and without commitment as to the necessity of certain historical patterns being duplicated in Africa – since the rate of acculturation at present is unusually rapid – it can be pointed out that most of the ingredients for full-fledged harmonic development do exist in this area.

However, such ingredients are still in a prenatal stage, and the attempt by some writers to adduce a full-blown "harmony" for African music can only be viewed as wishful thinking. Just as the English gymel and discant styles of the thirteenth century, with their movement in parallel thirds and 6/3 chords, respectively, [10] would hardly be considered evidence of fully developed harmony, the presence of parallel thirds,[11] ladders of thirds, [12] dovetailed or "zigzag" thirds,[13] the "leading" tone,[14] the completed octave,[15] in Central Africa do not in themselves constitute more than rudimentary harmonic tendencies. A true awareness of the vertical, involving relational use of chords within a closely knit framework of tension and relaxation encompasses much more than the above-mentioned tendencies. This is not to say that these tendencies are "accidental," that polyphony of this kind is not deliberate, but rather that the presence of all these elements points to a certain direction, a harmonic direction, but one nonetheless not fully pursued.

[9] An excellent case for the development of European harmony from rudimentary harmonic tendencies found in European folk music has been presented by Curt Sachs. See his *Rise of Music*, pp. 296 ff.

[10] In the gymel form, the intervals of a third were not always parallel, but often were approached in contrary motion, by way of a unison. See the example from the thirteenth century, "Jesu Cristes milde moder," in Gustave Reese, *Music in the Middle Ages* (New York, 1940), p. 389.

[11] E.g., *Mangbetu Choral Song* (Belgian Congo), Transcr. 1; cf. also Chapter IV, below, "Polyphony and Form."

[12] E.g., *Batwa Pygmies* (Ruanda), Transcr. 15; cf. also Chapter IV, below, "Ladder of Thirds" under "Melody Types."

[13] E.g., *Mangbetu Choral Song* (Belg. Congo), Transcr. 1; cf. also Chapter IV, below, "Octave Melodies."

[14] E.g., *Bongili Girls' Banana Work Song* (French Equatorial), Transcr. 36; cf. also Chapter IV, below, "Polyphony and Form."

[15] E.g., *Bongili Girls' Banana Work Song* (Fr. Eq.), Transcr. 36; cf. also Chapter IV, below, "Octave Melodies."

It should further be emphasized that, as is true of the music of non-literate societies, Central African music is not a written music, nor does it have any systems, theories, or scientific body of knowledge attached to it. Any true systematic approach to harmony is thus impossible at this musical stage. Of course, systems of music are rarely the catalysts that set a musical style into action, being rather, rational crystallizations of an already existent style, but it is worth noting that the general absence of systems is a trustworthy sign of the absence of the type of intricate harmonic superstructure developed in late European civilization. Even fifteenth-century European harmonic works, certainly part of a more sophisticated musical complex than the Central African one, are characterized by Gustave Reese as only "the first attempts at what we should call functional harmony." [16]

The problem of chronological priority with regard to the interval of the third (whether major or minor), is another debatable topic. Certain writers, among them von Hornbostel, have considered the African third a late European importation, a superimposition upon a more archaic intervallic structure of the fourth and fifth.[17] Other writers have, furthermore, assigned a "consonant" quality to the third, in opposition to the less consonant fourth and fifth, expressing at the same time surprise at the African "recognition" of the third in preference to parallel fourths and fifths.[18] These views assume a certain chronology with respect to the presence or absence of thirds, fourths, and fifths, a chronology which is by no means definite. Researchers have pointed to a very archaic European folk style in which the third is prominent rather than the fourth. Curt Sachs has, in fact, emphasized "an all-embracing European style" which featured the third, in speaking of medieval European music, particularly secular music.[19] Thus far, there is no reason to assume that the third is a highly sophisticated discovery, antedated by fourths and fifths.

As for the "consonant" quality of the third, it should be pointed out that not until the thirteenth century did a European theorist venture to pronounce the third a consonant interval.[20] Previously it had been considered dissonant, and not until Zarlino's time was it officially admitted as a consonant interval with full functional powers.

A FEW PRELIMINARY REMARKS at this point are also required with regard to Central African rhythms. It is quite misleading for one to approach these from the point of view of nineteenth-century European musical tradition. The person trained in an earlier tradition, that of the Renaissance for example, would feel more at home, in a sense, with the overall rhythmic style peculiar to Central Africa.

---

[16] Gustave Reese, *Middle Ages*, p. 424.

[17] Erich M. von Hornbostel, "African Negro Music," *International Institute of African Languages and Cultures*, Memorandum 4 (1928), p. 15.

[18] Arthur M. Jones, "African Music in Northern Rhodesia," *Rhodes-Livingstone Museum*, Occasional Papers, No. 4 (1949), p. 12.

[19] Curt Sachs, *Rise of Music*, p. 296. Examples of old Icelandic, Swedish, and other melodies featuring the third are given on p. 297.

[20] See Anonymous IV, in Charles E. H. Coussemaker, *Scriptorum de musica medii aevi nova series*, I, Facsimile ed. (1931), p. 358.

The present writer has employed the phrase, "African hemiola style," in describing the rhythms of this area, and it would seem that the phrase is a useful one.

As used in European musical tradition from the Renaissance onward, the term "hemiola" refers, of course, to the rearrangement or regrouping of note-values in two measures of triple time, more specifically, the interplay of two groups of three notes with three groups of two notes. This is accomplished without any durational change in the basic pulse unit, so that two groups of 3/4, for example, may become three groups of 2/4 without any metronome change in the quarter note. The important overall effect here is the quantitative alternation of two "conductor's" durations, one of which is longer or shorter than the other. This exchange of "long" and "short" is always in the ratio of 2 : 3, or 3 : 2, i.e., the longer duration is always one and one-half times the length of the shorter duration. Thus, the dotted-half note may be replaced by the half-note, or vice versa; the dotted-quarter by the quarter; the dotted-eighth by the eighth, etc.[21]

The African hemiola style is based on this play of two and three, which is much like the Middle Eastern additive [22] style of rhythm with its far greater diversity of durational contrasts. It appears to be difficult for the Western musician to refrain from seeing these rhythms in the light of his own equal-grouped rhythms. "Regular spacing" must somehow exist, he reasons ego-rhythmically, and, rather than look for a new analytic approach, he in the end comes forth with a theory of "superimposed elaboration," supported by the view that the regularity can be discovered with diligent aural application. Should he, hypothetically, be conducting these rhythms, he would continue steadfastly in 4/4 time regardless of what is happening musically.

This leads us to the heart of the rhythmic matter: It is the conductor's beat that is of the greatest interest, in comparing the two worlds of rhythm. The conductor's beat is an organizing agent and attempts to prove to the ear (and the eye) that one particular kind of note-grouping is the most important in the motley of durations existing in any piece of music. Thus, in a measure consisting of 64 sixty-fourth notes, his beat decides for us whether the basic grouping will result in two half-notes, four quarter-notes, eight eighth-notes, etc. He outlines the rhythmic vertebrae for us; the vertebrae happen to be equal in one style of rhythm, but unequal in the other style. The 64 sixty-fourth notes would in the second case inevitably be grouped as two dotted-quarters and a quarter, or four dotted-eighths and two eighths, or two dotted-eighths and five eighths, etc. The conductor's beat, accordingly, would not be uniform. To continue beating in 2/2, 4/4, etc., regardless of the irregular groupings, can become quite ridiculous, and in fact

[21] The ancient Greek "hemiolia" meant just this, "by 1 and 1/2," and referred to the paeonic or five-beat meter, which was realized in practice as a dotted-quarter plus a quarter (5/8), or a half plus a dotted-half (5/4). See C. Sachs, *Rise of Music*, p. 261.

[22] The term "additive" is Curt Sachs's and aptly refers to one of the two basic approaches to rhythmic organization, namely the non-symmetric. It is in the emphasis on the succession or addition of assorted lengths, e.g., 2/8 plus 3/8 (in the tradition of ancient Greek meters), that the term "additive" applies. In contradistinction, "divisive" rhythm is that which is equal-pulsed, wherein measures may be divided into underlying regular beats (e.g., 4/4 time). Cf. Curt Sachs, *Rhythm and Tempo, A Study in Music History* (New York, 1953), pp. 24–25.

impossible when the "measure" appears to have 65 sixty-fourth notes instead of 64.

To return to the hemiola: The phenomenon really belongs to the non-uniform kind of grouping, and in its African variety takes on an even greater quality of non-uniformity. While the traditional hemiola revolves about the grouping of six equal time-units, by two's and three's, the African hemiola style may effect any total number of such time-units, six included. *The essential resemblance to the traditional hemiola lies in the exchange of two- and three-unit "conductor" beats.* This exchange is realized both horizontally and vertically.

The horizontal hemiola style involves the two-three exchange within larger measure groupings running anywhere from two, three, or four time-units up. Thus, the time signatures may be 2/4, 3/4, 4/4, 5/4, 7/4, etc., and not necessarily the ternary one of the traditional hemiola. The change from two- to three-groupings may thus be accomplished within any kind of measure, involving any number of units.

The pacing of these 2–3 changes can be of two kinds, *immediate* and *sectional*. The immediate type of change, occurring within the measure (for example, the succession of 3/8 plus 2/8 plus 2/8 in a 7/8 measure[23]), is perhaps less typical of some areas than the sectional kind of change (for example, the succession of nine measures in 6/8 time, followed by two measures in 3/4 time[24]), but both pacing styles exist in Central Africa.

The vertical hemiola style results from the combination of several parts or lines, each line exhibiting its own particular 2–3 grouping. Such vertical polyrhythm may be quite complex, depending upon the number of lines combined, the intricacy of each line, as well as the timbre and dynamics of each line. It is not uncommon for one line to proceed in unvarying groups of 3/8, another line in combinations of 2/8 and 3/8, and still another in subdivisions involving sixteenths. The vertical hemiola style may be found in purely instrumental,[25] in vocal-instrumental,[26] and in purely vocal combinations.[27]

Many of these hemiola groupings are realized by means of variations in timbre and pitch, rather than dynamics. The true dynamic accent (so important in the Western even-pulsed rhythms), while existing in African music, plays a subservient role to the other types of accent. This makes for greater versatility and fluidity in the rhythmic patterning since, quite often, "neutral" running-eighths (i.e., without any accents) may be made to sound as groups of two's or groups of three's, depending upon the superimposed timbres and pitches of the other parts (or even, for that matter, upon the mental grouping projected by the listener).

Dynamic accent has traditionally been associated with the phenomenon of syncopation or, more to the point, syncopation has grown in a setting of equal-pulsed rhythms delineated by dynamic accent. The tie and the accented "upbeat" (i.e., offbeat or conductor's upbeat), the traditional signs of Western syncopation, may generally be

[23] See *Wasukuma Wedding Song* (Tanganyika), Transcr. 47.

[24] See *Babira Circumcision Drums* (Belgian Congo), Transcr. 4. Sectional hemiola is not simply the Western occasional time-signature alteration, but a special case of such occasional alteration, viz., involving the special beat-length contrast of 2 : 3.

[25] See, for example, the *Watutsi Royal Drums* (Belg. Congo), Transcr. 19.

[26] See, for example, the *N'Gundi Song* (Fr. Eq.), Transcr. 28.

[27] See, for example, the *Wameru Spell-Breaking Party Song* (Tang.), Transcr. 51.

looked upon with suspicion when found in a transcription of Central African music. (This holds particularly for the tie.) Such signs imply again the equal-pulsed downbeats and automatically assign a basic counter-rhythm of regularity to whatever pattern the upper "syncopation" appears in. In the African rhythmic concept, however, the upper "syncopation" should be considered as a basic pattern in itself, and not as an offbeat adjunct.[28] A transcriber may at times, despite the visual disadvantages, be tempted to divide an 8/8 measure into three measures marked 3/8, 3/8, and 2/8, in order to avoid any possible interpretation in favor of Western "syncopation."

CONCERNING SCALE STRUCTURE, both diatonicism [29] and pentatonicism [30] exist in Central Africa, and it is possible that these two scale forms exist here in some transitional or evolutionary relationship. This state might analogously be compared with that of the Chinese, wherein we find the movement from pentatonicism to diatonicism characterized by the use of auxiliary notes, the *pièns*,[31] or with the developments in ancient Greece, involving the pentatonic *enharmonion* and the diatonic Dorian, for example.[32] Such comparisons, of course, are not meant literally but broadly, and are mentioned in order to call attention to a probable morphological (and chronological) relationship existing between the two scale types.

Under no condition should the term "diatonic" be considered to mean "tempered," in accordance with the Western non-microtonic scale. Neidhardt's achievements have very little to do with indigenous Central African tunings, some of which are in fact related to Indonesia,[33] while others are probably peculiarly African. As applied to the African scene, the term "diatonic" will refer simply to a stepwise or "through" scale arrangement within any span – octave, sixth, fifth, or fourth. Such a scale generally involves whole and semitones, comparable to the diatonic tetrachord of Ancient Greece.

The term "pentatonic" will be used with reference to the octave only, designating five steps made up of seconds and unfilled thirds within the octave span. In some rare instances, the equal-stepped pentatonic scale (spanning an octave) would give prominence to the interval of 240 Cents, almost midway between a whole tone and a minor third. Although "pentatonic" has also been used by some writers with reference to smaller spans than the octave, e.g., "pentatonic tetrachord" composed of seconds and thirds, such usage will be avoided in the present work, since it is somewhat misleading

[28] This writer has avoided wherever possible the use of ties, although sustained notes at the end of a measure will of necessity be tied across the bar line (assuming the other parts do not permit shifting of the bar line). Also, when offbeat syncopation does unquestionably appear – both rhythmic styles may exist side by side occasionally – the tie is used.

[29] An excellent example of diatonicism may be found in the *Bongili Girls' Banana Song* (French Eq.), Transcr. 36.

[30] An excellent example of pentatonicism may be found in the *Mambuti Pygmies' Hunting Song* (Belgian Congo), Transcr. 14.

[31] Curt Sachs, *Rise of Music*, pp. 134, 220.

[32] *Ibid.*, pp. 220–221.

[33] Jaap Kunst, "A Musicological Argument for Cultural Relationship Between Indonesia – Probably the Isle of Java – and Central Africa," *Proceedings of the Royal Musical Association*, Session 62 (1935–36), pp. 57–76.

(implying five steps within the span of a fourth). To designate wide-stepped melody within any span, the present author introduces a term to counterbalance "diatonic," viz., *chasmatonic.*

THE AFRICAN CHORAL STYLE may generally be characterized as containing both antiphonal and responsorial elements,[34] stylistic phenomena easily found throughout the non-literate as well as the literate musical world. The intermittent choral drone [35] and drone-ostinato [36] are also prevalent in Africa, but attention at this point is being called to the first two features mentioned, in order to suggest clear-cut usage of the terms "antiphonal" and "responsorial." Throughout the present study "antiphonal" will mean the alternation (or overlapping) of two choruses, while "responsorial" will mean the alternation (or overlapping) of a solo and chorus.

THE DIFFUSION of certain types of instruments in various localities can be considered as important evidence in the tracing of culture groupings. But to attempt stylistic classification of the musical character through reliance upon the existence of similar names for instruments is a dubious procedure, particularly when divorced from musical analysis. However, when reinforced by, or better yet, preceded by a survey of the music proper, the tracing of similar instrument-names may well bring home a point or serve to put a final brick into place.

Note, for example, the name *kanbile* given to a circumcision-rite mirliton in the North Ituri Forest (northeast Belgian Congo),[37] and *kabile* (probably a different spelling of the same word), given both to a mirliton and to the circumcision rite itself, in the north central Belgian Congo.[38] Or note the name *enanga* [39] for a Uganda eight-string arched harp as well as for a trough zither; *nanga* [40] for a trough zither of Tanganyika; and *ingonga* [41] for a musical bow of the west central Belgian Congo. Such comparisons (and the similarity between Bantu languages should not be overlooked) may well prove meaningful when placed within some larger musical context, but in themselves cannot prove stylistic unity.[42]

---

[34] A characteristic example of responsorial singing may be found in the *Bapere Circumcision Bird* (Belg. Congo), Transcr. 8, while the example of antiphony may be found in the *Batwa Pygmies* (Ruanda), Transcr. 16.

[35] For example, see the *Bahutu Dance Chant* (Belg. Congo), Transcr. 17.

[36] For example, see the *Wameru Spell-Breaking Party Song* (Tang.), Transcr. 51.

[37] A. Moeller, *Les Grandes Lignes des migrations des Bantous de la province orientale du Congo Belge* (Brussels, 1936), pp. 317–18.

[38] John F. Carrington, "Notes on an Idiophone Used in *Kabile* Initiation Rites by the Mbae," *African Music*, I, 1 (1954), pp. 27–28.

[39] Margaret Trowell and K. P. Wachsmann, *Tribal Crafts of Uganda* (London, 1953), p. 394.

[40] Hugh Tracey, editorial notes to the record album, *British East Africa*, Columbia KL–213, No. 20.

[41] G. Hulstaert, "Note sur les instruments de musique à l'Équateur," *Congo*, II, 2, 3, Année 15 (1935), p. 190.

[42] A. M. Jones calls attention to an extreme case, similar instrument-names existing in two areas quite a distance apart, viz., *thomo*, the name of a single-stringed instrument of the Basuto of South Africa, and *thoum*, the name of a lyre of Uganda and the Southern Sudan; cf. "East and West, North and South," *African Music*, I, 1 (1954), p. 58.

SEVERAL SMALLER PROBLEMS, some linguistic, others musical, will be discussed as they arise in the course of the next chapters, and any necessary elaborations of the issues mentioned in the present chapter will, of course, be made at pertinent points. In addition, a section will be presented on a quite ignored topic – the singing styles of Central Africa (cf. Chapter V, below).

CHAPTER THREE

MUSICAL ETHNOLOGY OF CENTRAL AFRICA

MUSIC FOR THE CEREMONIAL

"And as the Corybantian revellers when they dance are not in their right mind, so the lyric poets are not in their right mind when they are composing their beautiful strains: but when falling under the power of music and metre they are inspired and possessed; like Bacchic maidens who draw milk and honey from the rivers, when they are under the influence of Dionysus, but not when they are in their right mind." Thus did Plato, in his *Ion*,[1] refer to the elements of trance and other-wordly contacts sometimes present in the making of music, dance, and poetry. The hypnotic, intoxicating atmosphere that is so integral a part of certain types of musical activity is as much engendered by the music itself as by the infusion of spiritual-mystical qualities formed in the minds of the participants. How vitally important, then, does the music belonging to ritual become in its double-duty character as emotional intensifier and as religious emblem.

That music should accompany the ceremonial is never questioned by the primitive for, without doubt, the intensification that comes with any of the arts – particularly the kinesthetic arts – appears to be intuitively recognized by him. The problem of musical accompaniment, in fact, would never take the form just mentioned, should he become self-analytical, but would appear in terms of ancestral heritage. What has occurred for generations would seem to be its own justification, and it is almost a truism that in a primitive society the view backward is a more potent factor in determining the daily life process than is the view forward.

Thus, the presence of music at the primitive ceremonial – and that it does exist in most cases can be almost categorically stated – is generically not a mystery. The particular *kind* of music – the form and mode of execution – is again another face of the same coin, for tribal tradition fixes details of musical style as much as it does the fact of the ritual itself. In the case ot style, the influence of tradition is of particular importance in that it makes itself even more restrictively felt wherever magico-religious factors are involved. The psychological etiology herein is of course that of potency and effectiveness. The tools of magic and religion – and music is such a tool – must needs have some permanent holy shape to perform their roles with the greatest efficacy. The

---

[1] Plato, *Ion*. B. Jowett, tr. (New York, n. d.), p. 287.

quality of permanence, thus, is surely expected of the unseen powers of the universe (is there any major theology positing an impermanent spiritual force?), and how perfectly logical to expect the same permanence of all prayer-like media touching at one end the immutable, granitic forces, and at the other end the dependent, ephemeral human.

Ceremonial music is of great importance to the ethnomusicologist, as may be seen from the above discussion, for, more than any other music, it may generally be depended upon to provide authentic clues to the musical nature of a particular group. Even in a society undergoing acculturation, and nearly all of Africa falls into this category, the ceremonial music would no doubt be the last musical stronghold of tribal tradition, withstanding almost to the last moment the onrush of foreign influences. Somewhat like the man running to his most importance possession when the house is burning, a group will tenaciously cling to its central and hence its most prized cultural artery: its mode of magico-religious expression.

The Healing Ceremonial

Music as a charm to insure health and to cure illness is well known throughout the world, both ancient and modern, and in Central Africa a fair portion of ceremonial activity is devoted to this phenomenon. Whether music is utilized in Central Africa with the specific consciousness that the ancient Greeks exhibited, i.e., a consciousness of the medicinal and psychologically permeative powers of music in its own right, apart from magical connotation,[2] is hardly likely. Such a consciousness is more fitting to a medium involved with theories of education and aesthetics – products of the highly abstract, intellectual activity found in high civilization. It can rather be said, when the Mambuti Pygmies of the Belgian Congo sing their special Lusumba [3] songs to their central deity, the "Great God of the Forest," in times of illness, that they are aware of their music as a mystic force and are utilizing it purely for prayer-like purposes, not as a psychosomatic palliative. That the music acts in the latter way as well is perhaps indirectly felt by some of the more clever shamans, particularly those who have developed the art of magical healing to a high degree and consider themselves specialists in the field. The quite advanced culture of the Watutsi of Ruanda, for example, boasts a distinct class of *bapfumu*, or healer-prophets, as well as a class of *abacumbi*, or exorcisers, in addition to their regular *impara*, or priest class.[4] The division of labor here makes for more subtle and differentiated development of skills, so that all the finer shades of shaman activity can be freely brought to the fore. No doubt in this case the pharmaceutical value of the

---

[2] The purely musical power utilized for healing among the ancient Greeks is discussed in Curt Sachs, *Rise*, p. 253 f.

[3] The Lusumba is a men's secret society among the Mambuti Pygmies. The term "Lusumba" is not original with the Pygmies but is borrowed from neighboring Bantu tribes, particularly from the large Bakumu group. Note, for example, Esumba, the name given by the Bakumu to all esoteric practices and to most taboo objects; also, Lusumba, used similarly among the Bapere. See Colin M. Turnbull, "Pygmy Music and Ceremonial," *Journal of the Royal Anthropological Institute*, LV (Feb. 1955), p. 24; also, A. Moeller, *Migrations des Bantous*, pp. 392 ff.

[4] R. Bourgeois, *Banyarwanda et Barundi*, Tome II, "La Coutume" (Brussels, 1954), p. 58.

music itself, in addition to its extra-terrestrial nature, may be an important part of the shaman's implements, used with some amount of conscious deliberation.[5]

Among the Wanyamwezi of North Central Tanganyika, the special task of healing is traditionally assigned to a secret religious sect, the Waswezi.[6] This is a cult composed of both sexes, in contrast to most secret societies; a large number of the members are Watutsi nomads who migrated to Tanganyika from the north. The quality of frenzy, the allusion to not being "in their right mind" that Plato spoke of, would seem to apply to the Waswezi ritual dance in general and the healing dance in particular. Since the cult is said to be a demon-worshipping one, paying homage to a very popular demon worshipped in this area, Lyangombe, it is quite understandable that the dancers should exhibit demoniac frenzy and claim to be possessed by a demon who speaks through them. The organization of the cult as a whole is quite developed and widespread, each community having its own representative division as well as priest, the *mutwale* or *mutware*, who organizes all ceremonials.

Most of these ceremonials involve the special *ngoma* (drum), a long, tubular membranophone, about one foot in diameter and about five and a half feet tall, which is hit with the flat of both hands. The *ngoma* serves as the rhythmic accompaniment to an all-night singing and dancing continuum known through most of Central Africa. The unusual ability to sustain an almost impossible pitch of explosive movement that the African exhibits in these dance rituals is no doubt a concomitant of the psychological state caused by the musical intensifying-factor mentioned previously. The intensification is realized not only in the form of excitement, but also in that of a hypnotic, trance-like insurgence pushed to unusual temporal lengths. The *ngoma* drum augments this "possessed" agitation.[7]

It ought to be added here that music as soporific or calming agent, apart from intensifier, also exists among primitive groups, but not specifically in this capacity. Rather, the effect is achieved inadvertently through repetitive, chant-like sections, causing more of a subdued hypnotic state than the calm aimed for by certain musics, e.g., David's playing and singing which caused Saul to be "refreshed and well, and the evil spirit to depart from him." [8] According to Curt Sachs, music for intensification or for excitement is older than music for soothing purposes.[9] This idea is in accord with the chronology of musical instruments, i.e., intensification generally stems from the "motor" instruments, the idiophones, which antedate the gentler "melody" instruments, the strings.[10]

---

[5] The division of labor is actually even more minute. The term, *bapfumu*, applies to the general group of healer-prophets, but this group is subdivided into the healers, or *abajiji*, and the prophets, or *abagare*. In Urundi, the "middle class" Bahutu are drawn upon for the healer group, while the aristocratic Bahima fill the prophet roles, significantly enough. See Bourgeois, *ibid.*, p. 58.

[6] Fritz Spellig, "Über Geheimbünde bei den Wanyamwezi," *Zeitschrift für Ethnologie*, LIX (1927), p. 64.

[7] For additional discussion of the Central African dance, see below, in this chapter.

[8] I *Samuel*, XVI, 23.

[9] Curt Sachs, *Vergleichende Musikwissenschaft in ihren Grundzügen* (Leipzig, 1930), p. 57.

[10] Curt Sachs, editorial notes to record album, *Man's Early Musical Instruments*, Ethnic Folkways P525 (1956).

When the regular "medicine man" fails to cure a patient, the Waswezi specialists are consulted,[11] at which time they usually remain in a village four or five days, close to the sick person. It is then that they set into motion these all-day and all-night healing ceremonials involving incessant dancing and drumming.

In Uganda, the healing ceremonial is just as elaborate. Among the Iteso tribe of central Uganda, the medicinal dance known as the *Etida* is of such a frenzied, almost maniacal nature that it has been banned by the government (although it still persists to date). Both men and women participate in this dance, which again is an all-day and all-night marathon. One observer comments on the "excesses" committed by the women particularly, as they dance in this mesmerized fashion: "In daylight, after only half an hour of the dance I have seen girls strip off the upper part of their clothing and roll in the dust stuffing dust and dirt into their mouths. Far more revolting excesses have been recorded from Usuka ..." [12] A quality of doomsday abandonment seems to run through these healing rituals, which involve nearly all of the senses as participants in a multifarious drama of *kinesis*.

The musical movement is just as pronounced, for voices and instruments more than match the physique in endurance ability. The *Etida* dance mentioned above is accompanied by a drummer playing two drums simultaneously, one a wide, tubular membranophone (about four feet long and three feet in diameter) called *etida*, and the other a minute membranophone (nine inches long and three inches in diameter) called *itelele*. The small one, actually a rattle drum since it contains two pebbles, emits a high-pitched note which is an indirect result of frequent heating of the skin over a fire.[13] Both drums are stick-beaten, in contrast to the hand-beaten *ngoma* drum of the Wany-amwezi healing ceremonial.

While the purpose of the healing ceremonial is to cure illness or to prevent it (and in this case the pharmaceutical intent may be said to be a "pre-healing" one), upon closer investigation it will be seen that the magico-religious factors involved are brought to bear not so much in the role of direct healing agents, as in that of warring adversaries of the "evil" magic. As such they are components of "good" magic activated to *break a spell* and indirectly cause the cure of the afflicted. The presence of illness, or any other misfortune, is never seen as the product of natural causes, but always as the result of magic malevolence. Hence, the ceremonial functions as a kind of agent to stir up an invisible match between the forces of good and evil. The present writer includes among the transcriptions an example of a spell-breaking song of the Wameru tribe of Tanganyika (a secular, party song).[14]

Initiation

The rites of initiation – puberty, secret-society, and royal rites – may be counted among the major celebrations of Central Africa. Most traditions, of course, dictate the existence,

---

[11] Fritz Spellig, "Geheimbünde bei den Wanyamwezi," p. 65.
[12] J. C. D. Lawrence, *The Iteso* (London, 1957), p. 166.
[13] *Ibid.*, p. 153.
[14] See Transcr. 51.

form, and execution pattern of the initiation phenomenon, but it is significant to note that a few tribes have never been over-concerned with initiation, historically, but have borrowed the custom, and often not too seriously, from neighboring tribes. The Mambuti Pygmies of the Belgian Congo are a case in point, for while they practice circumcision, or *nkumbi*,[15] which is an important form of puberty initiation, it appears to be a superficially grafted culture trait, since only the bare form of the Bantu ceremony appears. No doubt the loose societal organization of the Pygmies has some bearing on the lack of attention paid to initiation in general, which after all gains in importance in direct proportion to the prestige, strength, and clarity of outline of the club or tribe into which the initiation is being made. Circumcision is also absent in the highly developed kingdom of the Banyankole of Uganda,[16] and in fact throughout most of Uganda, as well as some parts of Tanganyika.[17] In these areas the form of puberty initiation is not as dramatic as the circumcision ritual, but involves other measures, notably physical endurance tests, flagellations, bodily markings, etc., which serve to emphasize the passage from childhood into adulthood. In many instances, among those tribes practicing circumcision, these measures are combined with the circumcision practices. An unusual case is that of the Wahehe of Central Tanganyika, who have no male circumcision but do have female clitoridectomy; [18] male initiation here takes the form of flagellation.[19]

Initiation is, of course, a means of gaining entry, and the status that comes with this entry is of prime importance to the initiate. Without such status, particularly the tribal status deriving from puberty initiation, the individual is literally a lost person. The uncircumcised male adult, among those tribes practicing circumcision, is always an object of derision and scorn, can never marry, and is eventually assigned something of the village-idiot role. Most of the Bantu of Central Africa practice circumcision as a means of initiating the young to bona-fide tribal membership and have highly elaborate ceremonials for the event.

Bantu circumcision, it ought to be pointed out, has little in common with Islamic or Judaic circumcision. The cultural motivations are entirely different. The Bantu practice does not exist as a monotheistic covenant (and is not performed at birth), but serves the tribal-entry purposes discussed above. The emphasis here is on instruction, discipline, and tests of endurance.[20] Several elements of male-female social division also

[15] Colin M. Turnbull, "Pygmy Ceremonial," p. 24.

[16] Kalervo Oberg, "Kinship Organization of the Banyankole," *Africa*, XI (April 1938), 2, p. 133.

[17] It is of interest to note that the puberty circumcision ritual, although widespread, is not a universal custom among primitive peoples. One culture without any puberty initiation whatsoever is that of the Samoans. See Margaret Mead, *Coming of Age in Samoa* (New York, 1928).

[18] G. W. B. Huntingford and C. R. V. Bell, *East African Background* (London, 1950), p. 74.

[19] A. G. O. Hodgson, "Some Notes on the Wahehe of Mahenge District, Tanganyika Territory," *Journal of the Royal Anthropological Institute of Great Britain and Ireland*. LVI (1926), p. 50.

[20] The cultural evolution of circumcision has been further described by one investigator as including involvement at one time with divine cannibalism and human sacrifice, i.e., cannibalism as the earlier tribal manifestation was assumed anthropomorphically to be a supernatural trait belonging to the deity and was transformed into human sacrifice and a lesser form of sacrifice, circumcision. See E. M. Loeb, "The Blood Sacrifice Complex," *Memoirs of the American Anthropological Association*, No. 30 (1923), pp. 3–28. Human

form part of the underlying dynamics, the strict social barrier between male and female and their class privileges becoming more sharply delineated as a result of initiation.

The theme of death and rebirth, so popular with cultures of all levels throughout history (note the ancient Egyptian legend of Osiris' death and resurrection, the Asia Minor myth of Adonis' rebirth, or the Greek Dionysus parable – all of which were realized as festival celebrations), is also interwoven through the Central African puberty ritual. Although the theme has usually been associated with the re-enactment of the vegetation cycle, in the case of the puberty ritual the idea finds expression as a purgation of childhood qualities and attitudes, with subsequent "rebirth" or renewal on a more advanced life-plane. Hence the existence of the various ordeals and tests of endurance.

The initiation ceremonies generally take place every five to fifteen years in Central Africa (the interval varies from tribe to tribe), and the age group may include eight- and nine-year olds as well as some over twenty (note the emphasis on social rather than biological puberty). The ceremonial is often quite elaborate, and the proceedings may last several weeks. Music and dance are integral parts of the activity and serve the magico-religious purposes outlined previously.

Among the Tuchiokwe of the Belgian Congo, a virtuoso dancer and drummer, the *tangishi*, is assigned the task of teaching the *tundandji*, the initiates, the esoteric songs and dances of circumcision.[21] One of these songs, for example, is concerned with the civetcat and is chanted by the initiates as they approach the village: *Shimba kulenga, shimba kulenga* (The civetcat is spotted). [22] Many of these circumcision songs refer to animals whose ferocity and strength are admired and symbolically emulated. (The magical osmosis of desirable traits appears to be one of the underlying motivations.) The imitation of and allusion to powerful, often fantastic, animals is expressed in the combined mask-and-cloak covering of feathers and fibres worn by the important dancers. Among the Babira and related tribes of the Ituri Forest this hooded costume is worn by the two virtuoso dancers called Kikulu and Ndukwu,[23] who participate in preparatory dances lasting approximately four days and four nights. The animal theme is further enlarged upon through the various bits of animal parts – horns, teeth, etc. – attached to or suspended from the cloak-mask.[24]

Animal emulation for personal invigoration is paired with another theme in these ceremonies, that of the terrorization of non-initiates (particularly women, in the case of male initiation). Several of the cries, noises, and audible animal imitations are speci-

---

sacrifice, however, has on the whole not been part of the Central African culture patterns, although cannibalism has. (Uganda history points up a notable exception; the older kingdom practiced mass human sacrifice in times of calamity.)

[21] Fr. P. J. Borgonjon, "De Besnydenis bij de Tutshiokwe," *Aequatoria, Revue des sciences congolaises*, VIII (1945), No. 2, p. 70 (footnote 6).

[22] *Ibid.*, p. 70.

[23] A. Moeller, *Migrations des Bantous*, pp. 323–327.

[24] The popular cloak-mask costume is found as far west as French Upper-Guinea, among the Kissi. Panther teeth appear to be a favorite mask appendage here. See André Schaeffner, "Les Rites de circoncision en pays Kissi (Haute-Guinée française)," *Études Guinéennes*, No. 12 (Paris, 1953), p. 15.

fically designed to instil awe and fear in the remote (and rigorously excluded) listener. The universal bull-roarer (the whirling fish-shaped board), for example, is rarely missing from these rituals, and it sounds sufficiently mysterious in its deep, "ghost-like" hum to serve as terrorizing agent. The screams of mythical birds are imitated among many tribes for the same purpose. This author includes an example of the cries of the *mukumo* circumcision-bird, sung by a member of the Bapere tribe of the Ituri Forest during the male-circumcision rituals. The example also includes the sounds of the *atuamba*, or bull-roarer, which is whirled about the head by a second man.[25] These sounds prevail throughout many points of the ceremonial, but particularly when the *baganja*, or initiates, have been served drugging drinks, after four days and nights of dancing and singing, immediately preceding the actual circumcision.

The strong emphasis on animals in the puberty ritual (as well as in other rituals) no doubt echoes the totemistic inclinations of the Bantu cultures. The totem, the binding factor in clan-organization, is of course not always an animal, but may be a plant or natural phenomenon (wind, rain, etc.). Nevertheless, animals play a major role in the religious patterns of these cultures and appear to be symbolically interwoven throughout the various ceremonials and secular activities. A sample Bantu puberty initiation for males, as found in the Ituri Forest of the Belgian Congo, may be briefly described as follows: [26]

In the forest clearing reserved for *gandja* (circumcision), an area of great taboo for non-initiates, two sheds which will house the initiates have been erected. Up to the time when the second boy has been circumcised, three or four days after the first, secrecy concerning the entire affair has prevailed. Now, however, the derisive cries of the spirit-birds are heard: of the *ebebe* in the hut of the master of ceremonies and of the *mukumo* in the forest.

At the end of about two weeks a gong is sounded in the village announcing formally that the ritual has begun. The drums then proceed to augment the ceremonial atmosphere with an endless barrage of sound, serving both as prelude [27] and as accompaniment to various dances.[28] Following the *alema*, a dance for women only, the master of ceremonies and one of the operators dance the *kobira*; additional dances, which women are forbidden to view, are danced by the hooded dancers, Kikulu and Ndukwu, who are painted red and white. These dances last about four days and nights, at the end of which time the subjects are completely shaven and covered with flour. About two hours after midnight on the fourth night, to the accompaniment of the cries of the mythical birds, the subjects are slightly drugged and caused to whirl about in a macabre-like dance. Circumcision at the river soon follows this, and on the way to the special

[25] See the *Bapere Circumcision Bird* (Belg. Congo), Transcr. 8.

[26] A. Moeller, *Migrations des Bantous*, pp. 323-327.

[27] The proclamatory circumcision drums of Babira Chief Kokonyange (North Ituri Forest) may be heard in Transcr. 4.

[28] Examples of circumcision dance music, with and without vocal accompaniment, are given in the Babira dances, Transcr. 5 (instruments only) and 6 (voices and drums), as well as in the Bapere dance, Transcr. 7 (voices and drums) (all of the Belg. Congo).

sheds in the forest gauntlets of men lie in wait to strike the initiates as they pass.[29]

During their three-week stay in the huts the newly circumcised undergo severe disci-plinary measures, deprived of most food and drink, commanded to perform various feats, and generally instructed in the important body of tribal lore and behavior.

Among the forbidden food, and this appears to be true of many Bantu tribes, is salt. Apparently salt has some phallic significance, as one writer points out concerning the Becwana of South Africa. The most important song of circumcision among this group is the "Song of the Salt," different varieties of which exist at male and female circum-cision rites.[30]

Finally, upon their return, the initiated sit in the center of the village, hiding their faces in order to avoid recognition by their mothers. Lavish gifts of money, pearls, etc., are bestowed upon them when they are eventually singled out, but all of the gifts be-come the property of the circumcision guardian. The entire proceedings then end with a baptismal dip in the river, and among some tribes this is accompanied by the re-trieving of a piece of wood thrown into the deepest part of the river.

The drum, the leading instrument in the initiation ceremonies, appears in several varieties. Apart from those which are struck, there are the friction drums, basically sexual symbols. In the Ituri Forest, for example, there is the *amahoto*,[31] a drum without a bottom and with a manually rubbed cord protruding from the skin. *Mabilango*, another friction drum, has a moistened skin upon which both a leaf and a perpendicu-larly held drumstick are placed. The drumstick is rubbed alternately by the player's wet hands, demonstrating sex symbolization involving both male and female charac-ters.[32] Other groups of instruments such as various mirliton pipes (closed at one end with a leaf), whistles and flutes of different kinds, rattles (including strung and gourd types), ankle bells, and the important tuned percussion-stick orchestra also play de-finitive roles (both musical and religious) in the ceremonies.[33]

The importance of color, often discussed in connection with Oriental cosmology, is not to be ignored in the African context. Visual elements – form, size, color, etc. – are as significant, magically, as are aural elements – linguistic, musical, or otherwise. Notice the emphasis on the color, red, painted on the bodies of the special circumcision dancers mentioned above. It is also the color painted on the circumcision drummers (Babira, Transcr. 4) and may be interpreted, generally, as being a "masculine" color

---

[29] An example of flagellation music among the Bapere is given in Transcr. 9. The lash of the whip may be clearly heard on the recording. The scene is a more public one than that described above; here the flagel-lation occurs before a large crowd and involves older men previously circumcised.

[30] J. T. Brown, "Circumcision Rites of the Becwana Tribes," *Journal of the Royal Anthropological Insti-tute*, LI (1921), pp. 419–427.

[31] A. Moeller, *Migrations des Bantous*, pp. 317–318.

[32] Curt Sachs discusses the sexual significance of the friction drum in connection with the North Rhodesia Ba-ila girls' initiation. See *The History of Musical Instruments* (New York, 1940), p. 40.

[33] Some Ituri Forest instruments of initiation are named as follows: *ntufu* and *kanbile* (mirliton pipes), *boti* and *akando* (wooden whistles and flutes with animal hairs introduced into pierced holes), *amita* (the percussion stick held under the player's armpit and struck with a mallet – generally occurring in tuned groups or "orchestras" of sticks), *ekulu* (jingles and leg bells of the chiefs), and *soli* (a bamboo pipe imitating antelope sounds). See A. Moeller, *Migrations des Bantous*, pp. 317–318.

associated with male rites.[34] The specific connection with circumcision is self-explana-
tory.[35]

The secret society in Central Africa appears, as a cultural organizing factor, most
prominently among the agricultural groups rather than among the cattle or dairying
tribes. Many societies function as semi-religious cults with special powers, in some cases
of a positive nature (note, for example, the Waswezi healing cult among the Wanyamwezi, mentioned above) and in some cases of a malevolent nature (note the cannibalistic
society, Anyota, practicing murder and black magic in many parts of Central Africa[36]).
Each society has its own secret formulas, passwords, dress and mask emblems, behavior
patterns, as well as initiation ceremonies. These are reminiscent, in many instances, of
the puberty initiations, particularly in the underlining of endurance and prowess tests;
instruction in esoteric, magical formulas and songs; bodily markings, etc. The societies
are highly exclusive, as may be seen, and are often regarded with fear, certainly with
great respect, by non-members, since informal judiciary powers are often appropriated
by these groups. In fact, one of the local names for "secret society" or "cult" is *ngoma*,
a word representing authority.[37] *Ngoma*, as noted above, is also the general Bantu
term for the membrane drum accompanying ceremonial dances, an instrument also
functioning in something of an "authoritative" capacity.[38] That many societies are
regarded as semi-professional, almost priestly in character, is demonstrated by two
other local terms of a multi-semantic cast, *mbina*, meaning both "dance" and "secret
society," and *moga*, meaning both "profession" and "secret society." [39]

The animal theme emerges again as an important base or binding agent in the organization of many secret societies. The "Sons of Sô," a secret society of the N'Gundi of
French Equatorial Africa, is built about the mythological being, Sô, uniting through
"blood brothership" all the members thereof. One of the signs of membership is a
tooth-mark shoulder tattoo. Among this writer's transcriptions may be found a Sô
song with sanza accompaniment,[40] an example of some of the secular songs "owned"
by the societies. The panther, emblem of ferocity, is the totemistic force behind a royal

[34] The diffusion of the ceremonial use of red cannot be checked at this point. Of interest, however, is the restriction of the color to "masculine" instruments, i.e., instruments of male sexual connotation and played only by men, as for example trumpets, flutes, etc. See Curt Sachs, *History of Instruments*, p. 50.

[35] Curt Sachs calls attention to the fact that "as late as the end of the middle ages European astrologers still grouped together the right nostril, the color red, blood, circumcision, the cardinal point south, and the planet Mars." *Hist. of Instr.*, p. 47. In Urundi, the king always carries a little shield painted red and white, which acts as an amulet as well as a sign of his military powers.

[36] See A. Moeller, "Aniota et Mambela," *Comptes rendus, Semaine de missiologie de Louvain* (1936–1937), pp. 50–69; also P. Schebesta, *Among Congo Pygmies* (London, 1933), pp. 263 ff.

[37] P. Fr. Bösch, *Les Banyamwezi* (Münster, 1930), p. 188.

[38] The general Bantu term, *ngoma*, appears to be one of those curious linguistic phenomena involving an assortment of meanings. The most widely used meaning is "drum" (membrane-drum). *Ngoma* also means "dance" among the Swahili, "ancestor spirits" among the Kikuyu, and, as mentioned above, "secret so-ciety" among the Wanyamwezi. *I-ngoma* is a membrane drum of the Ba-Ila as well as of the Barundi; among the Zulu, *i-ngoma* is a royal dance song and also a grain granary. *Ngoma na suma*, or "drum of iron," is a double bell of the Bangala. *Ngomo* is an eight-stringed harp of the Fang. See Harald von Sicard, *Ngoma Lungundu* (Uppsala, 1952), pp. 4 f; also Curt Sachs, *Real-Lexikon der Musikinstrumente* (Berlin, 1913), p. 271.

[39] P. Fr. Bösch, *Les Banyamwezi*, p. 188.

[40] See Transcr. 28.

secret society of the Kuyu of French Equatorial Africa. In the *likuma*,[41] the initiation ceremony of this sect, seven drummers proceed at first in a slow march, which the head drummer regulates by whistling through his teeth. The head drum, also called *likuma*, is supposed to represent the panther's voice.[42] The drums sound first successively and then simultaneously. Since each drum is of a different size (although the shape – long, conical – is the same) the tone produced by each is different and the musical result is of a rich, almost orchestral texture. Although the instruments and the context are not the same, the march of the seven calls to mind the biblical fall of Jericho preluded by the seven horn-blowing priests marching about the city.

The installation of a new chief in Central Africa is always accompanied by a major ceremony. Where the "chief" is actually a king, ruling what may be compared to the European medieval serfdom, the ceremony may take on the character of a coronation. Many of the eastern sections of Central Africa are organized as kingdoms boasting elaborate protocol and hierarchies of ruling personnel (earls, chiefs, administrators – all appointed by the king) and of courts. The Bantu term *mwami* is one of the common names for "king" in this area, appearing in somewhat different versions among different groups, e.g., *mwami* in Ruanda-Urandi, *moame* among the Ituri Forest Bakumu group, *memi* among the Wanyamwezi of Tanganyika, *nyimi* among the Bashongo of the central Belgian Congo, etc.[43] Can these terms be variants of "Mohammed"? Islamic influence in Central Africa can be traced on many levels – politically, artistically, etc. – and should not be underestimated in importance. The extent, however, to which the Arabs pushed into the interior of Central Africa (beginning with their early trading ventures before the birth of Christ and particularly following the flight of Mohammed in 622 A.D.) is still not fully explored. An example showing Middle Eastern influences (vocal style particularly) is given in the transcription of royal installation music among the Wanyamwezi of Tanganyika.[44]

It may be that an ancient Sumerian influence is present in the ceremonial importance attached to bulls in Ruanda-Urundi.[45] (Cf. Chapter I, above, for Sumerian-Bantu language ties.) The bull, symbol of virility and power, is especially esteemed in royal initiations. In Urundi the sacred bull Muhabura,[46] clothed in a robe of black and white, participates in all ceremonies pertaining to royal ascent to the throne. He also precedes the king in all his travels. Another sacred bull Semasaka is mounted by the *mwami* in the royal coronation ceremonies.

In continuing our exploration of music for the ceremonial in Central Africa, we may touch briefly upon some additional types of major events.

[41] M. A. Poupon, "Étude ethnographique de la tribu Kouyou," *Anthropologie*, XXIX (1918–1919), p. 62.

[42] *All* of the seven drums are actually symbols of panthers, the largest being a male panther, also known as *tata na kani* (father of the chief), and the rest being his wives. *Ibid.*, p. 65.

[43] R. Bourgeois, *Banyarwanda et Barundi*, p. 34.

[44] See Transcr. 48.

[45] The ritual of the Sumerian bull sacrifice is discussed in Curt Sachs, *History of Instruments*, pp. 78–77. Among the Watutsi, bull sacrifice takes place in the Kubandwa purification ceremony; see photographs by André Gauvin in *Pageant* (April 1949), pp. 94–100.

[46] R. Bourgeois, *Banyarwanda et Barundi*, p. 44.

Birth

The birth of twins is of particular interest, since it was often considered an abnormal event, generally of negative magical connotation. (Older practices involved destruction of one of the twins.) In Uganda, among the Iteso, a cylinder drum, the *emidiri*, used in pairs at twin-birth ceremonies, is covered at one end with lizard skin fastened down with studs.[47] Attention is called to the method of fastening since the nailed drumskin, prominent in the Far East and ancient Sumer, appears to be connected with some particular magic that is especially concentrated in the nails.[48] Women are often the principal musical performers at these ceremonies; one of the transcriptions included in our appendix is that of a Kuyu (French Equatorial) women's dance-song marking the occasion of the birth of twins.[49]

Marriage

The old European folk custom of bridal dowry-giving exists in reverse in central Africa. It is the prospective groom, here, who gives the dowry. Women are apparently considered of great value, since a man with a wife has double the work capacity of one man and, of course, may have an even greater work capacity with the addition of children. Exogamy is the general rule; marriages are usually forbidden within the same clan or kinship organization.[50] Both polygyny and polyandry are known (although the former is by far the more prevalent), and to a large extent these practices are regulated by the wealth and dowry-giving capacity of the persons involved.

In Ruanda, the marriage ceremony of the ruling groups has many Middle Eastern qualities. The Watutsi bride, for example, is veiled so that her head and face are completely covered.[51] The basic idea that women must never appear in public is certainly reminiscent of the Middle East. (The situation today, with respect to public appearance, is somewhat changed.) The Watutsi girl marries at fourteen or fifteen and is bought from her parents for three or four cows. (The bride-price is, in effect, a compensation

[47] J. C. D. Lawrence, *Iteso*, p. 154.

[48] Curt Sachs, *History of Instruments*, pp. 74; 173–174.

[49] See Transcr. 35.

[50] The almost universal incest taboo appears to be one of the factors governing marriage restrictions. However, among the Ruanda-Urundi and Ankole ruling classes a modified form of incest is practiced whereby brothers have access to each others' wives and fathers to their sons' wives. Some echoes of Ancient Egypt may even be discerned in the former Bahima practice of establishing the king's sister both as the queen and as his wife. The queen-sister custom (apart from incest) prevails in many of the east central kingdoms. The essentially patrilineal structure of the societies of this area would seem to explain the apparent acceptance of brother-sister incest only if some weight is given to a special form of bilateral descent whereby male children belong to the father's line and female children to the mother's line. Hence, brother-sister inter-marriage would be permissible and would not go counter to any taboo of exogamy. (In other words, the concept of incest would seem to be nonexistent in this area.) Culture patterns of the area do, in fact, suggest an earlier layer of matrilineal organization, a type of organization highly characteristic of the agricultural tribes further west. Freud, in his *Totem and Taboo*, James Strachey, translator (New York, 1952), p. 2, claims that patrilineal descent is a later manifestation than matrilineal descent, since exogamy was originally directed against son-mother intermarriage, and only the matrilineal society carries this type of taboo. This theory of chronology might be borne out by the fact that the patrilineal kingdoms of this area were established at a later date than the more primitive, matrilineal cultures – were, in fact, superimposed upon them.

[51] A. Pages, "Cérémonies du mariage au Ruanda," *Congo* (1932), p. 65.

to the parents for the loss of the girl's services. It does not mean that the bride becomes the chattel of the husband.)

Musical instruments appear on the marriage scene in both ceremonial and social roles. When a king of Urundi marries, the royal drums are steadily beaten until the marriage is consummated.[52] In the Stanleyville area of the Belgian Congo, prior to a marriage that has already been "contracted," the man may send a drummed message such as "my heart beats pit-a-pat" to his future bride.[53] The drumsticks have been previously rubbed with a potion, no doubt to insure sympathetic response. In one of this writer's transcriptions of the Wanyamwezi of Tanganyika, the sanza (a keyed, thumb-plucked idiophone) plays an *harusi* or wedding tune.[54] An unaccompanied wedding song for male solo and mixed chorus of the Wasukuma of Tanganyika is also included.[55]

Hunting

In preparation for a major hunt many tribes will sing, dance, and play special hunting songs, which may or may not be part of a ceremonial. The intent is, of course, to insure victory, and should the music and dancing occur after the hunt is over, then insurance of future victory, as well as immediate thanks, motivates the proceedings. Among the Kuyu of French Equatorial Africa a shaman's song, *Kabe*, used to attract alligators, is accompanied by a transverse antelope horn, drums, sticks, and handclapping.[56] That the alligators are attracted is no doubt hardly conceived by the Kuyu as being a direct function of the sound itself, but rather of the magic potency lodged in and stirred up by the song. Elephants, as well as okapi (small giraffes), are the major animals hunted by the Mambuti Pygmies of the Ituri Forest (Belgian Congo) and by the Babinga Pygmies (French Eq.). Although their celebrations are on the whole sporadic and meagre, quite logically the Pygmies have numerous elephant hunting songs. (The simple monotheism of the Pygmies of French Equatorial Africa even takes the form of a kind of elephant worship: their central deity is called the "elephant father of the world."[57]) A ritual hunting song called "Yeli" is sung by the Babinga Pygmies just before an elephant hunt (see Transcr. 30). After killing an elephant (the Pygmies are famous for their skill in tracking and downing the elephant with poisonous darts), a ceremonial for carving the animal may be performed. The feast music attending such a ceremonial is given in one of our Mambuti transcriptions.[58] The exuberant men sing in chorus and solo while the women wait in the background ready to prepare the meat. In the evening, after the meal, the Mambuti sit about the fire and sing of their day's hunt. This is not a ceremonial but a social song, and may persist all through the night. One of the men describes the successful hunt, singing against a choral ostinato executed in the charac-

[52] R. Bourgeois, *Banyarwanda et Barundi*, p. 48.
[53] John F. Carrington, *Talking Drums of Africa* (London, 1949), p. 57.
[54] See Transcr. 49.
[55] See Transcr. 47.
[56] See Transcr. 34.
[57] R. P. Trilles, *Les Pygmées de la forêt équatoriale* (Paris, 1932), pp. 332 ff.
[58] Transcr. 12.

teristic Mambuti interlocking style, i.e., each man sings one note at the correct time to form the melodic contour.[59]

Animal mimesis, discussed previously, takes on an immediate and practical character in many of these hunting songs and dances. The shrill cries of the elephant, *chigoma*, are imitated in a responsorial hunting song of the Wahehe of Tanganyika.[60]

The all-night dance discussed previously in connection with healing rituals may often form part of the hunting ceremonial. Among the Baya of French Equatorial Africa an elaborate cycle of nightly dances marks the beginning and end of the major hunt of the dry season.[61]

New Year and New Moon

Astral movement has an almost universal appeal, magical and non-magical, for the human mind. Celebrations involving imitations of the phases of the moon, the course of the sun, the changing seasons, etc., are common tribal phenomena, and appear in the forms of dance, song, instrumental music, and narration. The moon particularly, in its dramatic progress from crescent to circle, from dark to light, seems to offer rich material for symbolic imagery pertaining to female sex, death and rebirth, and fertility.

The Baya of French Equatorial Africa dance a circle dance the night of the full moon.[62] The royal *makondere*, or gourd-horn ensemble of the *Mukama*, king of the Banyoro of Uganda, is required to play on the first day of the new moon.[63] At the time of the new year, the Babunda of the Belgian Congo sing in mixed groups to celebrate the occasion.[64]

THE WORK SONG

The propulsive effect of certain types of music is taken advantage of by peoples of all civilizations in their daily attendance to details of livelihood. Physical labor, particularly, seems to benefit from the steady, insistent stimulus provided by certain kinds of musical accompaniment. Primitive groups do not deliberately project the "work music" upon the scene in the manner of modern factory psychologists. Rather, the music seems to be an expressive outgrowth of the labor itself. That the music also alleviates the burden of muscular monotony and spurs on to more energetic endeavors

[59] See Transcr. 14. The interlocking style may be compared to the European medieval hocket (the *quadruplex* variety, in the case of the particular example mentioned). The interlocking, or dovetailing, of tones also lends itself to certain instrumental musics, especially to the music of key- or phone-instruments (e.g., the sanza, xylophone, etc.). Vocally, this is not a "natural" style, in the sense that it is natural for the key-instruments. Nor is it "natural" to single instruments playing only one tone each (unless the instruments are bound together, like panpipes). Transcr. 13 is an example of Mambuti Pygmy flute music in the interlocking style. The single flutes probably are duplicating a vocal melody executed in the same style. (Cf. Chapter IV, below, "Tritone Melodies.")

[60] See Transcr. 52, meas. 23.

[61] Hermann Hartmann, "Ethnographische Studie über die Baja," *Zeitschrift für Ethnologie*, LIX (1927), p. 51.

[62] *Ibid.*, p. 51.

[63] See Transcr. 41.

[64] See Transcr. 22.

is an indirect concomitant, unconsciously sensed by the participants. The paddler who flexes his arms and bends his body in a symmetrical, purposeful rhythm begins to identify himself with the sounds and feel of paddling. The paddle cuts the water; the water swishes; his hands grip the handle of the paddle sending it forward, around, and back in some time relationship to the cutting and swishing; his muscles stretch and his bones may creak; the boat has a myriad of motions and counter-motions: all in some inter-related complex of rhythm which causes him to hear and sing something that seems to flow with the rhythm. The paddler's song comes into being.

The degree of originality is unimportant. No doubt each new crew that assumes paddling duties utilizes some older text and music as a springboard and may even duplicate the older song *in toto*. More likely, new elements deriving from each new situation are fused with some established tribal repertoire that is as enduring as the memory of its human repositories. A song of the Baduma paddlers of French Equatorial Africa, for example, contains the word *miseria*, which has been worked into the traditional musical framework.[65] At least here the foreign graft coincides in meaning and intent with the original text: the innovation, a bow to the white man's language, is an extension and not a meaningless adhesion. Spurred on originally by rhythmic motor elements of their work to make some musical sound, the paddlers very congruously joined the sounds to verbal attitudes. The hardships and tediousness of paddling are a fitting subject whether expressed entirely in a Bantu language or not. That the theme of hardship is often a literary adjunct of work songs may be seen from the quite dramatic text of another song, a song of the famed Wanyamwezi carriers of Tanganyika: "Work, dear father, the work is hard, my dear father; therefore will I sing, I the worker!"[66]

It ought to be added that the rigidity of musical form loosens in direct proportion to two factors: 1) the strength and obtrusiveness of surrounding or conquering cultures, and 2) the degree to which the particular music fits into the sacred or ceremonial category. It is understood that tribal life and all its expressive facets – musical, poetic, etc. – discourage innovation and change and are usually molded by the firm hand of tradition. However, this tenet applies to basic ingredients, to essences, mainly, and not so much to the particular realizations of the central matter. Each generation (each singer, in fact) will sing a song, despite its long-acknowledged place in the history of the tribe, with some slight and subtle modification (the logical concomitant of non-literate musical tradition). While the central mold is always recognizable, however, and basic stylistic elements are tenaciously clung to, over a period of years a certain number of songs may lose their identity and appear, in their new dress, as replacements of old material. Such change is, of course, superficial and, it should be noted, applies mainly to non-sacred music. However, where the natural conversion of secular music is combined with the press of foreign musical culture, the style and form may also be affected. It should be emphasized that sacred or ceremonial music is the most resistant to either ordinary, "executant's" change or extraordinary, acculturative influences.

[65] See Transcr. 37.
[66] Fritz Spellig, "Die Wanyamwezi," p. 251.

In the case of work music, certain stylistic elements – particularly rhythm – will automatically be conditioned by the nature of the work itself. The Baduma paddlers sing in a regular 4/4, obviously closely aligned with the symmetrical motion of paddling.[67] The Bongili girls of French Equatorial Africa pound their bananas with pestles, also in straight 4/4. The evenly spaced sounds of the pestle seem to shape and sustain the vocal rhythm.[68] The psychological problem of priority in regard to the relationship between work and rhythm, viz., to the problem of whether rhythmic patterns exist primarily in the work itself [69] or whether these patterns are superimposed by and due to the organizing capacity of the human mind, is not to be confused with the problem of expressional relationship between work and song, as discussed above. If the human mind does superimpose a rhythm upon the work motions of the body (i.e., if the second theory of rhythmic causality is to be accepted), it does so also with respect to music. The emotional-kinesthetic connection between work and song, however, exists above and beyond the more basic (almost ontological) problem of rhythmic origin. The two problems might be represented by a schema as follows:

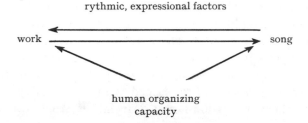

rythmic, expressional factors

work   song

human organizing
capacity

Since all teamwork implies a leader, or someone functioning in some kind of directive capacity, it is not unlikely that the leader will perform a dual role as work- and music-master, and it is not improbable that the responsorial musical form, so prevalent in work-music, owes something to this arrangement. The responsorial procedure is, of course, not confined to work-music but cuts across many categories, particularly those in which the presence of a leader (shaman, chief, etc.) insures some kind of directorial behavior. The degree to which the choral respond is conditioned by an imitative urge – which would probably be realized as canonic repetition – or by a desire for sustained intensification – which would probably be realized as refrain-ostinato – relates to matters of text and topic as well as of traditional style.[70]

[67] The straight 4/4 has a slight counter-rhythm, which would appear as offbeat syncopation if we could hear or feel the paddling motion (in 4/4). If the paddling is not aurally imagined, then the counter-rhythm appears in its own right as an additive pattern, viz., quarter, quarter, dotted eighth, dotted eighth, eighth.

[68] See Transcr. 36. Syncopation in the voices is marked as a result of the audible 4/4 pestle.

[69] Reference is here made to Karl Bücher's famous and much debated theory (1896) of the *inherent* or innate rhythmic nature of work and its influence upon human rhythmic thinking. The theory stands in opposition to the converse idea, viz., human superimposition of rhythm upon the outside world. (See above.)

[70] Canonic repetition is found in the *Bongili Girls' Banana Song*, and the refrain-ostinato in the *Baduma Paddlers' Song*. (See Transcr. 36, 37.)

MUSIC FOR ENTERTAINMENT

The renowned Gaelic bard of old was a product of the professionalism attendant upon high civilization with its stratification of people, skills, and labor. However, the Gaelic minstrel was only one historic link in a long chain of artistic professionalism. The first high civilizations of some 6000 years ago knew the social phenomenon of artistic special-ization, of purposeful dedication to the crafts of mental enrichment and stimulation, a dedication that could seemingly flourish only at the command and encouragement of an aristocratic, leisure class. The class system, so vital to the fostering of the arts, developed when tribe conquered tribe, when two groups merged their manifold cultural behaviors in disparate proportions; social strata began to form, first slowly and then with increasing impetus at each technological advance. At the arbitrary point of civili-zation that we call "high," strong social differentiation already existed, its specific realization taking the form of sharply defined leisure-ecclesiastic-artisan groups. Among the Sumerians the leisure or aristocratic class often overlapped with the ecclesiastic (priests, soldiers, and government officials usually comprised the aristocracy[71]), and it is to this composite group that much of the scientific and artistic achievement of the culture owed its existence, both directly and indirectly. The Sumerian priest was in-variably a skilled mathematician, astronomer, and music theorist as well as ecclesiastic leader and often developed and trained large corps of highly professional temple mu-sicians.[72] These were somewhat higher in rank than the secular musicians employed by the aristocracy, and it is to be noted here that even the professional-musician class did not escape differentiation and stratification.

Of course, the full-blown division of labor typical of high civilization is already foreshadowed in the primitive society. Not as sharply defined or as meaningful as that of high civilization, the specialization found in many non-literate cultures is nonetheless strong enough to warrant attention. In many instances the specialization is something more than rudimentary. Surely kings and shamans are all "specialists" to some degree, and in a highly developed political-economic structure such as that of Ruanda-Urundi or parts of Uganda the idea of specialization is certainly carried far beyond the rudi-mentary level. Here, too, the conquering Hamitic group – the pastoral Watutsi and Bahima – superimposed their culture upon the Bantu – the agricultural Bahutu and Bairu – forming, in the process, a quite rigid pattern of social, political, and labor division. Where the Pygmoid Batwa formed part of the cultural pattern, a more compli-cated triple-layer society arose.[73]

[71] This composite group was the highest class and was called *amelu*. See Ralph Linton, *Tree of Culture*, p. 306.

[72] Temple music is mentioned in extant Sumerian texts of the third millenium B.C. – among the oldest records of music theory. See Curt Sachs, *Rise of Music*, p. 58.

[73] See "Healing Ceremonial" in the present chapter, above, for an example of the priest-healer division of labor among the Watutsi-Bahutu group. Politically, the Watutsi are the ruling class; the Bahutu, the menial laborers and agricultural providers; the Batwa, some lesser echelon of the menial class. A sample division of labor would find the cowherds composed of Watutsi of good family, the menial sweepers com-

The degree to which the professional musician is esteemed in the non-literate society is a moot question. That his skills should be appreciated as much as those of the exorcist is hardly likely, despite the almost official capacity in which the musician sometimes functions. It is a strange corollary that even some of the ancient high civilizations often placed the skilled poet and musician in something of a lowly, almost "abnormal" social niche. Do the old myths of the "blind poet" or the "lame musician" signify something of this nature? [74] Aristotle was more explicit in his less than polite statement concerning the professional musician who "practices the art, not for the sake of his own improvement [of the mind], but in order to give pleasure, and that of a vulgar sort, to his hearers." Continuing, he states that "the execution of such [professional] music is not the part of a freeman but of a paid performer, and the result is that the performers are vulgarized, for the end at which they aim is bad." [75] Earlier he affirms that "we call the professional performers vulgar; no freeman would play or sing unless he were intoxicated or in jest." [76] To some degree, this extreme of attitude often finds its counterpart in the primitive society, probably for quite different reasons: The unique, the different (and the specialist becomes this) often arouses one emotional extreme or another – either respectful awe or cool disdain. The more distinctly creative the "specialization," the more pronounced may be the disdain. One writer speaks of the lowly role played by the "composer" among the Wabende of Tanganyika. Although the skilled performer, while not part of a special class, is held in "esteem" and "well fed," there is no particular merit to having created a popular song. "On l'ignore [the composer]. Personne n'a même le souci de le connaître." [77]

The traveling minstrel as well as the stationary "court" ensemble is an important part of Central African musical life. Often called upon to assist at ceremonial functions, these musicians are more likely to participate in secular music-making, acting generally as leaders in community "sings" (which, of course, are usually also "dances"). The itinerant minstrels often sing of their travels while accompanying themselves on some instrument (usually strings) and may also act in the capacity of minor magicians. Every major chief (and certainly every king) has some type of ensemble in his employ. For example, among the A-Lur of the Belgian Congo the official orchestra generally contains from eight to ten players (flutists, trumpeters, etc.) who proceed in a slow march when playing.[78] The Azande, also of the Belgian Congo, have an orchestra consisting of trumpets, whistles, rattles, and bells. At times xylophones and lutes are added, although these instruments are usually restricted to solo playing.[79] Reference was

posed of Bahutu, and the hammock-carriers composed of Batwa. See R. Bourgeois, *Banyarwanda et Barundi*, p. 58. (Cf. also Chapter I, above.)

[74] It might be pointed out that the N'Gundi singer of Transcr. 28 (French Equatorial) is blind. However, this may be, and probably is, an isolated instance.

[75] Aristotle, *Politics*, VIII, 6, 1341 b, 10 f, Richard McKeon, editor (New York, 1941).

[76] *Ibid.*, VIII, 5, 1339 b, 8 f.

[77] P. H. Molitor, "La Musique chez les Nègres de Tanganyika," *Anthropos*, VIII (1913), p. 718.

[78] Tervueren, Belgium. *Annales du musée du Congo Belge.* Série III. *Ethnographie et Anthropologie*, I (1902), fascicule 1, "La Musique," p. 17.

[79] *Ibid.*, p. 17.

made earlier to the *makondere* or royal gourd-horn ensemble of the Banyoro of Uganda that is called upon to play at each new moon.[80] Most of these groups are organized along informal lines in that the players are not divided into organized parts or "choirs," but are musically intermingled in a more or less free manner. Co-ordination, however, does exist in performance, although it is not the strict, rigid kind that has come to be associated with Western high civilization.

Since the music school obviously does not function in primitive society, instruction takes place by the age-old rote method which, it ought to be pointed out, consists more of a spontaneous and wholly informal imitation than of deliberate master-pupil instruction. The musical awareness implied by such instruction would more likely be found in advanced civilization with its crystallized and codified music theory.

Needless to say, the kind of person who steps into the role of official, professional, or semi-professional musician usually possesses some innate musical and kinesthetic aptitudes (although it should be remembered that the dancing-singing shaman probably owes his position as much to his forceful, possibly para-psychological personality traits as to his musical talents, if any). While men predominate in these roles, women occasionally take part – mostly in less official musical capacities, although the "virtuoso" female musician does appear sporadically, particularly where social restrictions have to some degree been weakened. According to one writer, many of the professional *adenden* or harp players of the Teso tribe of Uganda, whose services are employed for weddings and other large occasions, are women.[81] The bard-singer of historic songs among the Baganda may also be a woman, it appears.[82] With reference to the female harpist, the phenomenon might also be interpreted as the quite natural adjunct of any Oriental-flavored culture with its trained "music-girls," [83] rather than as the after-product of social "restriction-weakening."

The subject-matter and occasion for many of the professional musical performances relate to a broadly defined area of musical activity which might be called entertainment. This is not to say that the community as a whole does not engage in music-making for relaxation and entertainment; obviously it does. Note the community elephant-music of the Mambuti Pygmies, mentioned previously; or the famed choral songs of the Mangbetu of the Belgian Congo.[84] In fact, most of the transcriptions appended to the present work are of a secular, "social" nature and exhibit, in most cases, some kind of community or group participation. It should be remembered that the "professional" musician is the exception, not the rule. Most music-making, especially in the less organized, spread-out areas of Central Africa is a product of layman, community activity *en masse*.

[80] Transcr. 41.

[81] J. C. D. Lawrence, *Iteso*, p. 159.

[82] See Transcr. 45 (Uganda).

[83] The Middle and Far East have, of course, always encouraged the development and support of a professional "music-girl" class designed primarily for entertainment purposes. Ancient Egypt and Sumeria may well have played a part in the formation of the north-eastern cultures of Central Africa, as mentioned previously. (Alexander the Great's general captured 329 female musicians in the retinue of King Darius of Persia. See Curt Sachs, *Rise of Music*, p. 59.)

[84] Transcr. 1.

A number of the social songs are of a historic nature serving, no doubt, as substitutes for written tribal memory. Much of the folklore as well as actual tribal history is thus placed within a musical "transmitter" – the historic song – which serves the dual purpose of entertainment and recording device. Two such songs of the Baganda are included in the appended transcriptions, one a solo performed with typical, arched-harp accompaniment, an instrumentation reminiscent of Ancient Egypt,[85] and the other a female solo-chorus arrangement.[86] The first, in an intimate, chamber style with many Middle Eastern coloratura effects, relates the story of the king's executioner. Even the structure of the song, with its non-verbal introductory section, recalls the Middle East. The second, in the more outdoor, explosive style characteristic of the non-Oriental Bantu, tells of the behavior of a certain eccentric person.

Acting in a more official capacity, the bard may be attached to the king's retinue, serving as royal historian and general poet laureate. The Bakuba of the south central Belgian Congo, who in the sixteenth century ruled a large empire, boasted a royal court with a "master story-teller" and a "keeper of the oral traditions." [87] No doubt the method of expression involved both musical and purely verbal forms of narrative. Modern civilization has greatly influenced the present king of the Watutsi, Mwami Charles Rudahigwa Mutara the Third, who, in an attempt to make permanent the vast body of poetico-musical folklore of Ruanda, has founded the *Fonds Mutara, Caisse d'Éditions*, of which Volume I, "Inganji Karinga" (The Victorious Karinga) appeared in 1943.[88] Obviously, much of the material is drawn from the broad repertoire of the king's *abasizi*, or court bards. Some of this repertoire includes the Bwiru, a narrative trilogy of the royal dynasty.[89]

The long narrative form also appears among the Wabende of Tanganyika, particularly in their "hero" songs.[90] These epic-style songs, extolling the exploits of warriors and heroes, also form part of the Watutsi repertoire. In two of this writer's transcriptions a Watutsi bard, singing in the subdued, intimate, and quite florid Middle Eastern style – including the characteristic Middle Eastern free introduction, which the singer hums and which the Watutsi call *umerego* or tension [91] – tells of the victories of two Watutsi warrior groups, the Urwintwali and the Ibabazabahizi.[92]

---

[85] Transcr. 44. The eight-stringed *enanga* harp is similar to the arched harp depicted on Ancient Egyptian monuments. While the modern Central African harp has tuning pegs, the Ancient Egyptian harp featured stationary knobs for fastening the strings, not for tuning them. See M. Trowell and K. P. Wachsmann, *Tribal Crafts of Uganda*, p. 394; also Curt Sachs, *History of Instruments*, p. 92.

[86] Transcr. 45.

[87] *Les Beaux-Arts*, Belgian Congo issue (Brussels, 1955), p. 4.

[88] Alexis Kagame, "Le Rwanda et son roi," *Aequatoria*, VIII (1945), 2, p. 42. The Karinga is a royal-drum emblem. Fr. Kagame, incidentally, is the first native Ruanda priest.

[89] Marthe Molitor, *Danseurs du Ruanda* (Brussels, 1952), p. 17.

[90] P. H. Molitor, "La Musique chez les Nègres de Tanganyika," p. 715. The author states that the text of these songs is more important than the music. However, this opinion is open to question in view of what the author considers "important," musically, e.g., he speaks of the melody as "très primitive et non mesurée ...", p. 715.

[91] Leo A. Verwilghen, in album notes to *Songs of the Watutsi*, Ethnic Folkways Records, P428 (1952), p. 2.

[92] See Transcr. 20, 21; cf. also Chapter IV, below, "Descending Octave Melodies."

MUSIC FOR LITIGATION

Not within the category of "entertainment," but certainly of a secular nature, is the music for litigation and the airing of grievances. In a sense, such music might be termed non-religious ceremonial music, since it is set within a legal framework that partakes of the formal, ceremonial atmosphere, and since it generally contains little, if any, extra-human implications. It would indeed be strange to enter a United States courtroom and hear the participants of a legal battle cite details of pros and cons in singing voices. Whether their arguments would be enhanced by the addition of music might depend to a large extent upon the adeptness and skill with which the participants made use of personal musical gifts. (Is it not significant that the successful courtroom lawyer usually possesses a resonant, penetrating voice and some capabilities in the histrionics department, with which to impress his audience?) Apparently, musical intensification has some effect upon legal presentation in Central African courtroom scenes. Not only must the litigants sing, but they must be in full command of any poetic and rhetoric abilities they may possess, for the proceedings may follow a kind of oratory-song alternation process.

The litigants are usually members of the same community, come to plead some basic disagreement, some accusation, before the chief and the entire village. This is not an impromptu affair, for strictest formality is observed from beginning to end. The chief usually sets a day for the "trial" and in most cases opens court with his own rendition of a special drum signal. Among the Watutsi, it is one of the royal drums, Gatsinda-mikiko (he who makes game of jealousies and rivalries),[93] that is struck to announce the beginning of royal audiences. Another royal drum, Karinga (pledge of hope),[94] is given a light stroke by the king when he pronounces death sentences. A typical musical litigation, as occurring among the Bambala of the Belgian Congo, is described by one writer as follows: "The chief opens court by playing upon the small signal drum. Then each of the litigants, represented by an official, rises in turn and presents his argument. He attempts to confuse his adversary by proving he is wrong and that he contradicts himself. When he has finished his argument he sings an allegorical type of song in which the villagers and drummers join ... The litigants, with their supporters, face each other in two lines."[95]

Following are some excerpts from an actual Bambala litigation. (The purely verbal sections are sprinkled with supporters' responds in a kind of Greek-chorus commentary.)

FIRST PARTY: "I was in my house and would have liked to stay. But he has come and wants to discuss the matter in public. So I have left my house and that is why you see me here."

(sings) "I am like a cricket. I would like to sing, but the wall of earth that sur-

---

[93] R. Bourgeois, *Banyarwanda et Barundi*, p. 41.

[94] *Ibid.*, p. 41.

[95] Leo A. Verwilghen, in album notes to *Folk Music of the Western Congo*, Ethnic Folkways Records, P427 (1952), p. 2.

	rounds me prevents me. Someone has forced me to come out of my hole, so I will sing."
(continues argument)	"Let us debate the things, but slowly, slowly, otherwise we will have to go before the tribunal of the white people. You have forced me to come. When the sun has set, we shall still be here debating."
(*sings*)	"I am like the dog that stays before the door until he gets a bone."
OPPONENT:	"Nobody goes both ways at the same time. You have told this and that. One of the two must be wrong. That is why I am attacking you."
(*sings*)	"A thief speaks with another thief. It is because you are bad that I attack you." [96]

When the judges have finally pronounced sentence, the chief closes the proceedings with a drummed message, again using the same idiophonous slit-drum with which he announced the court's opening.[97]

In a less formal manner, music may be utilized for the expression of hidden, personal, or group grievances. The butt or "defendant" may be the government (central or local), the tax-collector, the white "boss," or simply one's mother-in-law. These songs-of-complaint are usually subtly phrased, replete with innuendo, and sharply satirical. They provide, of course, an indirect and sometimes noticeably effective way of expressing what is often legally or socially inexpressible and perhaps forbidden through more direct channels. At times, however, the veil of subtlety is abandoned in some daring and boldly-stated barb of criticism let fly by the "plaintiff" at the "defendant." For example, one writer cites some musical criticisms by Bashi girl-workers (of the eastern Belgian Congo), directed, with undisguised threats, against a plantation owner who has deprived them of their rations of oil: "We have finished our work. Before, we used to get oil; now we don't get it. Why has Bwana stopped giving us oil? We don't understand. If he doesn't give us oil, we will all leave and go to work for the Catholic Fathers. There we can do little work and have plenty of oil. So we are waiting now to see whether Bwana X will give us oil. Be careful! If we don't get oil, we won't work here!" [98] Is this a musical strike?

THE DANCE

Numerous travelers and explorers of the nineteenth century, viewing the various types of African dance, wrote of their impressions utilizing such terms as "lascivious," "contorted," "spasmodic," etc. The trained twentieth-century observer, while agreeing in his descriptive terminology, has usually discarded the centrifugal judgment-point characteristic of earlier evaluations and has also usually added a third dimension to his observations, that of the ethno-aesthetic. Not only does this mean that the African

[96] *Ibid.*, p. 3.
[97] See Transcr. 23.
[98] Alan P. Merriam, "Song Texts of the Bashi," *African Music*, I (1954), 1, pp. 51–52.

dance is to be viewed within its own cultural setting and to have applied to it at least its own aesthetic yardstick (in addition to others), but that deeper investigation into the relationship between the kinds of bodily movements and the kinds of ethnic forces producing them may be expected. This approach to the subject is, of course, desirable and in operation for all expressive aspects – music, sculpture, etc. – and not only for the dance.

Basic classification of primitive dance types has been extensively presented by Curt Sachs in his *World History of the Dance* (New York, 1937, 469 pp.), and the analytic treatment of dance-style has been further aided by the current, successful development of dance scripts and notations.[99]

The mimetic animal-dance, the convulsive shaman-dance of inner ecstasy, the fertility, marriage, initiation, war, and funeral dances (all realized in archaic circle or later file and couple forms) find their counterparts in Central Africa. While the subject-matter of these dances is rather uniform throughout the area, the styles and forms vary from region to region, even from tribe to tribe, obviously depending to a large extent upon psycho-cultural factors. Whether a group uses large, expanded movement (musical as well as kinesthetic) or small constrained movement would seem to be related to the social personality of its people. Broadly speaking, Central African dance styles exhibit the explosive, enlarged bodily movements so markedly missing from the Far Eastern dance world. The flinging up und out, the centrifugal leaping and kicking that bespeak an "outgoing," extrovert cultural temper appears definitely to belong to the dance-forms of Central Africa.

One notable exception to the extrovert mentality is the Pygmy group, particularly the branch or branches following nomadic life-patterns in the heart of the forest. The need for being quietly elusive, fast-moving, and sharply alert to the dangers – human and otherwise – of dark forest life, has no doubt played an important part in forming the Pygmy personality, which can best be described as shy, subdued, retiring. The Pygmies of French Equatorial Africa are described by one writer as being musically restrained. Noise is avoided among them in order not to arouse lurking dangers. Therefore, song, dance, and drumming during feasts are often very soft.[100]

However, it ought to be pointed out that the retiring artistic temperament is not characteristic of all Pygmies, that those groups living in close proximity to the larger Negroes have in many cases, depending upon the exigencies of the cultural association, quite outgoing characteristics. Thus, special musical skills are cultivated and brought

---

[99] Note, for example, the Labanotation of recent years (invented by Rudolph Laban, c. 1928), which is realized in vertical columns (read from bottom to top) placed to the right of and rhythmically aligned with a staff, also vertically arranged on the page, containing the accompanying music: viz., ⬚ | | | The central line, dividing the body (right, left), is the line for support; the lines to either side designate leg gestures; the spaces further on (divided by imaginary lines), body, arm, and hand gestures, in this order. Labanotation is probably the first successful dance notation that includes musical alignment and is being rapidly adopted throughout the Western world. Thoinot Arbeau's *Orchésographie* of 1588 contained one of the early known attempts at dance notation given with corresponding indications of musical rhythm. See Curt Sachs, *History of Dance*, p. 344 f; also Ann Hutchinson, *Labanotation* (New York, 1954), p. 12 f.

[100] R. P. Trilles, "*Les Pygmées de la forêt équatoriale* (Paris, 1932), p. 332.

to the fore among the Batwa of Ruanda who often function in the capacity of king's musicians, serving as professional entertainers for the Watutsi.[101] As "showmen," the Pygmies have made strong impressions on many observers whose reports often seem to contradict other accounts pertaining to Pygmy timorousness and reserve. The Ancient Egyptians, from the seventh millenium B.C. onward, seem to have had Central African Pygmies living among them,[102] and it was for their professional artistic skills that Pygmies from the interior were later presented as gifts to the Egyptian kings (for example, to Pharaoh Nefrikare, better known as Pepi II[103]). The Pygmies of Uganda were described by Harry Johnston as possessing highly developed dancing abilities in contrast to the almost monotonous movements of the larger Negroes,[104] while the Mambuti Pygmies of the Ituri Forest are considered "meisterliche Tänzer und Schauspieler," by still another writer.[105]

In vivid contrast to these accounts we hear of the quite introverted, almost inhibited character of Pygmy dance expression. The dance of the Mambuti is described as "unrhythmical, even stiff and constrained," as a shuffling "one-step" by the women, although the men are "more agile," [106] without any coordinated ensemble movement.[107] (See also the reference above to the "soft" and restrained musical sounds produced by the Pygmies of French Equatorial Africa.)

It would appear from these reports that no uniform kind of dance temperament exists among the Pygmies, but that in many cases both introvert and extrovert elements coexist, such elements being subsumed one within the other depending upon geographical-cultural placement of the Pygmies, e.g., their relationship to surrounding Negroes and white men. On the whole, it seems quite logical to presuppose some correlation between the sort of lives the Pygmies lead – and historically, they have generally been nomadic, displaying a kind of societal facelessness, pushed into the role of the pursued with its concomitant furtiveness – and their expressive temperament. The bold extrovert features mentioned by some observers may be allied to what modern psychology calls a "reaction formation," or the emphasizing of some level of behavior in its opposite form.[108]

Pursuing the line of observation pertaining to the outgoing, extrovert compartment of Pygmy artistic life, we find one dominant expressive form that is noticed by all who have come in contact with the Pygmies of Africa. This is the animal mimesis dance, which was mentioned previously in connection with initiation and hunting rites, and which is certainly not the exclusive property of the Pygmies, being widely favored

[101] Alan P. Merriam, in album notes to *Voice of the Congo*, Riverside RLP 4002.

[102] H. Lang, "Nomad Dwarfs and Civilization," *Natural History*, XIX (1919), pp. 697–713.

[103] Paul Schebesta, *Among Congo Pygmies* (London, 1933), preface.

[104] Harry Johnston, *The Uganda Protectorate*, II (London, 1902), p. 543.

[105] Oskar Eberle, *Cenalora* (*Leben, Glaube, Tanz und Theater der Urvölker*) (Breisgau, 1955), p. 33.

[106] Paul Schebesta, *Congo Pygmies*, p. 27.

[107] Tervueren, "La Musique," p. 18.

[108] In its pure form, the "reaction formation" might be exemplified by a person's antagonistic attitude towards something unconsciously favored. The Pygmy example given above would actually be a converse form, i.e., what is unconsciously disapproved (the shy, introvert behavior) is actively negated by means of bold, extrovert dance forms.

throughout Central Africa. Animal mimesis is, broadly speaking, a form of theatre, more pointedly, a special form of theatre that might be termed a *Gesamtkunstwerk*. All the senses are appealed to, multi-expression is aimed for (not deliberately, it is true, on the primitive level, for the intent is not aesthetic) so that song, dance, instruments, speech, and drama are brought together in one vast commingling. The term "commingling" is used advisedly, for this is not a *fusion* or integration of different expressive forms whereby each form is used to enhance the other and to make more potent the total stylistic effect; this is, in its *ur* or primeval state, simply an additive combination to make more vital both the extra-artistic (religious, power-assimilative) and sheerly muscular factors involved. Furthermore, this primitive "theatre" is not spectacle; that is, it is not designed for an audience, for, generally speaking, it is a collective affair, the "stage" being the center of the village or *kraal*, perhaps an uncleared forest nook, and the *dramatis personae* the initiates of the day, the worshippers of a certain totem, hunters, etc.

The "props" of such theatre often involve highly elaborate masks – among the larger Negroes rather than among the Pygmies [109] – which serve the dual functions of transfiguration and heightened realism. The dancers thus disguise their individuality, personal accentuation being taboo in totem-conscious societies, and at the same time try, paradoxically, to pin-point, to define the appearance and character of the animal they are portraying. Abstraction on the one hand, realism on the other – a significant blend that appears to be the key to the art-forms of an entire cultural complex.[110]

The masks, of course, are not confined to animal mimesis dances but are constructed and used for other dances related to imaginary and ghost-like powers – ancestor spirits, fertility, death, birth, harvest, and other incorporeal beings. In these cases, realistic resemblance is abandoned and the imaginary takes over, for the face of a spirit is secret and unknown. Dance pantomime, however, may be quite realistic, particularly in those dances involving fertility and harvest themes – where the idea of "inducement" or "request" prevails. The logic, of course, is readily seen: As in the case of hunting dances, the desired goal, through being dramatized, becomes more readily accessible, almost as if once a pictorial hint is given to nature it might be hard to erase it.

A particularly vivid mimetic dance called the *kutu*, combining three themes – farming,

[109] Sculptured masks, wood carvings, and other sculptured objects are generally not part of Pygmy artistic production, a fact no doubt due to their nomadic life-patterns as well as to the lack of strongly organized, elaborate religion and ceremonial. According to Ralph Linton, such sculptured works are, in fact, more characteristic of the agricultural societies (Belgian Congo, French Equatorial Africa, West Africa) than of the cattle societies (parts of Uganda, Ruanda-Urundi, Tanganyika), a circumstance originally noted in detail by Frobenius in his *Ursprung der afrikanischen Kulturen*. See Ralph Linton, *Tree of Culture*, p. 438. Since a large component of fetishim is involved in the making of sculptured objects, the absence of such objects in the cattle cultures might signify the presence of a more integrative, monotheistic religious attitude rather than the atomistic or piecemeal attitude implied by fetishism. Actually, there is a greater emphasis on the idea of a centralized, supreme deity among the cattle people; the Watutsi, for example, worship Imana (how close to Emanuel!) a supreme being whose creation of the Watutsi dynasty, eviction of an "Adam and Eve," sending of an emissary are strongly reminiscent of Christian theology. To forestall chronological evaluation of the two types of religious attitudes, it should be pointed out that the most simple and primeval African culture, that of the Pygmies, also includes belief in a central deity.

[110] See Chapter VI below for further discussion of this point.

death, sex – occurs among the Kuyu of French Equatorial Africa.[111] This is an excellent example of the blend of the abstract and the real, as well as of the confined, small gestures and the bold, outgoing movements. The confined, small movements are not peculiarly feminine (in the Asiatic world an entire culture dances this way), for in the *kutu* women are the main dancers and make use of both types of movements. The *kutu* dance is part of a larger ceremonial, that of planting and reaping. The dance is performed especially when a woman proficient in manioc farming has died. Three sections of the dance take form to the *a cappella* accompaniment of an ostinato choral melody, which increases in tempo with each dance section. This partnership of dance and music is quite dramatic, and it will be seen that the three dance sections are in themselves actually episodes in a mime-story that is both symbolic and realistic.

Part 1, which lasts through the night, is the sex-implantation theme. A circle of women with hoes in their hands and copper-ring rattles on their ankles move in a slow step, their hips gyrating in what has been called by many writers the "belly dance." The circle, according to Curt Sachs, is one of the most archaic dance forms and is usually connected with the abstract or imageless dance themes.[112] This part of the *kutu* does, in fact, suggest rather than depict, intermingling in a symbolic way ideas of the erotic with earth planting, which to the tribe appear to be magically if not logically related. The bodily movements are confined, restrained, "centripetal," the hip motion especially falling into this category. A woman (the oldest) soon enters the center and dances in imitation of an earth laborer, thereby infusing more realistic elements into the dance. This is theatrical pantomime, for a concrete image has caught hold of the dancer and is being projected by her. The slow hip-dancing circle continues meanwhile, and its suggestive message assumes more concrete form when a leaping man suddenly joins the old woman in the center. Convulsively kicking up both feet simultaneously, chest inclining backward in jacknife fashion and hip spasmodically brought forward, he very vividly mimes the sex act. "C'est le geste du coït debout, et très amplifié, qui est imité. Ce danseur se jette dans la vieille femme qui ouvre les cuisses." [113] This is realism carried to the far end of the scale where it borders on actuality. Not only is the sex theme connected with planting in this episode, but it also serves another and medicinal purpose – the negation of death.[114]

Part 2 of the dance takes place at dawn without any intermission. The circle of dancers now moves around the dead woman who has been placed in a central mound, and their movements become more animated, expansive. They, like the solo female dancer previously, are now dancing-actors and scrape the earth with their hoes in pantomime of farming labor. "Background" music, the chant of Part 1, is accelerated in keeping with the intensified atmosphere. This scene probably combines eulogy of

---

[111] M. A. Poupon, ". . . la tribu Kouyou," pp. 327 ff.

[112] Curt Sachs, *Dance*, p. 62.

[113] M. A. Poupon, ". . . la tribu Kouyou," p. 328.

[114] Curt Sachs points this out in connection with the high-kicking erotic dances of the ancient Egyptian music girls at funerals, the purpose again being to represent the counteracting force of the sex act. See *Dance*, Plate IX A (Egyptian funeral dance).

the dead with magic emphasis of the life principle (and possibly the magic transmission of the deceased's farming skill to the dancers[115]).

A kinesthetic crescendo is reached in the third episode when the dancers become enflamed, concentrate about the mound and jump upon it, stamping and crushing it. The chant accordingly reaches a maximum speed, becoming more intensified in rendition. This is the climax of the dance, a wild, frenzied, explosive kinesis directed at the corpse, at death. It is also, perhaps, a rewarding gesture towards the dead woman.[116]

The non-mimetic dance appears in several forms and situations. Two basic forms are the circle and the column, which may also be found in the mimetic dances, although the circle is essentially an abstract form more aligned with the imageless dances. Many of these dances derive simply from social-expressive urges, the collective desire to move, to exercise rhythmically, to entertain oneself. Thus, after an evening meal, a Mambuti Pygmy may casually strike a drum,[117] simultaneously hopping in place from one foot to the other, and eventually entice the entire camp to join him in an all-night affair. The women usually dance separately, in a circle about the men, while beating time with hands clapped at face level. The men may also play flutes as they dance.[118] Such dances are not meant to portray or depict anything, whether concrete or otherworldly. They are quite abstract in idea and intent, meant primarily for kinesthetic enjoyment. Where the motions become convulsive or frenzied, and some general magical purpose controls the dance, kinesthetic enjoyment seems to be overshadowed by an inner ecstasy of hypnotic dimensions. Here also, realism, mimesis, concrete imagery appear to be lacking or subsidiary to symbolic suggestiveness. The shaman solo dancers are particularly given to this kind of abstract ecstasy. A convulsive frenzy, it may be recalled, characterizes the *Etida* healing dance of the Iteso of Uganda, who dance in a circle about the drummer and finally in almost hypnotic hysteria roll on the ground stuffing their mouths with dirt.[119] Muscular jiggling, shaking, and convulsiveness appear to be allied to these ecstatic dances, whatever the occasion, entertainment, or religious ceremonial.

The *ngoma* drum-ceremonial of the Wanyamwezi of Tanganyika, which takes place every full moon, is a typical dance of the non-mimetic, convulsive type found in Central Africa. A proof of its abstract, non-realistic character is the fact that it is applied to different situations. The form, a closed circle, and the movements, ecstatic shaking and spasmodic contortion, appear in the different secret society initiations (whatever the animal totem) and in the dances of the demon-worshipping Waswezi cult of this area. For example, the dance of the snake cult, the Wajeje, is a typical *ngoma* cere-

---

[115] The circle with someone in the center may reflect some magic pattern of exchange of powers, according to Curt Sachs, *Dance*, p. 62.

[116] Many tribes do not bury their dead but leave them for the hyenas, or burn them.

[117] The drummer hits the skin with his left fist, while alternately striking drum and frame with a stick held in his right hand. See Paul Schebesta, *Congo Pygmies*, p. 27. The two timbres thus achieved seem allied both to the tonal language and to the hemiola-style rhythms with their two-three groupings (cf. Chapter II above and Chapter IV, "Rhythm," below).

[118] Paul Schebesta, *Congo Pygmies*, p. 27.

[119] See above in section on healing ceremonial.

monial dance also characteristic of the porcupine, the Wanunguli, and other cults. The dancers, men only, form a closed circle about a few skilled dancers and three to five drummers in the center. (Again the magic circle!) The central dancers (not more than three) wear short loin cloths, small black skin-capes, and iron rings on their feet. The circle moves about the inner dancers in a stamping motion, "keeping time with the drums." The eyes of the drummers are always on the dancers. Suddenly, to louder drumming, the central dancers begin to shudder, all muscles in play, shoulder-blades rolling, while they stand "like frozen statues" (except for the quivering muscles). At the climax of the excitement they fall to the ground and lie apparently unconscious. In a short while the dance begins again.[120] This is an excellent example of the non-realistic, inner-directed, ecstatic dance, far removed from the more style-conscious depictive dance.

The famed "belly movement" is part of this convulsive style and may take on quite realistic qualities in the courting dances. Often described by writers as "lascivious" and "improper," such movements appear to be an integral part of many Central African dances (cf. the Kuyu funeral-farming dance described above).

Most of the movements described above are contained, literally "down to earth." However, the large, expanded, leaping style is quite prevalent, as mentioned previously, and is particularly allied with mimetic dances – animal, war, harvest, etc. The Watutsi of Ruanda are especially known for this leaping, shooting movement in their dances. Most of these are war-like, in fact, and often involve a corps of forty golden-wigged dancers carrying lances and bows. Accompanied by a Batwa Pygmy band composed of drums and cowhorns, these dancers go through high jumps and flying leaps, miming the act of war. Vocal accompaniment in the form of shrieking cascades of declamatory sound that fade away on a low note is provided by two leaders.[121] This freely descending vocal style also appears in the quieter chamber singing of the Watutsi bards, in which it exists as an octave fall.[122] It is related to one of the two basic vocal styles outlined by Curt Sachs, the pathogenic or emotion-derived style.[123] The Watutsi octave-fall (and subsequent leap upward), together with the expanded dance motions (and also the athletic high-jump the Watutsi are famous for) would appear to be expressive aspects of the same underlying psychological make-up – that of the aggressive, extrovert kind. (Note also the strong fortissimos, sforzandos, and subtle diminuendos of the royal drum music, as well as the dramatic, almost developmental, form of this music.[124])

The evening shuffle dance of the Mambuti Pygmies is, on the contrary, quite lacking in dramatic, vigorous music. Intervals are small, tiny melodic nuclei are constantly repeated, rhythm is steady and symmetrical, while dynamics are unchanging.[125]

Dance and music styles are obviously related with regard to underlying social temper-

[120] Fritz Spellig, "Über Geheimbünde bei den Wanyamwezi," p. 62 f.
[121] Marthe Molitor, *Danseurs du Ruanda* (n. p., 1952), p. 20.
[122] See Transcr. 20; also discussion in Chapter IV below, under "octave-melodies."
[123] Curt Sachs, *Rise*, p. 41 f.
[124] See Transcr. 18.
[125] See, for example, the Mambuti flute music, Transcr. 13.

ament. Broadly speaking, there is a strong admixture of both in- and outgoing characteristics in the expressive outlets of Central African peoples, with a somewhat greater
emphasis on the dynamic, expansive features. Whether a cultural temperament is due
to some innate, racial predisposition or to social conditioning resulting from intertribal
status, contact, and prestige, is an open question still requiring much extensive research.

SPEECH MELODY AND THE 'TALKING' DRUM

In an effort to span the thick layers of forest air or the broad expanse of plateau, the
African Negro has devised an elaborate drum telegraphy fashioned to communicate in
almost speech-like tones the daily messages and announcements of each tribe. This is
accomplished by practically literal duplication by the drummers of the speech inflections and rhythms of the tribal languages. To communicate in this manner sentences
in English would be almost impossible, since there is no really distinguishing pitch
character to the English language that would make it feasible to send messages of pure,
non-cryptological sound. However, languages with distinct pitch levels, levels necessary to the conveyance of meaning, lend themselves quite readily to such a method of
speech duplication.

Among the best-known of these intoning languages is Chinese, a language whose
"sing-song" quality is not mere musical accident but an integral part of the semantic
structure. As a result of such structure, Chinese vocal music, in its alignment of pitch
levels with speech inflections and deflections,[126] mirrors the philological peculiarities
characteristic of parts of the Far East.

The languages of Negro Africa are also of a musico-semantic structure (cf. Chapter I
above), and where drum communication is an integral part of the social organization
the language structure is reflected not only in the song of the tribe but in the configur-
ation of drum sounds as well. The Bantu languages in particular, of which there are
some 150, are of the intoning kind, some possessing great numbers of pitch levels or
tonemes. Zulu and Kongo, for example, have nine such levels each,[127] and, in fact, most
of the languages of this area (the basin of the central and lower Congo River) are of a
complicated tonal character. The East and South Belgian Congo languages average
three tones, as do also the Bantu languages of Tanganyika.[128] A nasal and sonorous
consonant on the second syllable of many Bantu words [129] also appears to affect musical
expression, particularly vocal production.[130] Sudanic languages (mostly above 3° North
Latitude, in the Sahara region), although generally mono-syllabic, also have tone levels

[126] Curt Sachs, *Rise*, p. 137.

[127] K. E. Laman, *Musical Accent, or Intonation in the Kongo Language* (Stockholm, 1922).

[128] Clement Doke, *Bantu: Modern Grammatical, Phonetical, and Lexicographical Studies since 1860* (London, 1945), pp. 16 ff.

[129] H. Baumann and D. Westermann, *Les Peuples et civilisations de l'Afrique* (Paris, 1948), p. 462.

[130] The word *ba-ntu* is a good example. The second syllable is in fact the root and gives the basic meaning
of the word (man). The form of the prefix determines the singular, plural, "language of," or "country of."
In the example above, the prefix signifies the plural, "men." The importance of this kind of stem in Bantu
languages makes for an overall nasality in speaking and singing.

that affect the meanings of words. However, Bantu tonemes affect both grammatic tense and semantic meaning, while Sudanic tonal variation is essentially a semantic rather than a grammatic function.[131]

The visitor to Africa not familiar with Bantu-Sudanic tonal characteristics might very well find himself completely unintelligible in conversing with the natives solely on the basis of the written guide. Thus, for example, in Lonkundo, the bitonemal language of the Nkundo-Mongo group of the west-central Belgian Congo, the word *bokongo* has several meanings. If pronounced *bokongó*, with a high tone on the last syllable, it means "white sand"; if pronounced *bokóngó*, with high tones on the two final syllables, it means "vulva," etc.[132]

Speech tonality apparently has some bearing on musical expression. The flow of a melody very often depends on the pitch levels of the text.[133] Such music could almost literally be called a "word-born" or logogenic music and would seem to have no independent melodic life of its own. Actually, this is not the case, for several varieties of melody appear that possess strong individual characteristics pointing to stages beyond the simple two- or three-tone chant. The long-line descending melody of the Watutsi, the pathogenic melodic fall of the Batwa Pygmies, the elongated almost developmental melody of the N'Gundi of French Equatorial Africa are all cases in point (cf. Chapter IV below).

African telegraphy, particularly, rests upon the tonal language structure. The idiophonous slit-drum [134] is the most frequently used instrument for this purpose, but other instruments are also utilized. Antelope horns and ocarinas (bowl flutes),[135] membranophone *ngoma* drums and vertical flutes,[136] whistles and two-toned bells, [137] two-stringed stick zithers, and even the human voice employing a special conventionalized syllabary [138] – these may all be used to transmit messages over long distances. (The human voice usually shouts over a large body of water, which acts as an amplifier. Among the Lokele of the Belgian Congo, *ke* or *le* is shouted for syllables having low

[131] Joseph H. Greenberg, "The Classification of African Languages," *American Anthropologist*, L (1948) p. 24.

[132] R. P. G. Hulstaert, "Les Tons en Lonkundo (Congo Belge)," *Anthropos*, XXIX (1934), p. 79.

[133] In the Babira language, for example, a word like *kókó* (chicken) which has a high, even pitch in a sentence is usually placed high in a song; a descending word like *kapè* (visible) generally has descending musical tones; while a broken vowel sound would accordingly be broken up in the music, e.g., *htga* (hearth) gets two descending tones on the first syllable. See W. P. Maeyens, "Het inlandsch Lied en het muzikaal Accent met semantische Functie bij de Babira," *Kongo-Overzee*, IV (1938), pp. 250–259.

[134] The idiophonous slit-drum is *not* a "gong," as misnamed by some writers. Curt Sachs calls such incorrect usage "an intolerable abuse," (*History of Instruments*, p. 30) since "gong" refers to a bronze disk which is acoustically dead at the rim and alive at the center. The African bell is also misnamed "gong" by some. The bell, as opposed to the gong, is dead at the center and alive at the rim (*History of Instruments*, pp. 208, 456).

[135] R. P. G. Hulstaert, "Note sur les instruments de musique à l'Équateur," pp. 186, 188.

[136] G. Vancoillie, "Recueil de signaux claniques ou Kumbu des tribus Mbagani et du Kasai (Congo Belge)," *African Studies*, VIII (Mar.–June, 1949), p. 37.

[137] J. Jacobs, "Signaaltrommeltaal bij de Tetela," *Kongo-Overzee*, XX (1954), p. 409.

[138] J. F. Carrington, *A Comparative Study of some Central African Gong-Languages* (Brussels, 1949), pp. 37, 40–41.

tones and *ki* or *li* for high tones, rather than the actual words. Of interest here is the method by which drummer apprentices are taught their craft: They learn by rote the stylized vocal syllables representing the pitches of the drum messages as an aid in mastering the final form of the messages themselves. This syllabic method is reminiscent of the special *katakana* vocal method utilized by Japanese *Gagaku* players as an aid to instrumental memorizing.[139] The Western *do-re-mi* system is also, undoubtedly, part of the same "vocal-neume" approach to pitch designation.)

The messages used for telegraphy are really traditional sayings and proverbs, highly stylized for transmitting purposes and not characteristic of everyday speech. Such proverbs usually constitute the "classic literature" of the tribe, belonging to the treasured heritage of folklore, legend, and general accumulated wisdom that is passed on from generation to generation in a quite poetic medium. Unfortunately, some of this specialized language is dwindling today and going the way of all things acquiring the label of "archaistic." Where the successes of modern civilization have penetrated the wild forest, new methods of telegraphy are rapidly gaining ground and displacing the older, more elemental ways.

The poetic nature of these drum messages and their close relation to the pitch levels of the language may be seen from the following examples. In referring to the village chief, the Batetela (Belgian Congo) drummer will use the paraphrase "the cave termite-heap; the animals don't leap over it," and the pitch variations (as well as rhythm) of this phrase, *owánji; nkoi*,[140] will be literally duplicated on the drum, the second syllable of the first word receiving a high-pitched tone and the others low tones. Among the Lokele (Belgian Congo), the word "manioc" or *lomata* will be transmitted as "manioc which lies in the fallow ground";[141] announcement to a traveling father of the birth of his child (in the Stanleyville area) will be sent as "set the heart down (don't worry), the child has not set down his feet (has not remained) in the black body of the mother"; a message of death may be sent as "tears in the eyes, wailing in the mouth" together with the name of the deceased.[142]

The hollowed out slit-drum used for telegraphy is capable of emitting at least two pitches. This is due to the different thicknesses of the two lips surrounding the slit, the thicker giving a high tone and the thinner a low tone. Among the Lokele of the Stanleyville area, the low lip, *limiki lya otomali*, is the "voice of the female," and the high lip, *limiki lya otolomi* is the "voice of the male."[143] This seems to reverse the usual male-female characteristics, but actually the concept of "high" is not one of direction but of size and quality, and the same may be said of "low." Hence, "high" means large, strong, because of its more penetrating quality, while "low" means small, weak, because of its duller timbre. Such usage of the two terms is not limited to primitive groups, but

---

[139] Cf. the present author's review of Japanese *Gagaku* in *Journal of the American Musicological Society*, X (1957), pp. 39–44. The method is also related to the Hindu solmization method, in which special syllables are used for drum pattern memorizing. Cf. Curt Sachs, *Rise*, p. 187 f.

[140] J. Jacobs, ". . . de Tetela," p. 410.

[141] J. F. Carrington, "Drum Language of the Lokele Tribe," *African Studies*, III (1944), pp. 75–88.

[142] J. F. Carrington, *Talking Drums of Africa* (London, 1949), pp. 55, 57.

[143] J. F. Carrington, *Talking Drums*, p. 25.

appears in the Middle Eastern world – Arab and Hebrew – and was also probably characteristic of Ancient Greece.[144] Apparently, the concept that is based on direction is primarily a Western one.

The slit idiophone appears in a variety of shapes and sizes, one of the most popular being the bitonemal cylinder (averaging two to three feet in length). This is found particularly in the Stanleyville area, where it is struck with rubber-ball tipped sticks.[145] It is also found in the Kasai area (southwest Belgian Congo, where it is called *kiendú*) together with the wedge-shaped suspended slit-drum (the *kinguvú*) capable of emitting four tones.[146] The north Belgian Congo knows the footed slit-drum as well. (Note, for example, the giant, footed, animal-head drum of the Mangbetu.) When the membranophonous *ngoma* dance-drum is employed for signalling it is sometimes used in pairs in order to obtain the required pitch contrasts. Thus, the Ashanti and Ewe of West Africa utilize paired *ngoma* signal drums, one high- and one low-toned drum comprising the pair.[147] However, the double-toned single *ngoma* also exists and is found, for example, in the Kasai area, where it is called *gapimbi* or *gapagala* (the first name referring to a larger *ngoma* of c. 11″ by 29″, and the second referring to a smaller *ngoma* of c. 10″ by 20″).[148] It should be noted that membrane drums are generally struck by hand rather than by stick (although exceptions exist), such a method allowing for the greater rhythmic flexibility so necessary to dance accompaniments.

A Bambala (southwest Belgian Congo) drum message is given in one of the transcriptions appended to the present work.[149] Its subject is the termination of a tribunal and is delivered by the chief himself upon a small cylindrical slit-drum (struck with sticks). The tones are limited to two.[150]

[144] Thus, the highest note of the Greek scale was called *nētē* (low), the lowest, *hypátē* (high); the dark Hebrew vowel, o, is called "high," and represented by a dot placed *above* the consonant, while the brilliant vowel, ee, is considered "low," with a dot placed *below* the consonant; the Arabs use dashes instead of dots for similar designations, and also use the term "high" for a man's voice and "low" for a woman's voice. See Curt Sachs, *Rise*, pp. 69–70; also *History of Instruments*, p. 135.

[145] J. F. Carrington, *Talking Drums*, p. 26.

[146] G. Vancoillie, "... Kumbu... du Kasai," p. 37.

[147] J. F. Carrington, *Talking Drums*, p. 25.

[148] G. Vancoillie, "... Kumbu... du Kasai," p. 37.

[149] See Transcr. 23; also cf. "Music for Litigation," above.

[150] A trapeze-shaped slit drum, the *lukumbi* or *lokombé*, of the Batetela of the central Belgian Congo has as many as six tones, three on each side of the drum. Although the language is bitonemal, three to six tones are used for signalling. The six tones cover the span of a major ninth and run through a "scale" reminiscent of the last inversion of a dominant seventh chord. See Dorothy R. Gilbert, "The Lukumbi, a six-toned slit drum of the Batetela," *African Music*, I (1955), No. 2, p. 21; also J. Jacobs, "Signaaltrommeltaal bij de Tetela," p. 409. (The *lukumbi* drum is not to be confused with the *longombé* bow-lute of the Lake Leopold region of the Belgian Congo. See G. Hulstaert, "Note sur les instruments ... à l'Équateur," p. 193; also Joseph Maes-Tervueren, "Les Lukombe ou instruments de musique à cordes des populations du Kasai – Lac Léopold II – Lukenie," *Zeitschrift für Ethnologie*, LXX (1939), pp. 240–254.

CHAPTER FOUR

THE MUSIC

Several hints have been given in the last chapter concerning the vigorous, dynamic, outgoing nature of Central African musical expression. In specific terms, how uniform is this character and what does it mean? Do broad-leaped melodies, belligerent rhythms, and volcanic performance mark all tribal music? Furthermore, what does musical organization here signify in terms of pristine simplicity and sophisticated complexity, and what bearing, if any, does organization level have upon the leaping musical temperament?

  Some readers may be sorely disappointed to find a mousy, timid little tune almost concealing itself within the confines of a minor second and displaying no more rhythmic curiosity than a straight-laced 6/8; or a slightly bolder major-third melody without any particular rhythmic personality. Somewhere along the much-traveled forest paths lie concealed the atomic elements of any musical corpus and the more variegated and loosely bound this corpus the more apt are the elements to break free at the slightest provocation. In the course of our investigation, it will be seen that, while Central African music is indeed in a molecular rather than an atomic stage, basic particles often separate themselves from the parent body to exist independently or, what is more common, live rebelliously within the confines of the more developed parent network. This is particularly true of melody, although rhythm, polyphony, and form warrant occasional attention in varying proportions.

MELODY TYPES

One- or Two-Step Nucleus

The types ranging from the one- or two-step chant through the broader melody spanning an octave or more, may be found in nearly all areas, sometimes existing as extremes within the same tribe. Generally (although exceptions exist), the compressed, nuclear melody belongs to the sacred or ceremonial category of tribal expression, strictly guarded and reserved for only those occasions at which magico-religious factors come into play. Thus, the Bapere of the northeast Belgian Congo intone on a miniature phrase of three tones confined to a major third, when invoking the spirit of the fearful circumcision bird (Ex. 1, Transcr. 8[1]), but also have a more expanded vocal melody in

---

[1] "Example" refers to the music examples given in the body of this chapter (Chapter IV); "Transcription" refers to the transcriptions appended in Part II, from which the music examples are excerpted. The music example in the text may often be condensed from several lines in order to show the total effect.

the form of a pentachordal fanfare used for circumcision dancing (Ex. 2, Transcr. 7). Both types are related, however, in their emphasis on the interval of the third, limited compass, and chanted repetitiveness, the first melody being the more simple or primal. It is of interest to note that the expanded pentachord fanfare is a dance accompaniment, whereas the intoned major-third melody is a purely vocal recitation:

Ex. 1. Bapere Circumcision Bird (Belg. Congo)
        Transcr. 8, meas. 6 f

Ex. 2. Bapere Circumcision Dance (Belg. Congo)
        Transcr. 7, meas. 3 f

A "warming-up" device, calling to mind a Wagnerian melodic habit,[2] may be noted in Ex. 2, in the last three notes (a'–g'–e'), which precede a re-statement of the rising pentachordal melody with which the example begins. Such a rising melody is always prepared for with this kind of force-gathering link, which serves to emphasize and make more startling the first note of the melody. A momentum-gathering vocal device of this nature, appearing often in Central African music, is no doubt related to the physico-rhythmic factors involved in the general problem of tension and release. These physico-rhythmic factors have been discussed by various writers (notably von Hornbostel),[3] usually in connection with African drum beating, the central point of discussion being the importance of the single "upbeat." However, the preparatory cluster in Ex. 2, while connected here with the squarely rhythmic movement of the percussion (see Transcr. 7) and probably with the circumcision dance movement as well, is essentially a melodic device serving tonally structural purposes. The "warming-up" or momentum-gathering in this instance is therefore both directional and durational, since it counterbalances both melodically and rhythmically.

Von Hornbostel raised the question whether the rhythmical "upbeat" (i.e., offbeat or conductor's upbeat) is not really more important than the "downbeat" since, according to him, the "upbeat" appeared to be the point of stress or tension while the

---

[2] Note, for example, the introductory, momentum-gathering cluster of notes in the *Liebestod*, on the first syllable of the adjectives in the phrase, "Wonne klagend, alles sagend."

[3] E. M. von Hornbostel, "African Negro Music," *International Institute of African Languages and Cultures*, Memorandum 4 (1928), p. 52.

"downbeat" seemed to be a point of release or relaxation. (Note that this idea derives mainly from the physiological aspects of drum playing, as observed by him.) This question is valid for square or equal-pulsed rhythm rather than for the hemiola-like or additive rhythm, discussed in our Chapter II. Additive rhythm, it must be reiterated, in its basically unaccented, irregular configurations of "longs" and "shorts" does not lend itself to analysis involving concepts of "upbeat" and "downbeat," the identifying verbal labels of Western syncopation. However, since the circumcision music given above (Ex. 2) is clearly of the regular variety of rhythm and does involve equal-pulsed beats, von Hornbostel's question can be considered here. All evidence, nevertheless, seems to point to the fact that the "upbeat" (actually a vocal melody-cluster in Ex. 2) is of less psychological and mechanical importance than the "downbeat." The "preparation" (a'–g'–e') is just that: a passage preparing for another passage (Ex. 2, meas. 1) of greater dynamics, greater density (fuller vocal orchestration), greater tonal magnetism (greater scale importance), and greater vocal resonance (not necessarily the same as fuller vocal orchestration, but a qualitative change having to do with voice-production techniques[4]). It is this second passage rather than the preparatory one that is tension-filled. More accurately, somewhat like a volcano concentrating energy just before erupting, the preparatory passage possesses the stored, concentrated tension, but the second passage makes that tension mobile – it is here that the tension breaks bounds. The explosion is not a relaxation, whether considered psychologically or mechanically.

In returning to our melody types, we find an even more restricted chant-melody than the kind spanning a third – namely the one covering only a major second, examples being provided by the upper choral ostinato of a Kuyu shaman's alligator song (Ex. 3), as well as by the choral refrain of a Baganda women's historic song (Ex. 4):

Ex. 3. Kuyu Medicine Song (French Equatorial)
Transcr. 34, meas. 7

Ex. 4. Baganda Historic Song (Uganda)
Transcr. 45, meas. 2

This restricted, major- or minor-second melody-type is also found in instrumental music. Ex. 5 shows a four-measure melody composed solely of a minor second played on

[4] See Chapter V below for a detailed discussion of resonance.

a Mboko mouth bow; Ex. 6, a four-measure major-second melody found in the upper-most of the parts assigned to a group of royal xylophones (an ensemble belonging to the Kabaka, king of the Baganda); Ex. 7, a one-measure major-second ostinato repeated in the lowest line of a Bapere xylophone piece:

Ex. 5. Mboko Song on Mouth Bow (French Eq.)
      Transcr. 25

Ex. 6. Baganda War Song on Royal Xylophones (Uganda)
      Transcr. 46, meas. 21 ff

Ex. 7. Bapere Xylophone (Belg. Congo)
      Transcr. 11, meas. 11 ff

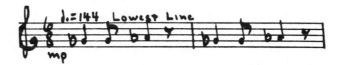

A brief horn ostinato (Ex. 8) spanning a minor third is part of the *Kuyu Medicine Song* shown above in Ex. 3:

Ex. 8. Kuyu Medicine Song (Fr. Eq.)
      Transcr. 34, meas. 1

What distinguishes these melodies encompassing a second or a third as a group, as well as from one another? Basically, they would all appear to originate from cantillation or psalmody – to represent what Curt Sachs calls the logogenic or "word-born" type of primitive music.[5] Such music serves as a vehicle for the recitation of text and is entirely secondary to it. Even the instrumental melodies (Exx. 5–8) fall into this cate-

[5] Curt Sachs, *Rise*, p. 41.

gory, as is shown in part by the fact that at least two of them are derived from vocal music (Exx. 5, 6). (African instrumentalists often use vocal music as a springboard; in fact, instrumental music is, in many cases, nothing more than the vocal melody transferred *in toto*. According to Curt Sachs, the two-tone instrumental ostinato often found in primitive music seems to be a vestige of vocal cantillation. [6])

Individually, the examples illustrate various degrees of melodic organization and pre-organization. The simplest and most primal kind of pre-organization is, of course, the one-note drone-ostinato (not given in the above examples). (The one-note drone is, in a sense, even more primal, but cannot be considered here, since a continuous note really has no organization.) However, such organization would be rhythmic rather than melodic. At least one leap or step is necessary for melody, or proto-melody to exist or be suggested. Now, assuming at least one step, it is obviously 1) the rhythmic manner of stating this step, and 2) the way in which a few of these steps succeed each other to form a larger unit, that determine melodic organization. The most rudimentary, nuclear type of organization takes place in the shortest amount of space (not time), that is, it involves the fewest number of notes put together (obviously two) and only one statement of the interval. This is illustrated in Ex. 7, a one-measure instrumental ostinato composed of three rather than two notes (♩ ♪ ♩𝄾) and depending for its identity on the rhythmic values of these notes. The major-second step is only stated once in this phrase. The most rudimentary organization is also illustrated in Ex. 3, a vocal ostinato on a major second. This type of proto-melodic organization – the very short, one-step kernel – is actually pre-organizational, for it functions on too small a level to be considered representative of melody proper. What happens once this fragment is stated further bears out the idea of rudimentary organization, for the immediate and constant repetition of this nuclear melody precludes any overall structural organization. To repeat is not necessarily to organize; it is mere seriation, suggesting a chain that may be cut at any point.

Longer patterns spanning four measures may be noted in Exx. 5 and 6. Both of these depend for identification upon the way the single step (a minor second in Ex. 5, a major second in Ex. 6) succeeds itself rather than upon rhythmic values. For example, the particular succession of f's and e's in Ex. 5 is always the same for any four measures. (Note that these longer patterns still involve only one melodic step or interval.)

The organized lengthening of the melodic nucleus may be achieved in several ways. Melodic inversion is one of these and is illustrated in Ex. 5: The last two measures of the phrase are actually an inversion of the first two. Or a phrase may be repeated with contrasting endings. Ex. 1 shows a choral phrase that is immediately repeated by the soloist (see Transcr. 8) with a different ending (i.e., where there had been an upward movement, a–b, of the choral ending there is a downward movement, c♯''–b', of the solo ending); thus, together the two statements form a larger melodic unit that seems to include something approaching partial and complete cadences. The inversion device of Ex. 5, mentioned above, serves a dual purpose, for it also contains partial- and com-

[6] Curt Sachs, *The Wellsprings of Music. An Introduction to Ethnomusicology*, MS. 1958.

plete-cadence suggestions: the first two measures end in an upward movement, e′–f′, while the last two measures end in a downward movement, f′–e′. Even Ex. 6 contains cadence suggestions, although it is not built on inversion: again the four measures are really a repeated two-measure phrase with contrasting endings, viz., d′–e′ for the first ending, e′–d′ for the second ending. These forms of inversion and cadence contrast are certainly seeds of more complex art devices.

Our examples of germinal melody are thus seen to range from the very shortest (one statement of a small interval, involving the fewest number of notes) to longer phrases involving four measures. In all of these cases, with the exception of Ex. 2, the interval is either a second or a third.[7] Now it would seem, at first glance, as if this primal type of melody is characteristic of a sizable part of Central African music. However, it should be pointed out that most of these examples are portions of more complex pieces wherein they function as either refrains or ostinatos to other melodic lines. That these refrains or ostinatos are more simple or primal than the rest of the pieces they are found in is undeniable; whether they are more *urtümlich* or chronologically earlier is perhaps not so definite. Certainly a chorus will tend to sing a simpler melody than a soloist if it is punctuating his song with a refrain or ostinato. Hence, a choral melody is not necessarily indicative of an earlier musical stage in a tribe's development.

Not all of the one- or two-step melodies, however, are refrain or ostinato sections within larger musical contexts. A few are actually the only or the leading line of a piece, and may be considered, in such instances, as representative examples of the very simplest melodic expression. The *Circumcision Bird* (Ex. 1) is one such example. Here the solo phrase, spanning a major third, is repeated by the chorus, and this alternation (with the exception of a few introductory notes at the beginning of the piece) comprises the entire song. The Mboko mouth bow melody (Ex. 5) is another illustration, for the entire piece consists of this minor-second melody, which is intermittently sung with slight variations by the soloist.[8] On the whole, however, such "pure" examples are not too common. Furthermore, it should be noted that the simplest one- and two-step melodies, whether found in more complex pieces (as is usual) or in isolated state, are spread out among all tribes and areas of Central Africa and cannot be exclusively associated with the Pygmy groups, ethnically the most primal people. The Babinga Pygmies of French Equatorial Africa, incidentally, sing in modified canon at the fifth (cf. Ex. 75 below in the present chapter), one of the most rare examples of non-unison canon among non-literate groups. (Unison canon is quite common throughout the world; cf. Chapter II.) The canon motif is constructed on the type of sparse, two-step germinal melody discussed above. Thus, strangely enough, a fusion of simplicity and complexity (of a polyphonic nature) is found in the music of the most simply organized people of Africa, the Pygmies.

[7] See Section 1 of Melody Chart, in appendix, for a larger listing of one- and two-step melodies.
[8] An entire section of a quite advanced song of the Mangbetu of the Belgian Congo (Transcr. 1, Section E) also consists of a very brief, reiterated phrase: a minor second in the chorus and a filled-in minor third in the solo part.

The Descending Tetrachord

The melody-types of Central Africa are of all varieties, as stated previously, the one-
and two-step chant melody spanning a second or a third being the least prominent
(except as part of a larger musical context). The broader scale-spans often bring with
them greater melodic organization, although not necessarily so. The short-lined motif,
reproducing itself in chain-like fashion, does not disappear when the melodic range
attains the interval of a fourth, for example. In fact, the broader-ranged one- or two-
step chant is almost as common as the chant limited to intervals of seconds or thirds.
Thus, there may be found the single leap of a fourth as a choral ostinato in a Wameru
spell-breaking party song (Ex. 9); or a two-step phrase spanning the interval of a
fourth in a choral ostinato of the Mambuti Pygmies (Ex. 10); or a two-step refrain
within a fourth in a N'Gundi girls' song (Ex. 11); or a two-step ostinato within a fourth
in a Yaswa xylophone piece (Ex. 12):

Ex. 9. Wameru Spell-Breaking Song (Tanganyika)
  Transcr. 51, meas. 3 ff

Ex. 10. Mambuti Pygmies (Belg. Congo)
  Transcr. 14, meas. 1 f

Ex. 11. N'Gundi Girls (Fr. Eq.)
  Transcr. 29, meas. 3 f

Ex. 12. Yaswa Xylophones (Fr. Eq.)
  Transcr. 32, meas. 28 f

These four examples still show the compressed, nuclear motif in its very primal state.
However, more deliberate melodic organization, constructed on the interval of the

fourth, may also be found. Such organization usually involves more notes (a longer melody) and greater rhythmic contrast among these notes. This is illustrated in two sections (Exx. 13 and 14) of a Mangbetu choral song which, as a whole, is of a more advanced style. The second section actually spans a fifth, but the fourth is the important base:

Ex. 13. Mangbetu Song (Belg. Congo)
　　　Transcr. 1, Section B

Ex. 14. Mangbetu Song (Belg. Congo)
　　　Transcr. 1, Section I)

Most of the tetrachordal melodies are descending (in fact, it will be seen later that, with the exception of those having a pentachord or pentachordal-octave structure, nearly all of the transcribed melodies are descending). Whether this phenomenon is allied to the natural tendency of the human voice to descend (assuming Central African music to be vocally based), particularly when singing emotional, longer-lined melody, or whether the tetrachord carries within it some innate, gravitational pull downward, cannot be categorically stated. The ascending pentachord and octave found in vocal music (that is, not instrumentally derived) must be accounted for, if the first explanation is accepted. Probably factors of psycho-ethnic make-up enter into the problem whether a group sings on an upward, increasing, explosive or on a falling, fading out, "resigned" movement.[9] (These are, of course, broad divisions. In practice, melodic contours are almost always combinations of rising and falling levels. Furthermore, a great deal of "explosiveness" exists in many African descending melodies, an explosiveness deriving from singing style rather than from direction.)

The Central African tetrachord is both partially and completely filled in. The partially filled, or chasmatonic [10] variety usually belongs to the very brief, ostinato type of

---

[9] It should be noted that an entire musical complex, that of the Far and Middle East, rests upon a tetrachordal structure, and that the music of this area is essentially a descending vocal music. See C. Sachs, *Rise*, p. 306 f.

[10] Cf. Chapter II above for discussion of *chasmatonic* (i.e., gapped melody) and *diatonic* (i.e., through or ungapped melody).

melody illustrated above. In fact, this type of melody is rarely completely filled in, or diatonic. When it *is* diatonic, the tetrachord is generally part of a more expanded melody pattern (note the two Mangbetu sections, Exx. 13 and 14). It would be fallacious, however, to deduce that diatonicism necessarily belongs to the more advanced, more organized melodies, and chasmatonicism to the primal motifs. While these primal motifs are generally chasmatonic (particularly when they are built on the tetrachord), the longer-lined, larger-ranged melodies are either chasmatonic (pentatonic when in octave form) or diatonic. Furthermore, the two types may exist side by side within the music of a single tribe, or even within the same piece (see the *Mangbetu Song*, Belgian Congo, Transcr. 1, Sections A and C). Apparently, diatonicism has become firmly established on the African musical scene, but without supplanting its precursor, chasmatonicism.

Whether a tetrachord is diatonic or chasmatonic seems to have no bearing on the kinds of seconds appearing within it. Both major and minor seconds, as well as shades in between, exist in various combinations. We find the old Greek Dorian prototype [11] – descending major third, minor second – in a more complex, long-lined melody of the Batwa Pygmies of Ruanda (Ex. 15). In this case, the tetrachord is part of a melody spanning a tenth:

Ex. 15. Batwa Pygmies Dance-Song (Ruanda)
　　　　Transcr. 16, meas. 3

The Bahutu, of the same community as the Batwa, also sing on a Dorian-like tetrachord in one of their dance-songs (Ex. 16). Here the tetrachord is subsumed within an octave structure: [12]

Ex. 16. Bahutu Dance-Song (Ruanda)
　　　　Transcr. 17, meas. 8 f

The non-hemitonic tetrachord – ancestor of the Greek Phrygian – appears to be more common, however, than the Dorian prototype. The intervals, a descending minor third

---

[11] Curt Sachs, *Rise*, pp. 220–221.

[12] Richard A. Waterman finds the Bahutu melody to be the same as the American Negro song "Run Old Jeremiah." See "African Influence on the Music of the Americas," in Sol Tax, *Acculturation in the Americas* (Chicago, 1952), II, p. 216.

plus a major second, may be joined in any order, but the most characteristic combination is the one just mentioned (viz., third plus second, descending). An excellent illustration of this is the Mambuti Pygmy choral ostinato, c′–a–g, of Ex. 10. This type of tetrachord is one of the most important skeletal bases of the many octave-melodies of Central Africa and generally appears at the lower end of the octave in what would be called a "plagal" form (in contradistinction to the Western "authentic" form, which displays the fourth at the upper end of the octave). Thus, many melodies seem to revolve about a central pivot point from which a fifth extends upward and a fourth, downward. It is not hard to see one possible genesis of this type of octave: a major-third nuclear motif disposed in an ascending fanfare to form a triad and extended below by a subsidiary ostinato tetrachord. The *Bapere Circumcision* music given above (Ex. 2) illustrates such a scheme.

The Rising Pentachord Fanfare

The nuclear motifs of seconds or thirds somehow seem to determine the manner of melody enlargement, broadly speaking. The tetrachord appears to rest on the second, despite the presence of the third. That the appearance is really a fact seems to be indicated by the manner in which our tetrachordal melodies behave: pivot points within these melodies feature the second. Thus, for example, the *N'Gundi Girls'* motif, c′–d′–a (Ex. 17), is chopped up by the solo line, which appropriates and emphasizes the upper second, c′–d′ (this being actually part of a nuclear motif of two seconds joined by the central tone, d′):

Ex. 17. N'Gundi Girls (Fr. Eq.)
      Transcr. 29, meas. 4

This point is further illustrated in a Banyoro xylophone melody built on the fourth, which also gravitates towards the second (Ex. 18):

Ex. 18. Banyoro Xylophone (Uganda)
      Transcr. 40, meas. 1 f

On the other hand, nuclear motifs built on the third tend to open out into the pentachord, and, quite often, in an ascending manner as already indicated. This drive upward is usually realized as a fanfare, i.e., as a large-stepped or chasmatonic type of pentachord, 1–3–5. The Bapere, Bantu of the northeast Belgian Congo (see Chapter I above), favor rising pentachordal melodies of the fanfare shape (*Circumcision Dance*, Ex. 19; *The Flagellation*, Ex. 20 – note the diminished fifths). A proximal and ethnically related tribe, the Babira, also have rising pentachordal melodies (*Circumcision Dance*, Ex. 21; *Choral Song*, Ex. 22).

May we speak of a "pentachordal complex" for this sector? Probably, but with several reservations. The Mambuti Pygmies also live in this area and musically show some tetrachordal orientation. The Mangbetu, who are not far off, have both penta-chordal and tetrachordal melodies. However, neither of these groups is of the Bantu family, the Pygmies belonging to their own nomadic stem, the Mangbetu to the Sudanic people. The question, therefore, might be altered to read, "May we speak of a Bantu pentachordal complex for this area?" The term "complex" is, of course, strong in its implications, calling forth images of vast, sweeping, all-embracing qualities. Actually we are searching for something of this nature when we attempt to classify, organize, generalize basic patterns and orders of things. When these basic patterns, however, are numerous and overlapping, and the picture multifarious, uncompromising classification is dangerous and the term "complex" too suggestive. Nevertheless, a little danger is unavoidable in the early stages of drawing up a schema, and it seems that we may speak of a "Bantu pentachordal complex for this area" if it is understood that this complex is not necessarily exclusive of others. That this is an important complex, an early or *urtümlich* one, cannot be doubted. The pentachord pervades a religious, traditional category of expression – the music of circumcision rituals.

Ex. 19. Bapere Circumcision Dance (Belg. Cong.)
    Transcr. 7, meas. 3

Ex. 20. Bapere Flagellation (Belg. Congo)
    Transcr. 9, meas. 2

Ex. 21. Babira Circumcision Dance (Belg. Congo)
    Transcr. 6, meas. 3 f

Ex. 22. Babira Choral Song (Belg. Congo)
         Transcr. 3, meas. 5 f

Pentachordal melodies are, of course, not confined to the northeast Belgian Congo. They are widespread, sometimes in the skeletal form of the pure pentachord, 1–3–5, but more often in octave and other enlargements. The top line of a Wanyamwezi wedding song adapted to the sanza, the thumb-plucked idiophone, again illustrates the behavior of the pure pentachord (Ex. 23):

Ex. 23. Wanyamwezi Wedding Song on Sanza (Tanganyika)
         Transcr. 49, meas. 3 f

Hexachordal Melodies

The larger-ranged melodies are quite common in Central Africa, appearing under all circumstances and in nearly all tribal areas. Such melodies are more numerous than the nuclear motifs of seconds and thirds which, as described above, are usually ostinato accompaniments or episodes within larger-ranged pieces. It would be fallacious, however, to expect greater melodic organization where just the span is increased. There is no logically (or musically) inherent necessity about the concomitance of the two factors. The short, immediately reiterated motif may exist as a second-span variety as well as in the form of an octave-span variety. (Of course, melodic line or *length* tends to be greater where range is increased, since an octave, for example, if it is not conceived as an open leap, has the possibility of more notes than a second-span melody.)

Among the wider-spanned types are the hexachordal melodies, which appear in Central Africa in several forms. Scale-genesis runs the gamut of pentachord plus second (Ex. 24), tetrachord plus third (Ex. 25; cf. also Ex. 14), or second plus tetrachord plus second (Ex. 26),[13] while melodic organization varies from the abbreviated chant-motif (Ex. 24) to more involved patterns (Ex. 25):

[13] Pentachord plus second is represented in Ex. 24 by c′–g′, g′–a′; tetrachord plus third in Ex. 25 by e′–a′, a′–c♯″ (the a′, while not too prominent in this choral example, appears as a strong focal point in the solo melody of Ex. 14, upon which the choral phrase is based); second plus tetrachord plus second in Ex. 26 by b♭–c′, c′–f′, f′–g′.

Ex. 24. Wachaga Chief-Praise Song (Tanganyika)
Transcr. 50, meas. 1 f

Ex. 25. Mangbetu Choral Song (Belg. Congo)
Transcr. 1, Section I

Ex. 26. Baganda Historic Song with Harp (Uganda)
Transcr. 44, meas. 3 f

The hexachord often seems to arise from variation techniques, e.g., a soloist may interject a second as an "upper auxiliary" in order to embroider a pentachordal choral melody (cf. Transcr. 6, meas. 5 f, *Babira Circumcision Dance*), or he may, upon repetition, vary his own melody with "addendum" notes to reach the hexachord range (Transcr. 7, meas. 4, *Bapere Circumcision Dance*). At this stage, the hexachord is still fluid, not being fully solidified, and may almost be considered of an ornamental nature. (The harp melody of Ex. 26 appears to fall into this category, the f pedal-note together with the c below it forming a hard center to which the other notes are attached. Note, incidentally, the syllables of the singer. These appear to be connected with the educational techniques discussed in Chapter III, under "Speech Melody and the 'Talking' Drum.")

Minor Seventh With Tritone Effect

A quality of intensity and suspense (what Western thinking would ally with the "unresolved chord") makes itself felt in a certain type of melody constructed on the tritone (i.e., the "augmented fourth"). The effect is entirely one of restless motion and anticipation that somehow are never satisfactorily terminated – as if a rousing theatre prelude continues indefinitely, blocking the rise of the stage curtains. Undoubtedly, these melodies impress the Western listener as being more emotion-charged than the others. Actually, there is no reason to assume that this is the case, for any structure, any style might carry with it something vital to the performer and native listener. Nevertheless, there does seem to be some innate quality to the tritone that implies bold dramatic tension, and the possible connection between Central African "extrovert" art-expression and the wide prevalence of this melody-type should not be ignored.

Specifically, these melodies usually cover or emphasize a minor seventh and are both diatonic and chasmatonic. The minor seventh further enhances the feeling of the "unresolved," sometimes evoking the quality of a "dominant seventh," an "incomplete dominant ninth," and other Western seventh-chords. There is, of course, danger in this kind of thinking, but it is mitigated by an awareness of the context with which we are concerned.

Most of our illustrations are instrumental, but it seems certain that on the whole they are vocally derived melodies. Thus, for example, the instruments of the *Bapere Horns* (Ex. 27) play one tone each to form what very strongly resembles the Circumcision dance-songs of this tribe and of its neighbor, the Babira (Transcr. 6, 7). The vertically combined sounds of all the horns span a minor tenth but most of the melodic movement revolves about the upper pentachord (c'–e'–g'). The tritone effect (allied to an inverted "dominant ninth") is unmistakable:

Ex. 27. Bapere Horns (1 note each) (Belg. Congo)
   Transcr. 10, meas. 5 f

The Mambuti Pygmies sing a long-lined tritonic melody at their elephant feast (Ex. 28), and for their flute dance after the feast have a related melody of a more terse, symmetric character (Ex. 29):

Ex. 28. Mambuti Pygmies Elephant Feast Song (Belg. Congo)
   Transcr. 12, meas. 1 f

Ex. 29. Mambuti Wooden Flutes (1-toned) (Belg. Congo)
   Transcr. 13, meas. 1

An example from French Equatorial Africa shows undeniably the instrumental-anticipation of a vocal melody, again of a tritone nature (note the one-beat quasi-canonic lag between voice and horns) (Ex. 30):

Ex. 30. Kukuya Ivory Horns (1 note each) (Fr. Eq.)
Transcr. 33, meas. 4

These tritone melodies seem to hint at two possibilities concerning their genesis: In the first place, a major-third nuclear motif, in its growth towards the pentachord, connects with the fifth by means of a raised fourth (e.g. c′–d′–e′–f♯′–g′), somewhat in the manner of the Chinese *pièn*.[14] This possibility is illustrated in another group of examples given later.[15] The later group, however, does not emphasize the tritone, either melodically or vertically, and the effect is not the same as in the examples given above, wherein the raised fourth is not treated as a passing tone but assumes a vital role in the melodic movement.

The second and stronger possibility is the extension of the major-third nucleus *downward* by a major second (e.g., e′–d′–c′–b♭). Superficially, the two explanations appear identical, since in both cases a major second is appended at different ends of a major third, but the scale emphases are quite different. The uppermost note of the tritone is not considered a filler- or passing-note, in the second explanation, but an important spinal note, the "3" of the scale in a hypothetical 1–2–3–5–7♭ structure. This would account for the strong emphasis on the tritone in the examples given. In practice, the hypothetical structure is, of course, inverted: The "7♭" appears at the *bottom*, i.e., 7♭–1–2–3–5, so that many of these melodies move downward towards the "7♭" (viz., e′–d′–c′–b♭). In *all* the tritone examples, without exception, the "7♭" – whether melodic or vertical – stands out as a vital focal point. As is hardly necessary to say, an harmonic function of the "7♭" as a "lowered leading-tone" should not be considered implied by the above discussion. The tone is neither lowered nor leading in this music and has no chord-progression character.[16]

Octave Melodies: Descending and Ascending

Octave melodies are found throughout most of Central Africa, appearing in so many different varieties that classification as to type (i.e., with regard to pentatonicism,

[14] Curt Sachs, *Rise*, p. 134.

[15] See the *Baduma Paddlers* (Fr. Eq.), Transcr. 37, 38, and the *Wahehe Elephant Hunt* (Tang.), Transcr. 52, under Octave-Melodies later in this chapter.

[16] The tritone also appears in other areas of the world, notably among the East-Florinese tribes. See Jaap Kunst, *Music in Flores, A Study of the vocal and instrumental Music among the Tribes living in Flores* (Leyden, 1942), pp. 35 ff.

diatonicism, length, inner organization, etc.) seems almost impossible. A broad division concerning direction, however, appears to be a likely starting point.

The descending octave-melodies are, on the whole, more numerous than the ascending ones, and the two types are not mutually exclusive, even so far as the music of a single tribe may be concerned (although this is not common). Nearly all of the melodies that have come to our attention are organized rhythmically (whether in regular or hemiolic patterns), only a few examples being of the freely flowing pathogenic type. Significantly, these are Arabic-influenced and belong to the Watutsi of Ruanda. The "pathos" or emotion underlying these pieces, however, is not of the raw, unleashed, elemental variety found in the primeval type discussed by Curt Sachs. In this type, "descending melodies recall savage shouts of joy or rage and may have come from such unbridled outbursts." [17] The chamber-like, subdued singing of the Watutsi bards is eons away from the convulsive, unrestrained eruptions of such expression. However, the root is the same: melody shaped by emotion rather than by text. Indeed, the Watutsi octave-fall, in its melismatic, spasmodic tumble from a boldly attacked peak, and the open leap upward again strongly suggest a transfigured, "aristocratic" realization of the primeval explosions (Ex. 31):

Ex. 31. Watutsi Epic Song of War (Ruanda)
      Transcr. 20, hummed introduction

The Middle East breathes through this music not only in the ecstatic ornaments and coloraturas, but also in the tetrachordal scale structure, something the unorganized melodic precursors hardly possess. The intimate (to the present writer) and enthusiastic (to Aristotle [18]) color of the ancient Greek Phrygian scale quite clearly pervades the Watutsi example in its flow downward. In skeleton form this emerges as: $e\flat''-d\flat''-c''-b\flat'$ $a\flat'-g\flat'-f'-e\flat'$, or two disjunct tetrachords. The *umurego* or hummed introduction further adds to the Oriental flavor, recalling the Hindu *ālāpa* and the Turkish *taqsīm* (and even the Indonesian *bebuka*), the free, introductory sections of most pieces.

---

[17] Curt Sachs, *Rise*, p. 41. The term "pathogenic" is used by Curt Sachs to describe one of the two basic musical styles, i.e., the "emotion-derived" style. The other of the two styles is the "logogenic" or "word-born" style.

[18] Aristotle, *Politics*, VIII: 5, 1340b.

The descending, emotion-propelled octave-melody is not limited to the Watutsi. In its more African, non-Arabic variety, however, it assumes greater symmetry and terseness of form as well as a bolder, physical vitality which somehow seems to represent a less personal and more communal emotion. The Mangbetu pentatonic, almost Gilbert and Sullivanesque excerpt (Ex. 32), the *Bongili Girls'* diatonic melody (Ex. 33), and the *Okandi Women's* diatonic melody (Ex. 34) illustrate the sheer straight-line drop down the octave, i.e., without significant direction change:

Ex. 32. Mangbetu Choral Song (Belg. Congo)
Transcr. 1, Section C)

Ex. 33. Bongili's Girls' Banana Work Song (Fr. Eq.)
Transcr. 36, meas. 2 f

Ex. 34. Okandi Women's Dance Song (Fr. Eq.)
Transcr. 39, meas. 2

The curving melody is more usual, however, and may assume several shapes, one of which is quite often present and is obviously strongly allied to the predilection for the third. In this type of melody the movement is distinctly zig-zag, conjuring up an almost exact picture of a jagged line, thus: \\/\\/\\. Such tertial melodic movement often is accompanied by parallel thirds, and the entire impression is that of an underlying

$$1\text{--}3\text{--}5$$

scale built on dovetailed (interlocking) triads, e.g., 2–4–6. In a sense, these double triads might be viewed as constituting the double pentachord fanfare (cf. "pentachord-fanfare" above in this chapter), except that the melodic movement here is not fanfare-like but zig-zag. It is in the extracted scale pattern that the fanfare lies. An excellent vocal example of the zig-zag melody with parallel thirds is found among the Mangbetu (Ex. 35),[19] while a Baduma song (Ex. 36) shows voice and sanza combined in a similar

[19] A vocal example of zig-zag thirds without "parallelism" may be noted in the *Wanyamwezi Chief Installation* (Tang.), Transcr. 48, meas. 14 f.

pattern, with the f♯ *pièn* included in the scale. (In effect, the raised degree is the result of the dovetailing of two *major* triads.):

Ex. 35. Mangbetu Choral Song (Belg. Congo)
    Transcr. 1, meas 5 f

Ex. 36. Baduma Paddlers with Sanza (Fr. Eq.)
    Transcr. 38, meas. 6 f

Other kinds of curving octave-melodies exist, none of which seem to adhere to any sharply defined type as does the zig-zag melody. Probably there are as many different melody-shapes as there are tribes in Central Africa. The combination of directions, in addition to adding variety to a melody, often results in the melodic sectioning and contrast of more diversified song-form. The rising and descending "question and answer" pair seems naturally to derive from a multi-directional approach. Typical of this more symmetrically balanced curve is the pentatonic Batwa Pygmy music of Ex. 37, which is the opening of a longer section marked by a completely descending motif (Ex. 15). The "authentic" scale organization of the octave, i.e., tetrachord *above* penta-

chord (a–c′–e′–f′–a′) is apparent in the melodic portion from the high point on:

Ex. 37. Batwa Pygmy Chorus (Ruanda)
    Transcr. 16, meas. 1

The true octave-rise is rare; only four modified examples come to our attention, and two of these belong to the same tribe, the Kuyu of French Equatorial Africa. This type of melody (Exx. 38, 39) apparently derives from the pentachord fanfare.

Ex. 38. Kuyu Medicine Song (Fr. Eq.)
   Transcr. 34, meas. 1 f

Ex. 39. Wanyamwezi Chief Installation Song (Tang.)
   Transcr. 48, meas. 38 f

The f♯ *pièn* referred to under "tritone melodies" and illustrated in the zig-zag octave-melody of Ex. 36 (*Baduma Paddlers with Sanza*) may be clearly seen again in its diatonic capacity in two other octave melodies, one a curving octave-ascent (Ex. 40) and the other an octave-descent (Ex. 41). (Note that two of the examples, 36 and 40 come from the same tribe, the Baduma, and that the f♯ is here used interchangeably with f♮):

Ex. 40. Baduma Paddlers (Fr. Eq.)
   Transcr. 37, meas. 1 f

Ex. 41. Wahehe Elephant Hunt (Tanganyika)
   Transcr. 52, meas. 11 f

Supra-Octave Ladder of Thirds

The piling of third upon third, a logical outgrowth of triadic orientation, often extends beyond the octave. Ladders of thirds appear not to have any starting point, or true tonic, melodic motion flowing almost indiscriminately from one triad to another. The thirds connect in alternate major and minor intervals, as they usually do in shorter-ranged melodies. (The double minor-third movement, i.e., diminished fifth, occasionally appears and has been pointed out in connection with the Bapere flagellation music, Ex. 20; it also appears in the tritonic melodies as a lower inversion of the augmented fourth.)

The Batwa Pygmies, who have distinct octave-organization, as demonstrated by the minor-like melody of Transcr. 16 (cf. Exx. 15, 37), also have the tertial ladder. This ladder seems to be fitted for climbing down rather than up (the overall movement is descending), and the effect is highly pathogenic, strongly marked by violent attacks at the peak and unrestrained catapulting downward. Four thirds, spanning a ninth, latch on to each other in this music (Ex. 42):

Ex. 42. Batwa Pygmies (Ruanda)
         Transcr. 15, meas. 3 f

Two other examples of the ladder of thirds come to our attention, one (bb′–g′–eb′–c′–a) in a song of the Wachaga of Tanganyika in praise of a chief (Transcr. 50, meas. 9f) and the other in a song of the Mangbetu of the Belgian Congo (Transcr. 1, Section J). The Mangbetu melody does not extend beyond the octave but is confined to the span of a minor seventh (b′–g#′–e′–c#′).

Non-tempered Intervals

The subject of intonation, or interval-tuning, seems to provide a logical finale to our investigation of melody-types. Central African chasmatonic, diatonic, small-ranged, and large-ranged scales found in the melody-types include intervals in a large variety of sizes. The equal-tempered twelve-tone octave of the West is definitely not a home-grown, indigenous African product. The 100-cent [20] minor second found on the Steinway piano and theoretically in the playing of a first-desk orchestral violin rarely appears in Central African tribal music, but instead is supplanted (actually heralded) by its multi-shaped fat and thin relatives, small and large minor seconds.[21] Concomitantly, there are all sizes of thirds, fourths, fifths, and other intervals.

[20] Reference is here made to the Ellis cent-system whereby the octave of 1200 cents is divided into twelve equal semitones of 100 cents each: the Western equal-tempered scale. Cf. Curt Sachs, *Rise*, p. 27 ff; also Jaap Kunst, *Ethnomusicology* (The Hague, 1955), p. 12 ff.

[21] The "just" or acoustical minor second is non-existent as a single entity, for there are different sizes of "just" minor seconds, depending upon where the second occurs in the octave. Thus, between e and f, the just interval is larger than the equal-tempered semitone; between c and c#, the just interval is smaller.

What are some of the tunings found in Central Africa, and how significant are these tunings from the point of view of norms? That is, may a xylophone tuning found in the northeast Belgian Congo be considered a theoretical standard for that area, or even tribe, consciously aimed at by local instrument-makers?

In an ethnically fluid and rapidly changing area like Central Africa it is difficult to speak flatly of the non-existence of musical theory. Mathematical, physical musical theory is, of course, easily excluded, for its existence in tribal, non-literate societies is quite incongruous with their make-up. However, musical norms do exist (what is tradition if not the subscription to a norm?), and there is evidence that scale intonation is a part of such norms, although the manner of cultural transmission is mainly one of musical memory. K. P. Wachsmann describes a three-hour xylophone tuning session in Uganda in which a "specialist-tuner" was called upon to "correct" by ear the builder's preliminary tuning.[22] Clearly, no two instruments could ever be tuned *exactly* alike by such a method, but the process does indicate some ideal pattern, no matter how flexible.

The result of the xylophone tuning session referred to above was an approximation of an isotonic octave of five steps, each step roughly 240 cents. This is, in effect, the *salendro* scale of Indonesia. Jaap Kunst has also shown evidence of Indonesian tunings in Central African xylophones: Of the 96 he tested, 69 were in the *pelog* scale (major third plus semitone, to the tetrachord), 15 in the *salendro* scale, and the remainder in mixtures as well as in pre-*salendro*.[23] Of the four xylophone transcriptions in the present work, only one, that of the loose-log xylophone [24] of the northeast Belgian Congo approximates Indonesian tunings; the effect is *salendro*-like in the middle range (a six-step isotonic octave is probably aimed at) and *pelog*-like at the extremes. The "whole-tone" scale of the middle range has one large "second" of 253 cents and mostly narrow seconds of *c.* 185 cents.[25]

The Uganda xylophones, on the other hand, appear to be tuned by Western-influenced ears, since most of the intervals (minor thirds and major seconds within a pentatonic octave) differ from their Western counterparts by a negligible number of cents.[26] The French Equatorial xylophone,[27] tuned pentatonically, has an assortment of seconds and thirds, some close to Western tunings and others approximating the *salendro* "neutral" intervals, e.g., 253 cents, 240 cents, 270 cents. The last two intervals appear

[22] K. P. Wachsmann, "A Study of Norms in the Tribal Music of Uganda," *Ethnomusicology, Jr. of the Society for Ethnomusicology,* I, 11 (Sept. 1957), pp. 9–16.

[23] Jaap Kunst, ". . . Cultural Relationship between Indonesia . . . and Central Africa," p. 66.

[24] Loose-log xylophones without resonators are the instruments of the Belgian Congo and Uganda transcriptions. A root name for the fixed-log xylophone of the Belgian Congo is *malimba* or *madimba,* for the free-log xylophone of the north Belgian Congo, *padingbwa*; the Uganda xylophone is called *madinda* (among the Baganda). See Olga Boone, "Les Xylophones du Congo Belge," *Annales du Musée du Congo Belge, Tervueren. Ethnographie,* Série III, Tome III, Fasc. 2 (1936), p. 97 f; also, M. Trowell and K.P. Wachsmann, *Tribal Crafts of Uganda,* p. 317.

[25] See Transcr. 11, Cent-Frequency chart.

[26] Cent-Frequency charts: *Banyoro Xylophone* (Uganda), Transcr. 40; *Baganda Royal Xylophones* (Uganda), Transcr. 46. The 240-cent interval does not appear here.

[27] Cent-Frequency chart: *Yaswa Xylophones* (Fr. Eq.), Transcr. 32. These xylophones have calabash resonators.

in a prominent tetrachord, b–a–f♯, and suggest attempts to equalize the degrees within the fourth and to blend seconds and thirds.

Two of the three sanza [28] transcriptions again show Western tuning influence.[29] The third example,[30] however, has a somewhat different intonation, e.g., it includes a minor second of 71 cents. The voice, incidentally, also makes use of this small minor second in its melody.

The winds, particularly, show distinctive interval-tunings, not one of which is Western (playing techniques, e.g., lip adjustments, may have something to do with this, rather than the instruments themselves). The one-note horns of reed of the Bapere (Belgian Congo) include, when answering one another in hocket, a large major second of 214 cents (Transcr. 10); the royal *makondere*, gourd horns of the Banyoro (Uganda), play a major second of 228 cents and an open "fifth" of 643 cents (Transcr. 41); the bamboo flute ensemble of the Bamba (Uganda) plays a "fifth" of 661 cents and an augmented "fourth" of 578 cents (Transcr. 43); while the one-note ivory horns of the Kukuya (French Equatorial Africa) play, in ensemble, a large major second of 227 cents and small minor thirds of 283 and 279 cents (Transcr. 33).

A cappella vocal intonation is, of course, flexible, as all human singing is, but occasionally the intonation is markedly "different" and apparently deliberately so. This is true, for example, of the *Mambuti Pygmy Elephant Song* (Belgian Congo, Transcr. 12, meas. 9 ff) where the solo quite consistently, at certain places, sings in *salendro*-like intervals of *c.* 240 cents, viz., a–g̿, f–d̥–c; it is also true of the Arabic-influenced Watutsi singer, who includes sharpening and flattening of sustained notes as well as an occasional large major second (Ruanda, Transcr. 20).

RHYTHM

The rhythmic personality of Central Africa is, in one of its aspects, quite pronounced. For the Western listener it is what is "different" that draws attention and that he tends to consider the important identifying characteristic of any non-Western musical style. Hence, it is the unfamiliar hemiola-like rhythms (defined in Chapter II above), comprising an exceedingly strong part of Central African rhythmic style, that usually command most interest. However, equal-pulsed, square rhythms (as well as occasional rhythmic freedom) also appear on the scene and should not be entirely ignored.

---

[28] The sanza has keys of iron or rattan. Curt Sachs, in conversations with the present author, has pointed out that the sanza is not a "thumb-piano" as misnamed by some, but a thumb-plucked idiophone. *Mbira* is a general native name for the instrument, also known locally as *lukembe* (Ituri Forest, Belgian Congo) and *malimba* (among Wanyamwezi of Tanganyika).

[29] Cent-Frequency charts: *Baduma Paddlers* (Fr. Eq.), Transcr. 38; *Wanyamwezi Sanza* (Tang.), Transcr. 49.

[30] Cent-Frequency chart: *N'Gundi Song* (Fr. Eq.), Transcr. 28.

The African Hemiola Style

The additive,[31] irregular-pulsed rhythms of Central Africa, featuring the exchange of "longs" and "shorts," have been termed *hemiola-like* by the present writer and have been discussed in Chapter II above. Without duplicating all of that discussion, let it be reiterated here that the African hemiola style is strongly allied with the Middle Eastern and Hindu rhythmic style – a complex style and one that is metric (in the Ancient Greek sense) – rather than with late-Western regularity and its precipitate, syncopation.

Syncopation (again cf. Chapter II above) takes its cue from or rather depends for its identity upon stressed downbeats in a context of equally divided measures, i.e., measures with regularly spaced conductor-beats (for example, the four equal beats of 4/4 time). The stressed downbeat implies an offbeat, and when the offbeat becomes antagonistic or is prominently featured, syncopation exists (e.g., 2/4: ♪ ♩ ♩ ♪ or ♪ ♪ ♩ ♪ or 𝄞 𝄞). Thus, an "offbeat music," i.e., a rhythmically regular or divisive [32] music, is always a generating ground for possible syncopation.[33]

To what extent an "upbeat music" – having phrases beginning on the offbeat – was foreign to early Western civilization cannot be fully stated at present. However, there may be a clue in the early disinclination towards preparatory upbeats – at least in the very first phrase of a composition. Where the text of a polyphonic piece began with a syllable that looked as though it should be treated as an upbeat, composers would often circumvent such treatment: "they extended the initial short and stressless syllable backward so that it began on a first beat and filled out a whole measure." [34]

Furthermore, what to the modern eye might appear as a *stressed* offbeat creating syncopation (cf. the examples two paragraphs above) in a Renaissance polyphonic work barred according to the original mensuration signature, quite often may be interpreted as a shift in downbeat – as nothing else but the result of a succession of unequal beat groupings, a kind of succession that is characteristic of an additively oriented music. Gustave Reese illustrates this idea in connection with the fifteenth-century composer Isaac, showing, in the piece *Et qui la dira*, that "the greater length or height of certain notes in relation to those about them produces a particularly fine counterpoint of rhythmic accents." [35] These accents, instead of being strait-jacketed within a modern 4/4 barring, appear to better advantage with appropriate change of measure-length.[36]

---

[31] Cf. reference to Curt Sachs, in connection with this term, in Chapter II above.

[32] Cf. reference to Curt Sachs, in connection with this term, in Chapter II above.

[33] The term "syncopation" has also been used by the present author elsewhere in a second sense, i.e., with reference to additive music with its alternation of unequal beats. However, the first and more basic definition of syncopation – as an "upbeat" phenomenon – is the one adopted for the present work. Cf. Rose Brandel, "Music of the Giants and the Pygmies of the Belgian Congo," *Journal of the American Musicological Society*, V (1952), pp. 16–28.

[34] Curt Sachs, *Rhythm and Tempo*, p. 261; also see p. 113. The initial upbeat did, however, appear in folk and instrumental music, particularly in the *estampie* and *basse* dances of the fourteenth and fifteenth centuries. Cf. *Rhythm and Tempo*, p. 262.

[35] Gustave Reese, *Music in the Renaissance* (New York, 1954), p. 212.

[36] Two barring versions of Isaac's piece are given in Gustave Reese, *Music in the Renaissance*, p. 213. The top voice, for example, instead of being "syncopated" as in the 4/4 version, appears in the other version as a succession of 4/4, 3/4, 6/8, and 4/4 measures.

Similarly, African hemiola rhythms could be misinterpreted as being syncopated. Should a notation within a symmetric [37] context showing a basic undercurrent of regular beats be utilized, the stressed offbeat would make its appearance. (Here stress is essentially a function of length, pitch, and particularly timbre, rather than of intensity.) The subsuming of an independent, asymmetric line under a "counter" line of regularity, however, would be a falsification of the rhythmic intent of the music.

To illustrate this idea briefly, two ways of notating the same material are given below (Ex. 43):

Ex. 43. Mangbetu Choral Song (Belgian Congo)
     Transcr. 1, Section I

1. Notation implying syncopation

2. Notation showing hemiolic content

The second version is the one adopted by the present author. This version, incidentally, also illustrates one of the two pacing categories of change, namely *close-paced hemiola*. To reiterate, African hemiolic change refers to the succession of unequal conductor-beats in a 2 : 3 length-ratio (e.g., ♩ and ♩. or ♪ and ♪.). The essential resemblance to the traditional European hemiola is in this 2 : 3 beat-length contrast (and not necessarily in the number of units involved – viz., six units in the traditional hemiola). The five-unit *hemiolia* (meaning "by one and one-half") of Ancient Greece also contained this 2 : 3 conductor-beat contrast. In the second version of Ex. 43 the music is distinguished by *immediate* exchange of such conductor-beats (i.e., many changes occur within a short space, usually within the measure). Further illustrations of this condensed hemiola style may be noted in the following (Exx. 44–48), all of which display the close-paced exchange of two unequal conductor-beats in a 2 : 3 ratio:

[37] "Symmetry" refers to the equality or balancing of parts of a whole and is being used above in this sense. The "parts" are the conductor-beats; the "whole" is the measure or a group of measures. "Asymmetry" refers, of course, to the lack of symmetry, viz., unequal conductor-beats within the measure or measures.

Ex. 44. Wasukuma Wedding Song (Tanganyika)
      Transcr. 47, meas. 1 f

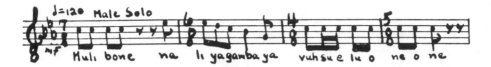

Ex. 45. Babunda New Year Song (Belgian Congo)
      Transcr. 22, meas. 1 f

Ex. 46. N'Gundi Humorous Love Song (French Eq. Afr.)
      Transcr. 28, meas. 1 f

Ex. 47. Mboko Riddle Song (French Eq. Afr.)
      Transcr. 26, meas. 8 f

Ex. 48. Babira Choral Song (Belgian Congo)
      Transcr. 2, meas. 1 f

These examples are highly suggestive of the Hindu rhythmic style with its *tāla* configurations, not only in the immediate exchange of unequal beats (2/8, 3/8) but also in the arrangement of these beats within a larger "period" or section (several measures) comparable to the Hindu *vibāgha*.[38] Such African periods are usually repeated immediately, generally with the same melody, but occasionally with a new one, in isorhythmic fashion. The repetitions are rarely exact, however (owing to text requirements in vocal music), although the overall length of the period is usually the same. A good illustration of period patterning is the *Wasukuma Wedding Song* (Ex. 44), which contains a twenty-two note rhythmic pattern (four measures containing twenty-two eighths arranged in beats of 2/8's and 3/8's) that never varies in the total number of eighths during the course of its constant statements throughout the piece. When the melody changes (cf. Transcr. 47, Section B) the twenty-two eighths remain intact, although the inner groupings are slightly altered. Thus, in the new-melody section the inner rhythmic pattern appears as 7/8 plus 4/8 plus 7/8 plus 4/8, instead of the 7/8 plus 6/8 plus 4/8 plus 5/8 of the first melody (Ex. 44). Is it too much to regard this as a species of isorhythm, since the twenty-two eighths are retained entirely?

Period patterning also characterizes the *Mboko Riddle Song* (Ex. 47). The pattern shown here (5/8 plus 4/8) is exactly repeated (although not with a new melody) not only in total length but also with regard to the inner grouping of two's and three's. Incidentally, note the almost universal *dochmiac*, 3/8 plus 3/8 plus 2/8, in the *Babunda New Year Song* (Ex. 45).[39]

On the whole, however, Central African hemiolic patterns of the close-paced kind are, when repeated (whether the melody is the same or not), slightly varied in their inner groupings, while kept intact in their overall length.

The second type of pacing found in the hemiola style, namely, *sectional hemiola*, is illustrated in several examples, two of which are drum pieces. One of these has elsewhere been referred to by the present author as a "twin-topic prologue" in reference to the dual rhythmic nature of the work.[40] A quality of dramatic partitioning is indeed evident in this type of hemiolic structure, which is characterized by a homogeneous section of some length succeeded by a contrasting homogeneous section. The contrast lies in the hemiolic change from a two-grouping to a three-grouping (or vice versa) by sections, the sections themselves being internally homogeneous in that no or little hemiolic change occurs within them. In the *Babira Circumcision Drums* (Ex. 49), used to announce the beginning of the circumcision rituals, the "twin topic" is evident as a series of 3/8 groupings (organized in 6/8 measures) followed by a series of 2/8 groupings (organized in 4/8 plus 2/8 measures). This particular example, incidentally, illustrates the true European hemiola.

[38] Cf. Curt Sachs, *Rise*, p. 186.

[39] The Ancient Greek *dochmiac* meter has appeared in all times and places. Cf. Curt Sachs, *Rhythm and Tempo*, pp. 65, 136.

[40] Rose Brandel, "The Music of African Circumcision Rituals," *Journal of the American Musicological Society*, VII (1954), pp. 52–62.

Ex. 49. Babira Circumcision Drums (Belgian Congo)
Transcr. 4, meas. 1 f

The *Watutsi Royal Drums* (Ex. 50) shows the sectional change in reverse, i.e., from the two-grouping to the three-grouping. Here the 2/8 groups are organized in 3/4 measures (17 measures in this section), and the 3/8 groups are organized in 3/8 measures (22 measures in this section). Again the true hemiola is evident, provided two 3/8 measures are combined:

Ex. 50. Watutsi Royal Drums (Ruanda)
Transcr. 18, meas. 16 f

More rapid change, from measure to measure, may be seen in the *Wameru Spell-Breaking Party Song* (Ex. 51) as well as in the *Babinga Pygmy Dance* (Ex. 52):

Ex. 51. Wameru Spell-Breaking Party Song (Tanganyika)
Transcr. 51, meas. 3 f

Ex. 52. Babinga Pygmy Dance (French Eq. Afr.)
Transcr. 31, meas. 5 f

THUS FAR, the hemiola style has been discussed in its *horizontal* or one-line realization. The *vertical* hemiola style, however, a logical concomitant of our African polyphonically oriented music, appears in quite intricate manifestations, strongly commanding the listener's interest. The vertical hemiola style is, in effect, vertical polyrhythm in its basic sense, that is, it features the combination of parts or lines each of which maintains a certain degree of rhythmic independence.

Referring again to European Renaissance music for a parallel, we find that the problem of accented or pseudo-offbeats ("pseudo" when considered in reference to regular barring) and shifting bar lines (discussed above) is even more intensified when we consider simultaneous independent rhythms. If the pseudo-offbeat is actually a downbeat, then it is obvious that the vertical coexistence of independent rhythms may result in overlapping of downbeats, that is, what consists of a downbeat for one part may be an offbeat for another part.[41]

Similarly, it may be seen that the multi-lined African hemiola rhythms are, in one sense, realizations of overlapping downbeats.[42] But this is not the entire story. Overlapping downbeats could conceivably exist in a square, equal-beat rhythmic style as well as in the hemiola style. Thus, two lines of contrasting rhythms may retain their downbeat independence in either of the two rhythmic styles (Exx. 53, 54):

Ex. 53. Independent Lines in Equal-Beat Style

Ex. 54. Independent Lines in Hemiola Style

As may be seen from Ex. 54, the vertical hemiola rhythms are, together with the horizontal hemiola, distinguished by the two-three groupings, i.e., two unequal conductor-beats in a 2 : 3 length ratio. The problem here, however, is which two-three grouping is to predominate where several lines are concerned. In the equal-pulsed, divisive style there is no problem of this kind, for the beats of all the lines are of equal length, regardless of different entries. Even a strong offbeat is considered a subdivision of a steady, uniform basic beat. The vertical hemiola rhythms, on the other hand, would seem to demand as many conductors as there are lines. (Note in passing that the

---

[41] Again, Isaac's *Et qui la dira* illustrates the overlapping of downbeats in its four voice parts. A rhythmic abstract of the top two lines of the "b" version in G. Reese, *Renaissance*, p. 213, would look like this:

[42] Arthur M. Jones emphasizes the idea of "staggered points of entry" in "African Rhythm," *Africa*, XXIV (1954), pp. 26–47.

American composer, Charles Ives, requires two conductors for one of his works.) However, two things become apparent: 1) that the coincidence of hemiolic lines inevitably carries with it some kind of *Gestalt* effect, almost as if a new rhythmic pattern, resulting from the composite interplay of all the lines, emerged; and 2) that very often the preponderance through timbre, pitch, etc., of one line over the others makes for "single-line listening," no matter how complex the entire work.

The second point is well illustrated by certain music for drum ensemble, wherein a leader-drum plays a running monologue of "neutral" eighths throughout the piece, eighths that appear now as 2/8, now as 3/8, depending upon the strength of the dominant line or lines. In the *Watutsi Royal Drums* (Ex. 55), for instance, a soprano ostinato is played by a leader-drum in groups of 2/8. However, these 2/8 groups are so inconspicuous that they are easily overshadowed by the two-three groupings of the deeper toned drums in the ensemble. In Ex. 50 these deeper toned drums were shown in their change from the two-grouping (3/4) to the three-grouping (3/8). The leader-drum, at that point, actually continued its 2/8 figure (shown in Ex. 55), but because of its lesser obtrusiveness (dynamic accent in this drum is almost lacking, the 2/8 grouping being achieved by means of very subtle timbre contrast), the listener does not really hear the total counter-rhythm – he merely feels it.

Ex. 55. Watutsi Royal Drums (Ruanda)
     Transcr. 18, meas. 17 f

The same situation, i.e., the near-obliteration of the ostinato rhythm, occurs in another Watutsi example (Ex. 56). Here, however, the leader-drum   plays in groups of 3/8 instead of the 2/8 of Ex. 55.

Ex. 56. Watutsi Royal Drums (Ruanda)
     Transcr. 19, meas. 9 f, 15 f

Distinct opposition of lines may, however, be heard earlier in the same piece (Ex. 57). Despite the galloping strength of the lowest line, the three-grouping of the top line somehow makes itself quite apparent, and the eventual result is a complex pull in two directions.[43]

Ex. 57. Watutsi Royal Drums (Ruanda)
          Transcr. 19, meas. 4 f

The "neutral," running notes of an ostinato (that becomes a middle line later in the piece), grouped now as 3/16, now as 2/16, appear again in a xylophone ensemble of the Yaswa (Ex. 58).

Ex. 58. Yaswa Xylophones (French Eq. Afr.)
          Transcr. 32, meas. 1 f

[43] The Royal Drums of the *Mwami* of Ruanda were recently swept up by western impresarios and deposited at the Brussels World's Fair to hypnotize visitors with a touch of the "exotic." To one western visitor, however, the 24 drummers made, in essence, "an insistent, horrendous banging . . ." and "after a while the din overcame one's power of concentration." See *New York Times*, August 17, 1958, music section.

The vertical hemiola style also appears in purely vocal as well as in vocal-instrumental music. The *Babinga Pygmy Dance* (Ex. 59) and the *Wameru Spell-Breaking Party Song* (Ex. 60) illustrate the former, while the *N'Gundi Song* (Ex. 61), the *Wanyamwezi Chief-Installation Song* (Ex. 62), and another portion of the *Babinga Pygmy Dance* (Ex. 63) illustrate the latter.

Ex. 59. Babinga Pygmy Dance (French Eq. Afr.)
　　　　Transcr. 31, meas. 1 f

Ex. 60. Wameru Spell-Breaking Party Song (Tang.)
　　　　Transcr. 51, meas. 3 f

Ex. 61. N'Gundi Song (French Eq. Afr.)
　　　　Transcr. 28, meas. 1 f

Ex. 62. Wanyamwezi Chief-Installation Song (Tang.)
     Transcr. 48, meas. 12 f

Ex. 63. Babinga Pygmy Dance (French Eq. Afr.)
     Transcr. 31, meas. 33 f

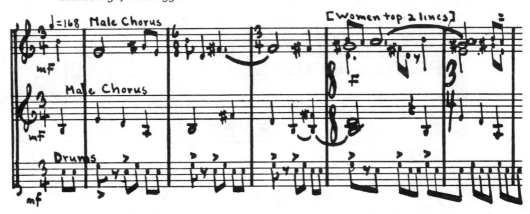

A FEW BRIEF REMARKS concerning *tempo* are in order at this point. The problem of tempo is a delicate one owing to the varying attitudes that exist concerning the nature of tempo. Is it a product of the basic beat, or does it derive from the smallest subdivisions within this beat? The present writer is inclined towards the first possibility since, generally, the "conductor's beat" will adapt itself to a note-sign (or signs, in the hemiola style) fairly close to the smallest subdivisions. Hence, for example, the possibility of considering ♩ = 30, 𝅘𝅥𝅯𝅘𝅥𝅯𝅘𝅥𝅯 𝅘𝅥𝅯𝅘𝅥𝅯𝅘𝅥𝅯 as a slow tempo is practically nil since, despite the metronome designation, it will probably be beaten in eighths, at ♪ = 120. In the transcriptions included in the present work this problem has been avoided through the use of appropriate notation rather than subdivision of metronome beats. Sixty-fourths and thirty-seconds rarely, if ever, appear, inner values being usually designated by eighths or sixteenths no matter how fast the conductor's beat. On the whole, the present transcriptions point to an African inclination for rapid tempo. The beating of two's and three's is usually accomplished at an average of ♩ (♪) = *c.* 120 to *c.* 195, ♩. (♪.) = *c.* 80 to *c.* 130.

To what extent the African hemiola style derives from the complex rhythmic world of India, or of the Middle East, is an open question. Certainly, the interpenetration of the cultures of these areas at various points in history would seem to suggest some musical interpenetration as well. That traditional Africa is basically more of an Oriental than an Occidental culture is almost certain. Whether it is more Oriental than "African" – and here is assumed a substratum of something "pure" and primeval – is not easily resolved. Suffice it to say, at the present, that the African hemiola style belongs with the rhythmic style of India and the Middle East, even of Ancient Greece, broadly speaking. While not as strict and formalized as the styles of these areas, the African hemiola style rests upon the same musico-kinesthetic premise – that of the inclination for unequal groupings, or the play of long and short beats: essentially an attitude of asymmetry.[44]

POLYPHONY AND FORM

The most striking phenomenon about Western musical civilization is the development of a unique kind of polyphony, namely, functional harmony. This type of harmony may be defined as the setting up of relational chords (a process allied with concepts of tension and relaxation) within a context of major and minor scale systems. As such, functional harmony is a special subdivision of polyphony which theoretically refers simply to the coexistence of more than one musical line. Historically, Western early polyphony was distinctly of a horizontal nature, the simultaneity of lines being considered secondary to individual line movement.[45] Only with the growth of chord hierarchies was there a shift to true awareness of the vertical.

In its preharmonic stage, Europe revealed musical signs that were probably indica-

[44] Rather than discuss what is an already familiar phenomenon to Western readers, namely, symmetric, equal-beat rhythm, the present author simply points to several transcriptions exhibiting such rhythm:

4/4 – *Kuyu Medicine Song* (Fr. Eq. Afr.) – Transcr. 34.
4/4 – *Bongili Girls' Banana Work Song* (Fr. Eq. Afr.) – Transcr. 36.
4/4 – 2/4 – *Bahutu Dance Chant* (Ruanda) – Transcr. 17.
2/4 – *Mambuti Pygmies Song* (Belg. Congo) – Transcr. 14.
2/4 – *Wanyamwezi Sanza* (Tang.) – Transcr. 49.
2/2 – *Banyoro Xylophone* (Uganda) – Transcr. 40.

Free rhythm (i.e., containing much rubato, accelerando, and fermata-like sustained notes) appears in only two examples, both of which come from the Watutsi. (See *Watutsi Historic Songs* – Transcr. 20, and 21.) However, hemiolic patterns may be distinguished within the apparent rhythmic freedom of the first example. See the comparison of Watutsi freely rhythmic hummed introduction with the Hindu *ālāpa*, the Turkish *taqsīm*, and the Indonesian *bebuka* under "Descending Octave Melodies," above. Curt Sachs draws a parallel between all of the modern Oriental free introductions and the Ancient Babylonian free instrumental solo introducing the *sumponiāh*, i.e., instruments playing together. *Rhythm and Tempo*, p. 95; Sachs also relates these introductions to the Ancient Greek free introduction, the *anápeira*. *Rise*, p. 252.

[45] Pietro Aron wrote with admiration, in his *De institutione harmonica* (1516), of the new method composers were using of writing all voice parts simultaneously rather than successively, "a very difficult thing that requires long training and practice." Cf. Curt Sachs, *Rhythm and Tempo*, p. 93; also, Gustave Reese, *Renaissance*, pp. 181–182.

tive of a protoharmony. Since the essence of Western traditional harmony is the interval of the third, particularly within a triadic setting, it may be expected that such early harmonic signs featured this interval. Several appearances of parallel thirds, both in early art music and in folk music (cf. Chapter II above), confirm this expectation.[46]

The third as a melodic phenomenon in Central African music has already been demonstrated above (cf. "Pentachord Fanfare," zig-zag thirds under "Octave-Melodies," and "Ladder of Thirds," in the present chapter above), while its "harmonic" occurrence has been hinted at. It may be shown now that parallel thirds are an integral part of Central African polyphony.[47] Whether the presence of vertical thirds indicates the type of harmonic structure present in Western music is a question that can at present be answered only in the negative, since full-fledged Western harmony is in one sense the product of a theoretic, scientific attitude. However, if early European musical signs are of any significance, then African parallelism of thirds may analogously be considered the precursor of a true harmonic music [48] quite different from the tetrachordal music of the Orient with its emphasis upon the horizontal.

Parallel thirds are found in the music of the Mangbetu (Exx. 35, 64), the Babira (Ex. 65), the Bapere (Ex. 66) – all of the Belgian Congo –, and the Wahehe (Ex. 67) of Tanganyika, the Baduma (Exx. 40, 68, 69), the Mboko (Ex. 70), and the Okandi (Ex. 71) – all of French Equatorial Africa. With the exception of Exx. 69 and 70, which represent music for a sanza and a zither, respectively, all of the examples are vocal:

Ex. 64. Mangbetu Choral Song (Belgian Congo)
         Transcr. 1, Section D

Ex. 65. Babira Choral Song (Belgian Congo)
         Transcr. 3, meas. 5 f

[46] Regarding parallel thirds in early European art music, see Gustave Reese, *Middle Ages*, pp. 388 ff; regarding parallel thirds in early European folk music, see Curt Sachs, *Rise of Music*, pp. 296 ff.

[47] In addition to examples to be given above, parallel thirds appear in examples by George Herzog (Angola) and W. Heinitz (Tanganyika). See Herzog in Wilfrid Hambly, "The Ovimbundu of Angola," *Chicago: Field Museum of Natural History*, Anthropological Series, XXI (1934), pp. 217–223; also, W. Heinitz, "Zwei Phonogramme aus Rutenganyo," *Vox*, XXII (Dec. 1936), pp. 50–56. Parallel thirds among the Bemba of Northern Rhodesia are pointed out by A. M. Jones in "East and West, North and South," *African Music*, I, 1 (1954), p. 60.

[48] The third is *not* a recent "foreign" importation. Chronological comparison of the third with the fourth and the fifth has been presented in Chapter II above. Cf. also the tuning in thirds of an ancient zither of Madagascar, in Curt Sachs, *Les Instruments de musique de Madagascar* (Paris, 1938), p. 53.

Ex. 66. Bapere Flagellation Song (Belgian Congo)
   Transcr. 9, meas. 19 f

Ex. 67. Wahehe Elephant Hunting Song (Tanganyika)
   Transcr. 52, meas 10

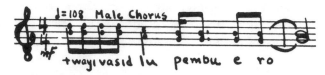

Ex. 68. Baduma Paddlers' Song (French Eq.)
   Transcr. 37, meas. 11

Ex. 69. Baduma Paddlers with Sanza (French Eq.)
   Transcr. 38, meas. 7

Ex. 70. Mboko Riddle Song (French Eq.)
   Transcr. 26, meas. 5 f

Ex. 71. Okandi Women's Dance Song (French Eq.)
   Transcr. 39, meas. 2

Parallel thirds in vocal music cannot be attributed to heterophony, in which vertical combinations result fortuitously when different performers intend to sing the same melody but do not attempt to do so in strict unison.[49] If men and women sing together the result is generally in parallel octaves, while voice-range variations within the same sex may perhaps result in parallel fifths and fourths. However, the smaller intervals cannot be accounted for in this manner, particularly when the parallelism is consistently of a certain pattern – for example, one in which major and minor thirds are alternated.

Even with regard to parallel fourths and fifths, it cannot be stated with complete assurance that the presence of the intervals is always due to voice-range variation. Certainly, in the type of rhythmically sophisticated structure found among the Wasukuma of Tanganyika, the presence of parallel fifths appears to be more than the result of mere chance (Ex. 72):

Ex. 72. Wasukuma Wedding Song (Tanganyika)
       Transcr. 47, meas. 17 f

The mixture of parallel thirds, fourths, and sixths in the *Okandi Women's Dance Song* (Ex. 73) again seems to be deliberate rather than the by-product of range variation. This likelihood is strengthened by the fact that, despite the presence of mature and immature voices in the performance of this piece, some of the parallels are produced by voices of the same type.

Ex. 73. Okandi Women's Dance Song (French Eq.)
       Transcr. 39, meas. 8 ff

The question whether parallelism results fortuitously from the combination of different voice types hardly arises where instrumental music is concerned: Parallelism would

---

[49] Medieval organum may be considered a species of heterophony, since in organum there is concern with only one melodic line. However, here the polyphony (parallel fifths, for example) is deliberate and not fortuitous.

obviously not be an accidental result of voice ranges here, but a deliberately employed musical device. Parallel fourths are shown in Ex. 74, a section of a Wanyamwezi sanza melody:

Ex. 74. Wanyamwezi Wedding Tune on Sanza (Tang.)
Transcr. 49, meas. 11 f

Type distribution of parallel intervals through Central Africa may, on the basis of evidence thus far available, be tentatively stated to be as follows: Parallel thirds are quite widespread, occurring, for example, in French Equatorial Africa, the Belgian Congo, Tanganyika, Angola, and Northern Rhodesia; parallel fourths and fifths, however, appear in greater concentration towards the east, notably among the Wanyamwezi and Wasukuma of Tanganyika. Erich von Hornbostel, in his transcriptions of Wanyamwezi music, also shows this predilection for parallel fourths and fifths.[50]

Parallelism is, of course, not the only type of polyphony found in Central African music. The co-sounding of tones often appears as the result of antiphonal or responsorial overlapping, ostinato or drone-ostinato accompaniment, or distinct contrapuntal juxta-position whether of a double-melody type or of an interjection-variation type (cf. description before Ex. 84 below).

Choral antiphonal and solo-choral responsorial singing – almost universal phenomena – are enormously favored in tribal Africa. Quite often, the "answering" musical section will start before the first section is completed, and if the "answer" is imitative, then canon may result; if the "answer" is not imitative, then it may constitute a cadential elongation of the phrase. A rare example of modified canon at the fifth (unison and octave canons are the usual types found in the music of non-literate peoples [51]) may be seen in a responsorial yodelling song of the Babinga Pygmies (Ex. 75), also, the continuous choral ostinato of a Mambuti Pygmy song occasionally lends itself to canonic passages at the fifth (Ex. 76). The Babinga yodel-canon (the canonic motif is in the three lowest-sounding tones of the solo yodeller) gives rise to vertical intervals of thirds and fifths, and the Mambuti ostinato-canon to the vertical interval of the second, among others. (The tetrachordal structure of the Mambuti melody – cf. "Melody Types" above – seems to be connected with the type of canonic imitation utilized in the song: the two disjunct tetrachords of the octave arise naturally from imitation at the fifth):

[50] Erich M. von Hornbostel, "Wanyamwezi-Gesänge," *Anthropos*, IV (1909), pp. 781–800, 1033–1052. (See particularly, Exx. 3 and 7.) Also see transcriptions in P. H. Molitor, "Nègres de Tanganyika," Ex. 17, p. 725, and Ex. 28, p. 730.

[51] For an excellent example of *unison* canon deriving from responsorial overlapping, see the *Bongili Girls' Banana Work Song* (Fr. Eq.), Transcr. 36.

Ex. 75. Babinga Pygmy Elephant Hunting Song (Fr. Eq.)
Transcr. 30, meas. 4 f

Ex. 76. Mambuti Pygmy Song (Belgian Congo)
Transcr. 14, meas. 13 f

Antiphonal overlapping giving the effect of an elongated cadence may be noted in the following excerpt from a Batwa Pygmy chorus (Ex. 77). The vertical intervals resulting are the fourth and the fifth:

Ex. 77. Batwa Pygmies (Ruanda)
Transcr. 16, meas. 3

The ostinato and drone-ostinato, resulting in vertical intervals (including the major seventh), are illustrated in the three following examples (Exx. 78, 79, 80) as well as in the canonic Mambuti excerpt above (Ex. 76), which is part of an ostinato accompaniment to a soloist's melody (Transcr. 14).[52]

Ex. 78. Bahutu Dance Chant (Ruanda)
Transcr. 17, meas. 2 f

[52] Cf. also *N'Gundi Girls* (Fr. Eq.), Ex. 11 and Transcr. 29; *Baganda Historic Song* (Uganda), Ex. 4 and Transcr. 45; *Baganda Historic Song with Harp* (Uganda), Transcr. 44; and the *Wameru Spell-Breaking Party Song* (Tang.), Ex. 9 and Transcr. 51. The first two pieces illustrate the intermittent ostinato, while the last two illustrate the continuous ostinato.

Ex. **79.** Batwa Pygmies (Ruanda)
    Transcr. 15, meas. 3 f

Ex. **80.** Kuyu Medicine Song (Fr. Eq.)
    Transcr. 34, meas. 1 f

Distinct contrapuntal movement of a dual- or triple-melody type is vividly illustrated in the *Banyoro Royal Horns* (Ex. 81), in the *Babinga Pygmy Dance* (Ex. 82), and in the *Mambuti Pygmy Elephant-Feast Song* (Ex. 83); [53] brief contrapuntal interjection for variational purposes (generally by a vocal soloist) may be noted in the *Babira Circumcision Dance* (Ex. 84). The vertical intervals resulting from these two kinds of melodic counterpoint range from the strong major seconds of the Mambuti music (Ex. 83) through fourths, fifths, and minor sevenths in the Banyoro music (Ex. 81), as well as thirds and fourths in the Babinga music (Ex. 82):

Ex. **81.** Banyoro Royal Horns (Uganda)
    Transcr. 41, meas. 1 ff

Ex. **82.** Babinga Pygmy Dance (Fr. Eq.)
    Transcr. 31, meas. 1 ff

[53] Cf. also the N'Gundi song for voice and sanza (Fr. Eq.), Ex. 61 and Transcr. 28.

Ex. 83. Mambuti Pygmy Elephant-Feast Song (Belg. Congo)
    Transcr. 12, meas. 1 f

Ex. 84. Babira Circumcision Dance (Belg. Congo)
    Transcr. 6, meas. 36 ff

Simultaneity of tones often results from an occasional "chord," neither contrapuntally caused (in the dual-melody sense just explained) nor due to parallelism (although close to this), nor due to antiphonal overlapping. Such "hanging chords" are illustrated in the Wachaga excerpt (Ex. 85), where they appear to consist of simple tones surrounded by less important or accompanying tones, and in the Babira excerpt (Ex. 86), where the two notes of the sustained major second simply stand in equal force (dynamically, at least, for the pentachordal flow of the melody suggests that the c'' is structurally more important):

Ex. 85. Wachaga Chief-Praise Song (Tang.)
    Transcr. 50, meas. 10 f and 12 f

Ex. 86. Babira Choral Song (Belg. Congo)
    Transcr. 3, meas. 7 f

Quite often, especially in "orchestral" works featuring instruments and voices, or in works featuring a non-monophonic instrument (e.g., a keyed or multi-stringed instrument), the polyphonic forms are blended so that "harmony" may, for example, appear as the resultant of double-melody combined with ostinato accompaniment. In the Bapere xylophone piece (Ex. 87), the three lines consist of a dominant upper melody, a subordinate lower melody (which becomes an ostinato later in the work), and an ostinato middle (entering at the ninth measure):

Ex. 87. Bapere Xylophone (Belg. Congo)
    Transcr. 11, meas. 3 f

Although the raised leading tone, as a functional component of relational harmony, is not common, three examples containing it may be noted: the *Bongili Girls' Banana Work Song* (Cf. Ex. 33), the *Wanyamwezi Chief-Installation* (Transcr. 48, meas. 34), and the *Batoro Dance Song* (Ex. 88):

Ex. 88. Batoro Dance Song (Uganda)
    Transcr. 42, meas. 1 f

CONCERNING OVERALL MUSICAL FORM in Central Africa, the most characteristic structure is immediate melodic repetition (not necessarily exact) – in effect, the litany form: A, A, A . . . This is the general principle, although the length of the melody may make for inner subdivision (brought about by segmentation with or without cadences) so that the "melody" is actually a period, e.g., A(abc), A(abc) . . . (cf. *Batwa Pygmies*, Transcr. 16). The litany form encompasses all of the polyphonic devices discussed above, viz., antiphony and response (which may be continuous and not necessarily overlapping), giving, for example, the form A(ab), A(ab) . . . (cf. *Kuyu Women's Dance*, Transcr. 35); the ostinato and drone-ostinato, giving the form A, A . . ., although a soloist's line added to the ostinato may be of a more complex form (cf. *Mambuti Pygmies*, Transcr. 14); multi-melody, usually giving the subdivided form A(ab), A(ab) . . . (cf. *Babinga Pygmy Dance*, Transcr. 31).

Occasionally a more complex structure appears, as in the following rondo-like form: A(abc), B(de), A$_1$(bc), B(de), A$_1$(bc), B$_1$(d), A(abc), etc. (Cf. *Batoro Song*, Transcr. 42).

The text of this music is always the same, except for the "e" phrase, which has a new text with each statement. (A soloist sings "a" and "e"; the remainder is sung by a chorus.)

Another complex form, like the European medieval sequence or lai, may be noted in the *Wanyamwezi Chief Installation* Transcr. 48). The long-lined melodies in this piece group themselves with the text as follows (letters for melody, numbers for text-lines):

```
‖:    A(ab)     A(ab),*    B(cd)     B(cd'),    C(efg)    C(hfg),
      1          1          2          2          3         3

      ┌─────┐              ┌──────────────┐
      1st end.             second ending
      D(ij) :  ‖           D(ijj'j'j'j')                    ‖
      4                    4 da capo al segno
```

(The soloist sings the entire pattern the first time; the chorus joins the soloist the second time, entering on "b"; after the second ending, all voices complete two more "A's," and drums alone finish the piece, retreating in staggered fashion, as they had entered.)

The melody that is truly developed is rare, appearing strictly as a solo phenomenon generally over an ostinato accompaniment (cf., for example, *N'Gundi Song*, Transcr. 28, or *Batwa Pygmies*, Transcr. 15), while overall structural development is still rarer (but cf. the *Watutsi Royal Drums*, Transcr. 18[54]). "Development" here is not strictly variational, but refers to distinctly integrative, dramatic *enlargement* rather than to *seriation*, which belongs to all other forms discussed above. (Variation techniques, of course, definitely exist in the "litany" forms, although such techniques are usually the property of a soloist rather than of a chorus. [55])

Finally, one highly complex form draws our attention. This form is still seriational, but within larger as well as within smaller units. Several large contrasting sections of considerable length are strung together and are unified by a short refrain-like solo-call, thus (vertical strokes mark off the insertion of the solo-call): |AB|CD|EF|GHI|JD| (cf. *Mangbetu Choral Song*, Transcr. 1).

[54] For detailed analysis of this piece cf. Rose Brandel, "Music of the Giants and the Pygmies . . .," pp. 17–22.

[55] An exceptional instance of a chorus varying a soloist's melody may be noted in the *Mangbetu Choral Song* (Belg. Congo), Transcr. 1, Section C. The choral response is mainly a rhythmic variation, although a small melodic "coda" is grafted, by the chorus, onto the soloist's melody. The variation does *not* seem to be caused by text change.

CHAPTER FIVE

SINGING STYLE

When we listen to a Zulu singing, we know he sounds quite different from a Japanese folk singer, and we may wonder at the reasons for this difference. Is it just the contrast in music – different melodies, rhythms, harmonies – that causes us to react differently to each singer, or is there something additional?

Actually there is. The music may be reproduced on paper and performed by any of us, but without those essentials of vocal style – timbre, range, dynamics, etc. – which are characteristic of a culture, the sounds we make would not resemble anything (except our own normal type of vocal expression).

Identification of the factors that cause a particular style to take form obviously poses a problem. Such causative factors may be the result of variation in physical make-up. Although all people possess the usual things that exist in a throat – a larynx, with its vocal cords and two groups of muscles to control the cords, a space or pharynx, a tongue, etc. – certain minor differences do exist. The size and shape of the throat components will affect the type of sound produced, as will also the sex of the individual, but these differences, like the similarities just mentioned, belong to people the world over. (Racial variation in physiology, of course, is not part of this common dissimilarity, which encompasses only individual and sex differences. Thus, racial physiology may be pertinent to the search for causative factors in singing style.)

Since *basic* human physiology is the same, it must be something beyond and in addition to this that produces a vocal style. What it is, is a question for which an answer is not readily provided, but at least two factors must be included – the dictates of the music itself and that strong shaping phenomenon, tradition.

Each culture has its own tradition, so that a *geisha*, for example, sings in a certain style mainly because she was taught to sing that way and because her teachers were taught to sing that way. In a non-literate culture there is less formal instruction, perhaps, and more imitation, but the idea is the same: It is the inherited or accepted manner of singing that influences each singer.

Sometimes a particular kind of music contains many runs and rapid scale passages, perhaps large melodic leaps, grace notes, etc. Such musically structural factors require the singer to make certain vocal adjustments. For example, the yodel leap requires a lightning adjustment in the laryngeal muscles. It is such an adjustment that is responsible for what we hear as two distinct timbres, popularly associated with so-called "chest" and "head" registers, although these have little to do with the chest or head. These two registers, lower and upper, exist in both men and women and are used in different cultures according to the requirements of the music (as well as of tradition).

BEFORE the particulars of Central African singing style are discussed, definitions of the basic physio-acoustical terms to be used in the discussion are presented as follows: [1]

1) *Registration:* This refers to the use of the two laryngeal groups of muscles (the *arytenoid* and the *thyroid*) actuating the vocal cords (which are two bands of flesh), that is, controlling the length and the tension of the cords by stretching or shortening them, in order to produce sound. There are *only two* groups of laryngeal muscles. The two registers (i.e., the two timbres resulting from the use of the two groups of muscles) are the *upper* (also called "falsetto" [2] or "arytenoid register") and the *lower* (also called "thyroid register") and they exist in both men and women. (Note that there is no "middle" register.) These registers are not to be confused with pitch ranges; they are concerned with the two tone qualities caused by muscular action in the larynx. Both sets of muscles may be active simultaneously throughout the entire pitch range of the human voice. However, the arytenoid-register muscles are more active at the higher pitches, and the thyroid-register muscles are more active at the lower pitches. In addition, the loudness or intensity of vocal sound is in part controlled by these muscles. Thus, soft singing is primarily a function of the physiological apparatus of the upper register (at any pitch level), while loud singing is primarily a function of the physiological apparatus of the lower registeı (at any pitch level).

2) *Isolated Register:* It is possible to use the apparatus of one register (one group of laryngeal muscles actuating the vocal cords) without the other at any one pitch (particularly at the extremes of pitch range). In isolation each register will sound quite different in quality from the other. The isolated upper register will sound somewhat flute-like, colorless, while the isolated lower register will have a strident, heavy quality. Actually, in most singing the apparatuses of both registers are used simultaneously and in certain proportions depending upon the intensity (loudness) required at the particular pitch level. The tone e♭" (for all voices) is the first tone at which the upper register may be used with greater maximum intensity than it is possible to achieve in the lower register.[3] That is to say, at full voice the tone e♭", when sung in pure upper register, will sound louder than the tone a half-step below it (d"), also at full voice and sung in pure lower register. Physiologically, this means that in a rising scale the tension-

---

[1] Definitions are based upon the researches of Douglas Stanley at Bell Telephone Laboratories, at the New York University Physiology and Physics Departments, and at Electrical Research Products, Inc. (subsidiary of Western Electric Co.). Cf. *The Science of Voice*, third edition (New York, 1939), 384 pp.; D. Stanley and J. P. Maxfield, *The Voice, its Production and Reproduction* (New York, 1933), 287 pp.; *Your Voice* (New York, 1945), 306 pp.

[2] "Falsetto," as used above, means not only the upper register of men, but also the upper register of women, i.e., the term designates the use of the arytenoid muscles by either men or women.

[3] Douglas Stanley, *Your Voice*, pp. 16, 103. Cf. footnote 5 below.

balance between the two groups of muscles changes proportionately, until at e♭″ the loudest possible sound has a greater percentage of arytenoid than of thyroid tension.

3) *Resonance:* This refers to the enlargement or amplification of sound in a tuned cavity. The main cavity used for resonance is that part of the throat called the *pharynx*. The pharynx is composed of three sections – the *nasal pharynx* (area behind the nose), the *oral pharynx* (area behind the mouth), and the *laryngeal pharynx* (area behind the larynx). As the vocal cords produce a tone, the pharyngeal cavity is immediately adjusted (tuned) to the pitch or frequency band (vibrations) of this tone, and the volume is thus increased.

Resonance also influences the quality of the tone, as well as the volume, since certain partials (harmonics) may be emphasized to the exclusion of others, depending upon the pharyngeal adjustment.

Other cavities may also be used for resonance, but not as successfully as the pharynx. Among these is the mouth, which may be tuned to the desired tone. However, in acting as a resonator, the mouth replaces the pharynx, a much larger and more efficient cavity, as prime resonator and partially or completely blocks off the pharynx with the back of the tongue. In this case, the back of the tongue is pushed back towards the rear wall of the oral pharynx, an action leading to throatiness. (In pharyngeal resonance the back of the tongue is pulled away from the rear wall, so that the pharynx is completely open and can resonate freely.)

The nose is not an adjustable cavity and hence cannot be utilized as a true resonator. (Only one pitch – that to which the fixed cavity of the nose is tuned – probably receives any fair amount of amplification from the nose.) This applies as well to the brain cavity.

IN MOST FOLK and primitive styles of singing (except for Italian and perhaps Russian) the two registers and their muscular apparatuses are generally undeveloped or at least not equally developed. This is probably connected with the fact that vocal pitch range is, in such music, rather limited. The registers and their muscular apparatuses tend to develop fully when large ranges are employed, for it is at the extremes of pitch level that the two muscular groups are put to maximum use.

Depending upon the pitch gamut peculiar to the musical style, as well as upon the preferred intensity levels, singers, therefore, will bring those laryngeal muscles into play that are most appropriate physiologically. Central African registration illustrates this point. Since women generally sing at the lower pitch levels with fairly high intensity, they primarily make use of the lower register apparatus. (The upper register apparatus cannot be used with great intensity at the lower pitches. Cf. above in the present chapter.) Hence, the timbre is usually the strident one characteristic of the lower or thyroid register. However, since *extremes* of low pitch are rarely used, full development of this register is not apparent, nor is it used in isolated state. The recorded performance of the *Kuyu Women's Dance Song* (French Eq., Transcr. 35), celebrating the birth of twins, is an excellent illustration of combined registration with the lower register greatly predominating. The soloist's *forte* melody lies between c♯″ and b (the transcription is transposed one-half step down), a range at which the lower register sounds particularly raucous at high intensities.[4]

THE MEN OF CENTRAL AFRICA generally sing at the high pitch levels (i.e., "high" for the male voice, which is naturally an octave below the female voice). Although also usually favoring the greater intensities, they mainly employ the *upper* register for these intensities, with the result that most male singing sounds "tenor-like." (The true "bass" voice is rare among primitive singers.) But owing to the limitations of the intensity levels obtainable in the upper register, the intensities sought and achieved – greater than would be obtainable in the upper register alone [5] – actually result from a *combination* of registers (i.e., upper plus lower) in which the proportion of falsetto or upper register is nearly always at maximum (arytenoid tension is at maximum) and the lower register at minimum (thyroid tension is at minimum). As a result, the total timbre is of a tense, somewhat hoarse nature. This characteristic timbre may be noted, for example, in the recording of the *N'Gundi Song* (French Eq., Transcr. 28), in which the soloist's melody extends from b♭' down to f (actual pitches) at generally high intensities. Occasionally, an example of pure or isolated male falsetto appears, as in the *Wahehe Elephant Song* (Tang., Transcr. 52, meas. 16) or in the *N'Gundi Song* (French Eq., Transcr. 28, end of piece not shown). In the latter song the falsetto is part of a yodel, which, as mentioned above, ordinarily consists of a lightning alternation of isolated lower and upper registers. The N'Gundi singer, however, alternates between his regular voice (combined registers) and isolated upper register. (Genuine isolated-register contrast may be heard in the yodelling of a female Babinga Pygmy; see the ritual hunting song, French Eq., Transcr. 30.) In addition, Richard A. Waterman has pointed out examples of pure male-falsetto singing in West Africa.[6]

THICKNESS OR GUTTURALNESS is another characteristic of Central African male singing. This quality derives partly from the combination of high intensity and upper register, but also from another factor. At unusually loud musical sections, the tension threshold of the upper register muscles (the arytenoids) is reached and cannot be exceeded (for

---

[4] According to Douglas Stanley's researches, there is a physio-acoustical proportion of lower and upper registers which is *natural* (i.e., physiologically tension-balanced) for each pitch level (at each intensity through which that pitch level may run). Hence, at a middle tone, e.g., g' sung *mezzo-forte*, the amount of lower register is *c.* 56% and the amount of upper is *c.* 44%; at *forte*, the amount of lower register is *c.* 75% and of upper register, *c.* 25%. At a higher tone in *mezzo-forte*, for example c♯", the natural proportions are *c.* 50% for each register; at *forte*, they are lower register *c.* 60% and upper register *c.* 40%. Cf. fig. 14 and 15 in *Your Voice*, pp. 88–90; 184 f. When these *natural* proportions are departed from, a physio-acoustical state of imbalance results. In the Kuyu song, the c♯" at *forte* contains more lower register than is required for that pitch and intensity, with a resulting timbre composed of the characteristic stridency of the lower register plus noise elements (irregular upper partials).

[5] The written note e♭''' (above high c''') represents the first tone (e♭'' actual pitch) at which the male voice can utilize the upper or *falsetto* register with any great intensity. Cf. "Isolated Register" above in the present chapter; also *Your Voice*, pp. 16, 103.

[6] Richard A. Waterman, "African Influence on the Music of the Americas," p. 215.

those pitch levels used). Since very little lower register action is being utilized by the singer, the greater musical volume must be produced by another means. This is accomplished by the singer's use of the constrictor muscles (i.e., neck muscles such as the sterno-mastoid[7]). These muscles press against or squeeze the vocal cords to produce the greater volume necessary. Such extra-laryngeal action plays a large part in causing the guttural quality.

The particular use of the tongue also contributes to the gutturalness and, judging from the type of singing, is probably just as important as the use of the constrictor muscles. In extreme gutturalness the back of the tongue (hyoid muscle) is pushed towards the rear pharyngeal wall, almost touching it. (No sound or a kind of choking would result if the wall were actually touched.) The degree to which the pharyngeal passage is blocked is the degree to which the voice sounds guttural. An example of extreme gutturalness at *mezzo-forte* intensity may be noted in the recording of the *Mangbetu Song* (Belgian Congo, Transcr. 1), particularly in the male soloist's singing, while gutturalness at *forte* intensity (the constrictor muscles are working very hard here) appears in the N'Gundi soloist's singing (French Eq., Transcr. 28), particularly at the top of his phrase near b♭' (actual pitch).

BECAUSE OF THE TENDENCY towards gutturalness, *resonance* in the African male voice is essentially of the mouth rather than of the pharyngeal variety (cf. "Resonance" above in the present chapter). The movement of the back of the tongue towards the posterior pharyngeal wall succeeds in greatly reducing the resonating capacity of the pharynx and in introducing the oral cavity as prime resonator. Since pharyngeal resonance is more efficient (acoustically) than mouth resonance, the resulting tones are relatively weak (i.e., "weak" when compared to pharyngeally resonated tones) and also "bodiless" rather than brilliant. (A resonance chamber tuned to the desired tone or frequency not only magnifies amplitude or volume, but also affects "color," since the more accurate the tuning, the better the selection by the chamber of those upper partials of a tone that determine richness or color.) The small, so-called"natural-sounding" voice that most people use is, in fact, essentially a product of mouth resonance.

Thus far, the typical Central African male voice has been characterized as being 1) *"tenor"-like* and *tense-hoarse* (deriving from a predominating upper register plus high intensity at a certain pitch range); 2) *guttural* (deriving from extension of the hyoid muscle of the tongue towards the posterior pharyngeal wall, as well as from prominent action on the part of the neck or constrictor muscles), and 3) *bodiless* and *not fully resonated* (deriving from the use of mouth resonance).

The typical Central African female voice has been characterized as being *strident* (caused by a predominating lower register plus high intensity at a certain pitch range). It may also be added that gutturalness exists but is not as pronounced as in the male voice, and that resonance is also of the mouth variety.

[7] Douglas Stanley, *Your Voice*, pp. 132 ff.

TYPICAL of both male and female singing is the *absence of vibrato*. (The vibrato is a-coustically a slight and regular pitch variation at the rate of *c*. six changes per second. The pitch variation depends upon the intensity of the tone: from almost zero variation at *pianissimo* to *c*. a major second at *fortissimo*. Deep or diaphragm breathing is used for the vibrato. [8]) Such characteristic steadiness or lack of movement – caused by steady tension on the thorax (chest) muscles, particularly on the expiratory muscles – is es-pecially noticeable on long, sustained tones. (Cf., for example, the sustained seconds in the *Babira Choral Song*, Belgian Congo, Transcr. 3, meas. 8.)

While the vibrato is entirely absent, an occasional tremolo appears (although rarely). (The tremolo is much faster than the vibrato – having seven to eleven movements per second – and of a narrow pitch variation. While the vibrato involves laryngeal pulsation essentially, the tremolo mainly involves fluttering of the tongue. Furthermore, while the vibrato is actuated by deep thorax, or diaphragm, movement, the tremolo does not involve the thorax muscles. [9]) In the *Wachaga Chief-Praise Song* (Tang., Transcr. 50) a rapid and shallow tremolo is heard in the chorus on certain sustained tones (meas. 11, 14, 16, 17). This tremolo is almost bleat-like and appears to be caused by rapid glottal interruption of the breath pressure as well as by tongue flutter.[10] In its somewhat stac-cato quality, the Wachaga tremolo calls to mind the medieval European *notae vinnulae* (neighing notes), which may have been represented in neumes by the *strophicus*.[11]

AS ALREADY STATED ABOVE, both men and women generally sing at high intensity. Allied with this is the fact that accents, shouting, and even screaming are sprinkled throughout the singing. While the accents are at times caused dynamically, the timbre-accent is more prevalent. The dynamic accent is physiologically a sudden, sharp in-crease of breath pressure against the glottis; in the *Kuyu Women's Dance Song* (Fr. Eq., Transcr. 35) this accent appears in the soloist's melody as a kind of "Scotch-snap,"

♪ ., on a major second. The timbre-accent (which may occur on a group of successive notes as well as on a single note) often takes the form of excessive breathiness (*breath expulsion* and not *breath-pressure* increase) as at the end of the *Mangbetu Song* (Belgian Congo, Transcr. 1), or, more often, of unusual gutturalness, as in the *N'Gundi Song* (Fr. Eq., Transcr. 28, meas. 12), or even of excessive nasality [12] (*N'Gundi* Song, Fr. Eq., Transcr. 28). Shouting and screaming qualities (i.e., tones with large noise ad-mixtures, acoustically deriving from the presence of very irregular partials) appear in almost all the recorded examples. This emphatic, explosive, full-voice singing style is

[8] Douglas Stanley, *Your Voice*, p. 32.

[9] *Ibid.*, pp. 30 ff.

[10] The *glottis* is the opening between the vocal cords and is closed during phonation. It is the breath pressure against the closed glottis that actuates the voice. Cf. Stanley, *Your Voice*, pp. 4 f.

[11] Cf. Willi Apel, *Gregorian Chant* (Bloomington, 1958), p. 116. The medieval staccato-tremolo, however, did not have pitch variation, while the Wachaga tremolo does have such variation to a slight extent.

[12] A light nasality appears in most Central African singing, probably caused by the sonorous "m" or "n" found in the Bantu languages. Excessive nasality is sometimes used for disguise, as in the *Bapere Circum-cision Bird* (Belg. Congo, Transcr. 8). Nasality is caused by extreme muscular tension on the outside of the face, particularly in the jaw and nose regions. It is not "nasal resonance" (the nose is not a true resonator; cf. above).

quite obviously allied to the fact that most Central African singing is of the free, outdoor variety involving community participation.

Such "gusto" singing is generally punctuated by frequent breathing (i.e., intake of breath), since vocal phrases (not necessarily musical phrases) must be short at the full-voice intensities applied.

ORNAMENTS are not very common, except where the singing is Arab-influenced. The single grace note, sung before the beat and usually of a different pitch than the main note, occasionally appears, sounding sob-like. This effect is produced by a sudden blast of air against a nearly closed glottis, accompanied by an abrupt register alteration to introduce momentarily more upper register with hardly any lower register. (Cf. *Kuyu Medicine Song*, Fr. Eq., Transcr. 34, meas. 2.) The Arabic Watutsi singing, however, has many more ornaments, in addition to the one just described, viz., the sob-like grace note before the beat but of the *same* pitch as the main note, the "Scotch-snap," the "mordent" (on the beat, i.e., ♪♩♩), and the throbbing double-mordent (on the beat, i.e., ♫♩). Note clusters connecting two tones also appear. (Cf. *Watutsi Historic Songs*, Ruanda, Transcr. 20, 21.) The Watutsi style is a more subdued, chamber style; also, less gutturalness and hoarseness are apparent. Some Arabic influence may also be noted in the *Wanyamwezi Chief Installation* (Tang., Transcr. 48, meas. 17, 24, 27), in the sob-like double notes with pitch change ♪♩ before the beat. This ornament may also be observed in the *Baganda Song with Harp* (Transcr. 44, meas. 39 ff).

SPECIAL EFFECTS may also be found in Central African vocal music – effects such as *yodelling* (cf. definition above in the present chapter; also, *Babinga Pygmies*, Fr. Eq., Transcr. 30, and *N'Gundi Girls*, Fr. Eq., Transcr. 29, meas. 12 f); *humming* (phonation with closed mouth; cf. *Watutsi Historic Songs*, Ruanda, Transcr. 20, 21); *Sprechstimme* (semi-speech singing; cf. *Wameru Spell-Breaking Song*, Tang., Transcr. 51); *melodic interlocking* or hocket (in which a melody is broken up into minute fragments, sung in turn by different individuals; cf. *Mambuti Pygmies*, Belg. Congo, Transcr. 14, and also Chapter III above, "Hunting" section); *glissando* (pitch slurring through undefined larynx tension; cf. *Bahutu Dance Chant*, Ruanda, Transcr. 17); and *whistling* [13] (produced by breath blown through pursed and tensed lips, with no laryngeal participation).

Finally, a special species of "vocal" effect ought to be noted, that of drum duplication of the singing voice (Cf. Chapter III above, "Talking Drum," for drum and *speaking* voice.) In the *Okandi Women's Song* the drums, at one point, imitate both the rhythm and the pitch direction of the singer's melody (Fr. Eq., Transcr. 39, meas. 5).

IN CONCLUSION, it may be stated that Central African singing is highly syllabic (i.e., there is usually one syllable to a note), a circumstance making for musical consonant-emphasis and obviously contributing to the overall dynamic, emphatic vocal style. Where Arabic influences appear, however (cf. the ornaments of the Watutsi, Wanyam-wezi, and Baganda songs just discussed), some melismatic singing (i.e., with several notes to one syllable) becomes apparent.

[13] Mentioned by M. A. Poupon, ". . . la tribu Kouyou," p. 63.

CHAPTER SIX

CONCLUSION

In attempting a summary of our discussion of Central African musical style, it would appear expedient to answer the following questions:

1) What are the most common, widespread style-elements?

2) What elements appear sporadically, and where?

The "musical map" that begins to take shape, as we answer these questions and consequently go through a kind of sorting and integrating process, may be compared with a living organism that is constantly changing while yet retaining some basic, identifying elements.

The most widespread elements seem to be those of hemiolic rhythm, tempos inclining towards the rapid, the melodic and "harmonic" third, large rather than small scale spans, both diatonicism and chasmatonicism, overall descending melodic direction, some kind of polyphony, seriated form, non-tempered instrument-tuning, antiphonal and responsorial singing, and an emphatic, syllabic vocal style (combined registration with upper register at maximum intensity, for the men; combined registration with lower register at maximum intensity, for the women).

The term "widespread" should not be misinterpreted as meaning necessarily occurring in every square mile. If there is reasonably sufficient "spread" of a musical characteristic, without enormous gaps, then the term "widespread" is applicable and may be justifiably used.

Elements appearing sporadically, or confined to certain areas, seem to be the one- and two-step nucleus (appearing by itself and not – the usual thing – as ostinato accompaniment to another part), parallel fourths and fifths, melody and form of a developmental nature, the "leading tone," free rhythm, intimate "chamber-like" singing, and melismatic, ornamented melody. The last three may belong together and are found among the Arabic-influenced Watutsi bards.

The areas where these elements appear are as follows:

1) *One- and Two-Step nucleus (not as accompaniment):* in ceremonial music of the Bapere (northeast Belgian Congo) and of the Babinga Pygmies (French Equatorial); in social music of the N'Gundi (Fr. Eq.), of the Mboko (Fr. Eq.), and of the Mangbetu (Belg. Congo, although in this instance the element appears only as a small section within a more complex song).

CIRCUMCISION CEREMONY: UNCLE COMFORTS INITIATE
WHILE ALL THE BOYS SING INITIATION SONGS
MAMBUTI PYGMIES, Congo Republic (Formerly Belgian)
Courtesy of Colin M. Turnbull

Hunting Bow Used As Musical Bow; Mouth Is Resonator; Right Hand Taps
String With Arrow; Left Finger Mutes String
Mambuti Pygmy, Congo Republic (Formerly Belgian)
Courtesy of Colin M. Turnbull

YASWA SUSPENDED XYLOPHONE WITH CALABASH RESONATORS
(SEE TRANSCRIPTION 32), Congo Republic (Formerly French)
Courtesy of Folkways Record Corp., New York

N'Gundi Singer with Sanza; Blind Musician at Right Plays Percussion Sticks
(See Transcription 28), Congo Republic (Formerly French)
Courtesy of Folkways Record Corp., New York

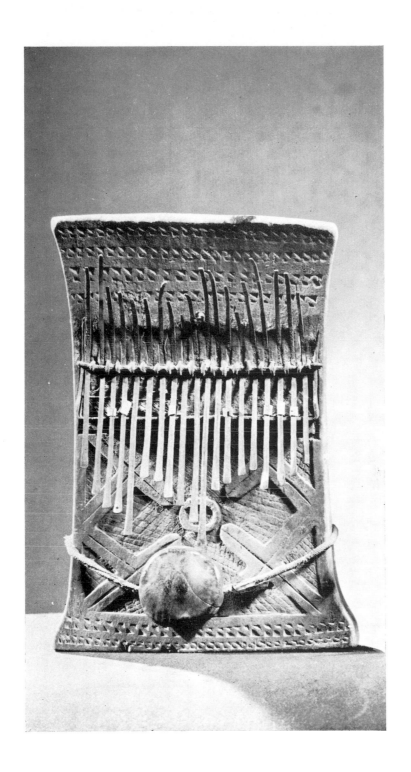

BACHOKO SANZA (LUKEMBE), Congo (Kasai)-Angola border
Courtesy of American Museum of Natural History

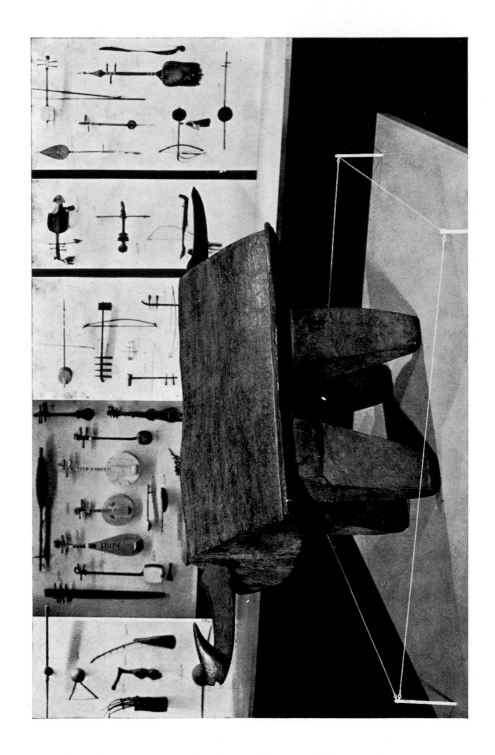

Mangbetu animal-shaped Slit Drum, "Nemurambi," Used for Signalling
Congo Republic (Formerly Belgian)
Courtesy of American Museum of Natural History

BAMBALA DRUMMER, Congo Republic (Formerly Belgian)
Courtesy of Folkways Record Corp., New York

Watutsi Royal Drummers, Ruanda
Courtesy of Folkways Record Corp., New York

WATUTSI DANCER, Ruanda
Courtesy of Folkways Record Corp., New York

SOCIAL CIRCLE-DANCE, MAMBUTI PYGMIES
Congo Republic (Formerly Belgian)
Courtesy of Colin M. Turnbull

2) *Parallel fifths and fourths:* mainly towards the east, viz., in music of the Wanyam-wezi and of the Wasukuma of Tanganyika.

3) *Development in melody:* in social music of the N'Gundi (Fr. Eq.) and of the Batwa Pygmies (Ruanda); in ceremonial music of the Wanyamwezi (Tang.).

4) *Development in form:* in music for royal drums of the Watutsi (Ruanda).

5) *"Leading tone":* in work-music of the Bongili (Fr. Eq.); in ceremonial music of the Wanyamwezi (Tang.); in social music of the Batoro (Uganda).

6) *Free Rhythm:* in bard songs of the Watutsi (Ruanda).

7) *Intimate, chamber-singing:* in bard songs of the Watutsi (Ruanda); also found among the Mboko (Fr. Eq.).

8) *Melismatic, ornamented melody:* in bard songs of the Watutsi (Ruanda), of the Baganda (Uganda); in ceremonial songs of the Wanyamwezi (Tang.).

It may be seen that the first stylistic category (i.e., "widespread elements") cuts across the social categories of both language and culture-area. The second stylistic category (i.e., "sporadic elements") coincides in part with the social category of culture-area (parts of the cattle-area, specifically), although such coincidence applies mainly to elements 2, 4, 6, 7, and 8 above.

From a musico-cultural point of view, it is obvious that non-literacy and the most simple music are neither logically nor actually concomitant. The first category of style-elements given above, in any systemic hierarchy of musical structure, can be deemed non-primal: the most rudimentary or simplest type of music has in Central Africa been superseded by a relatively complex style. The tribal cultures of Central Africa are, of course, non-literate (although in many instances signs of high civilization other than literacy have appeared). The significance of this situation is hard to gauge at present. While some studies have pointed to the possibility that the musical art of a people is the last to develop – other cultural and artistic achievements generally lead the way when historical points of concentrated change are reached – the Central African musico-cultural condition appears, in one sense, to be an exception. This "one sense," which has to do with the state of non-literacy, however, may not be important enough to warrant consideration. If so, we may summarize by saying that the Central African cultures are comparatively "advanced" (with exceptions, of course) and that the musics are also comparatively "advanced."

THE PRESENCE OF SYMMETRY and asymmetry in the musical art of Central Africa leads to a final deduction.

The case for symmetry appears to be a strong one, in view of some of the musical traits our investigation has revealed – for example, the African predilection for the litany form and the application of rhythmic "period"-patterning. Symmetry as found in the litany form occurs most clearly in the species of that form that has been described earlier as "subdivided." We have defined symmetry as "the equalization or balancing of parts of a whole." Subdivision is naturally easier to discern if the melodic line that is repeated is of fair length and does not itself consist largely of repetitions of a small nucleus. The immediate repetition of a tiny melodic nucleus, to be sure, gives a kind of symmetry, but such symmetry exists on too small a level for the ear to perceive it as of overall structural significance. In fact, the small-sized series – while fitting the definition of "symmetry" in that it contains a "balance of parts" – is almost like a straight line in which the fragmentation into "parts" is discernible only under the microscope. It is in the series of large-sized components – in the "subdivided" litany – that symmetry becomes more readily apparent. In its overall succession of A's, the litany form presents serial symmetry (the outcome of an addition of similar parts). In its inner subdivisions, the form may reveal directional symmetry (produced by a contrast of parts that have some apex in common, e.g., the rise and fall ⋀ of the Batwa Pygmy melody of Transcr. 16, or the cadential contrast within the Baganda xylophone melody of Transcr. 46). Another type of inner subdivision may bring about intermediate symmetry (the result of the regular reappearance, from one statement to another, of a refrain, or of a phrase ending, or of an intermittent ostinato, or even of an orchestral "texture" such as the antiphonal or responsorial alternations).

Rhythmic "period"-patterning is, of course, a direct correlate of the melodic litany and may appear under all of the categories of symmetry discussed above (except that of directional symmetry).

Allied with the musical symmetry is the obvious symmetry of the circle and file dance-forms, and the indisputable symmetry present in the plastic art-forms of Central Africa. (Some strong similarities have even been noted between European Romanesque and Belgian Congo painting and sculpture.[1] Such similarities are both literal and formal, particularly with regard to symmetry.)

The case for asymmetry may be stated as follows: Hemiolic rhythms are by very definition asymmetric (in their succession of "longs" and "shorts"). The variational techniques employed during the course of immediate melodic repetition also ally themselves with asymmetry. Both of these devices have been found in the music under study. Development, in melody and in overall form, is asymmetric. The development-technique is, as stated above, rare in Central African music. Free rhythm – and this too has been shown to appear infrequently – belongs with asymmetry.

In the sphere of the dance, the convulsive shaman dances, the mimetic animal dances, and all of the "theatre" or story-telling dances are basically of an asymmetric nature.

The overall vocal style, in a sense, also belongs under the category of asymmetry, specifically with regard to changes in "texture" or color, changes especially involving strong nasality, gutturalness, shouting, etc., and aligned with the dramatic-expressive requirements of text and music.

Clearly, both symmetry and asymmetry exist in Central African art forms; and clearly, the logical correlates of these two elements, namely staticism and dynamism, or station and progression as Curt Sachs puts it,[2] are also present. Furthermore, this ambivalent character becomes even more apparent in the tracing of abstraction, non-

---

[1] *Les Beaux-Arts*, Belgian Congo issue (Brussels, 1955), p. 36. Note, for example, the great similarity in Romanesque and Congolese stone masks.

[2] Curt Sachs, *The Commonwealth of Art* (New York, 1946), p. 296.

realism, and magical remoteness, on the one hand, and of emotionalism and realism, on the other. The strong, restraining influence of magic and other-worldly symbolism sets its vivid stamp upon African expressive forms (the sculptured "portrait" of even a king may not resemble him[3]), but an inner vitality, a drive towards dramatic, extro-vert expression permeates and countershapes the same art.

[3] Note the impassive, non-realistic, symmetric statue of a former king of the Bakuba of the Belgian Congo, as pictured in *Les Beaux-Arts*, p. 5.

PART TWO

PREFACE TO THE TRANSCRIPTIONS

Fifty-two transcriptions are appended to the present work. These transcriptions have been made by the present author from the following recordings:

1) *Reeves Sound Studios*, Belgian Congo and Ruanda music recorded on the Denis-Roosevelt Expedition, 1935–1936, 78 RPM.

2) *Folkways Records Co.*, P402 (Music of Equatorial Africa, recorded by André Didier); P427 (Folk Music of the Western Congo, recorded by Leo A. Verwilghen); P428 (Songs of the Watutsi, recorded by Leo A. Verwilghen), 33 1/3 RPM.

3) *London*, LB 832 (Music of the Uganda Protectorate, recorded by Hugh Tracey), 33 1/3 RPM.

4) *African Music Society: International Library of African Music*, DC 158, GB 1311, GB 1315, GB 1553, GB 1561, GB 1331 (music of Tanganyika, recorded by Hugh Tracey), 78 RPM.

The equipment used included the following:

Phonograph: Webcor.

Monochord: Constructed in the Netherlands according to specifications by Jaap Kunst; calibrated in frequencies from 210 to 500 cycles per second.

Tuning Fork: c' at 256 cps.

The *Cent-Frequency Charts* refer to the instrumental works and were derived as follows:

1) The frequency of every instrumental note was obtained. This involved (a) tuning the monochord (with the tuning fork), so that c' = 256 cps; (b) obtaining the pitch of the instrumental note in question on the monochord; (c) reading off the frequency number on the calibrated scale on the monochord.

2) Once the frequency of every note was obtained, the distance between two notes, or the interval ratio, was then computed into cents.* A combination of Von Hornbostel's table plus the direct logarithmic method was used in the computations. The second method was employed as a check against the first.

Von Hornbostel's table, as given in Jaap Kunst's *Ethnomusicology*, p. 133, is used with the following formula:

$$\text{Cents of } p/q = (\text{cents of } p/n) - (\text{cents of } q/n),$$

---

* In the Alexander J. Ellis cent system (1884), the octave equals 1200 cents and is divided into twelve equal semitones of 100 cents each.

where p and q are the two frequency numbers of any interval, and n is an arbitrary frequency number lower than either p or q. Von Hornbostel's table gives the cent numbers of any interval up to a tenth above n, i.e., any interval x/n, where n = 340 cps, and x = (n + 1), (n + 2) ... (n + 469) cps. Thus, to find the cents number of the interval p/q, where p = 420 cps and q = 366 cps, find the cents number of the interval p/n (420/340), which is given on the chart as 365 cents; find the cents number of the interval q/n (366/340), which is given on the chart as 127 cents; according to the formula above subtract these two cents numbers to obtain the cents number of the interval p/q (i.e., 238 cents, or a very large major second).

The logarithmic method involved the obtaining of the log of each of the two frequencies of an interval, subtracting these logs from each other, and then working with the Ellis Log-Cent table, as given in Kunst's *Ethnomusicology*, p. 13, to obtain the cents number. Thus, to find the cents number of the interval p/q, e.g., 420/366, subtract log 366 (or 2.5635) from log 420 (or 2.6232). The log difference (.0597) is then converted into cents by using the Ellis chart: On the chart the next lowest log or .05017 = 200 cents; subtract this log from previous log = .00953; on chart, next lowest log or .00753 = 30 cents; subtract this log from previous log = .00200; on chart .00201 = 8 cents; add all cents numbers = 238 cents total, or a very large major second.

SPECIAL SIGNS USED IN TRANSCRIPTIONS

     $\overset{+}{\flat}$ = sharp note
     $\flat$ = very sharp note
     $\bar{\flat}$ = flat note
     $\flat$ = very flat note
     ＼ = glissando
     ♪ = grace note sounding before the beat
     ' = indefinite pause
UR = upper vocal register
LR = lower vocal register
     ♩ = half-spoken; indefinite pitch
     ⓰ = sounds an octave lower *
CF = Cent-Frequency chart; respective chart numbers are given at the bottom of transcriptions.

In the transcriptions of vocal works, text syllables have been notated wherever possible. In nearly all instances, the subject matter of the text has been explained at the bottom of each transcription. In several cases, a literal translation (in English) of the first line or phrase of the text is also given at the bottom of the transcription (this material being quoted from the annotation accompanying the recordings used by the

* All transcriptions, unless otherwise indicated, sound as written.

author). The text syllables, unless hyphenated, are not necessarily grouped into words. It is hoped that future linguistic investigations will reveal further details in connection with matters of text structure. Attention is called to the fact that the letter "b" is not, in the Bantu languages, pronounced like the English "b," but sounds midway between a "b" and a "v," or between a "v" and a "w."

BELGIAN CONGO
(Rungu)
Transposed up
Major 3rd

1. MANGBETU
CHORAL SONG

Denis-Roosevelt
Reeves Sound Studios
Side I

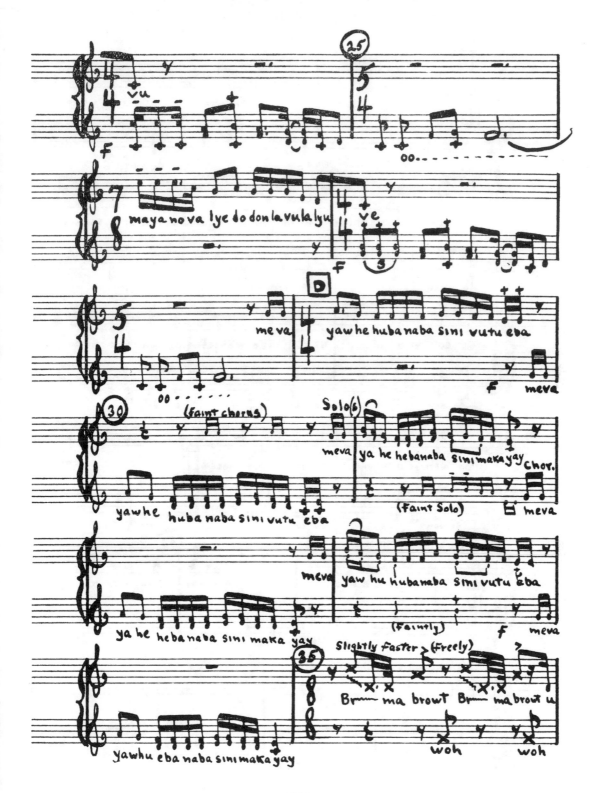

113

115

116

BELGIAN CONGO
(Ituri Forest
near Mambasa)
*Transposed
down min. 2nd*

2. BABIRA
CHORAL SONG

Denis-Roosevelt
Reeves Sound
Side 2 – Song 1

BELGIAN CONGO
(Ituri Forest
near Mambasa)
*Transposed
down min. 2nd*

3. BABIRA
CHORAL SONG

Denis-Roosevelt
Reeves Sound
Side 2 – Song 4

4. BABIRA CIRCUMCISION *
DRUMS OF CHIEF KOKONYANGE

Denis Roosevelt
Reeves Sound
Side 11 – Band 1

* Transcription published in *Journal of the American Musicological Society*, VII (1954), p. 59.

121

5. BABIRA CIRCUMCISION *
CEREMONIAL DANCE
Kokonyange's Village

Denis-Roosevelt
Reeves Sound
Side 11 – Band 2

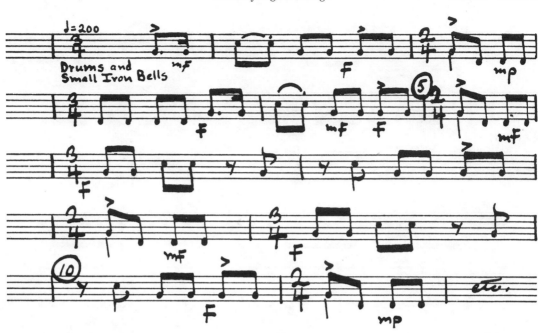

* Transcription published in *Journal of the American Musicological Society*, VII (1954), p. 59.

BELGIAN CONGO
(N. Ituri Forest)
*Transposed
down min. 2nd*

6. BABIRA CIRCUMCISION *
CEREMONIAL DANCE
Chief Omande's Village

Denis-Roosevelt
Reeves Sound
Side 11 – Band 3

* Transcription published in *Journal of the American Musicological Society*, VII (1954), p. 60.

BELGIAN CONGO
(Moto-Kolia)
*Transposed
up min. 2nd*

7. BAPERE CIRCUMCISION *
CEREMONIAL DANCE

Denis-Roosevelt
Reeves Sound
Side 12 – Band 1

* Transcription published in *Journal of the American Musicological Society*, VII (1954), p. 61.

BELGIAN CONGO
(Moto-Kolia)

8. BAPERE CIRCUMCISION BIRD *
WITH BULL-ROARER **

Denis-Roosevelt
Reeves Sound Studios
Side 12 – Band 2

* Transcription published in *Journal of the American Musicological Society*, VII (1954), p. 62.

** The magical cries of the "bird" are made by a man pinching his nose; another man whirls a bull-roarer. The chorus "repeats" the bird's insults to the women.

BELGIAN CONGO
(Moto-Kolia)
*Transposed
down min. 2nd*

9. BAPERE CIRCUMCISION *
THE FLAGELLATION

Denis-Roosevelt
Reeves Sound
Side 12 – Band 3

* The music accompanies the whip-lashing of adult, circumcized men whose courage is being tested.

129

BELGIAN CONGO
(Ituri Forest:
near Wamba)
*Transposed
up min. 2nd*

10. BAPERE
HORNS *

Denis-Roosevelt
Reeves Sound Studios
Side 3 – Band 2

* CF 1. Music accompanies social dance of Chief Karumi's people.

etc.

BELGIAN CONGO
(Lubero)
*Transposed
up a major 3rd*

11. BAPERE
XYLOPHONE *

Denis-Roosevelt
Reeves Sound Studios
Side 4

* CF 2.

BELGIAN CONGO
(Ituri Forest)

12. MAMBUTI PYGMIES
ELEPHANT FEAST

Denis-Roosevelt
Reeves Sound
Side 5 – Band 1

136

137

138

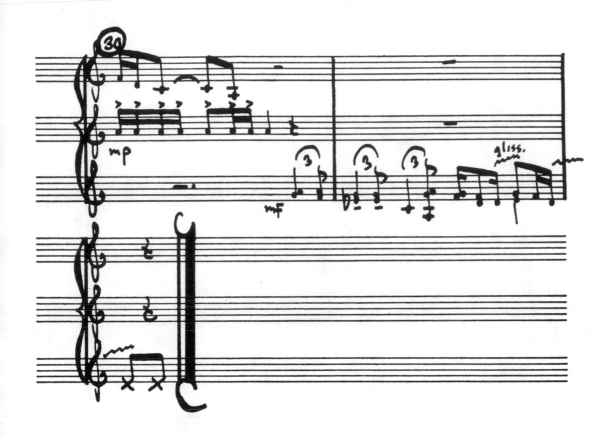

BELGIAN CONGO
(Ituri Forest)
*Transposed
down min. 2nd*

13. MAMBUTI PYGMIES
FLUTES AND DRUM *

Denis-Roosevelt
Reeves Sound Studios
Side 5 – Band 2

* CF 3. Flutes (wooden, vertical) play one note each; music accompanies single file shuffle dance.

etc.

BELGIAN CONGO
(Ituri Forest)
*Transposed
down min. 2nd*

14. MAMBUTI PYGMIES
HUNTING SONG *

Denis-Roosevelt
Reeves Sound
Side 5 – Band 3

* In this all-night song the solo tells about hunting in the forest.

143

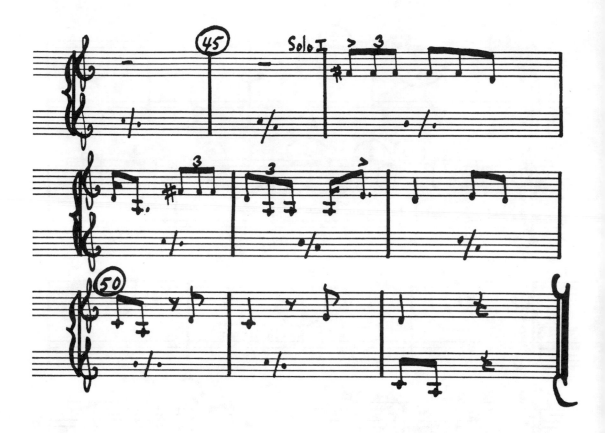

RUANDA
(NGoma)
*Transposed
up min. 2nd*

15. BATWA PYGMIES *
DANCE

Denis-Roosevelt
Reeves Sound
Side 6 – Band 1

* Transcription published in *Journal of the American Musicological Society*, V (1952), p. 25.

RUANDA
(NGoma)
*Transposed
up min. 2nd*

16. BATWA PYGMIES *

DANCE

Denis-Roosevelt
Reeves Sound
Side 6 – Band 2

* Transcription published in *Journal of the American Musicological Society*, V (1952), p. 26.

RUANDA
(NGoma)
*Transposed
up min. 2nd*

17. BAHUTU *
DANCE **

Denis-Roosevelt
Reeves Sound
Side 10 – Band 3

* Transcription published in *Journal of the American Musicological Society*, V (1952), p. 22.
** The music accompanies a circle dance in which the men stamp vigorously on the ground.

RUANDA
(Kigali)
*Played by King
Rudahigwa and
Chiefs*

18. WATUTSI *
ROYAL DRUMS

Denis-Roosevelt
Reeves Sound
Side 7

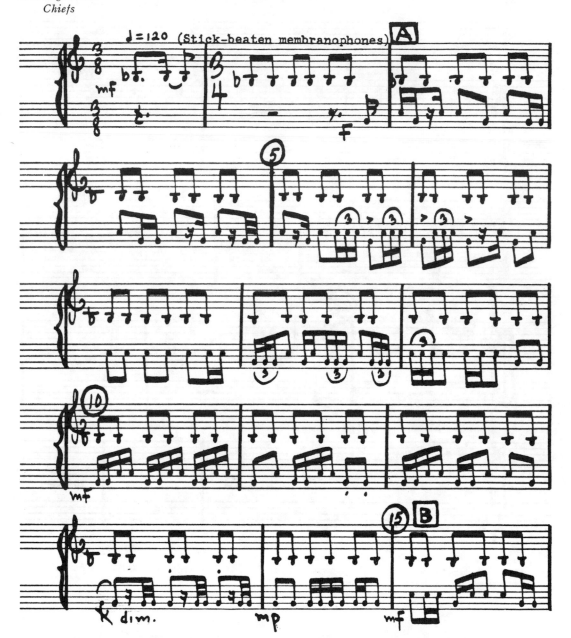

* Transcription published in *Journal of the American Musicological Society*, V (1952), p. 18.

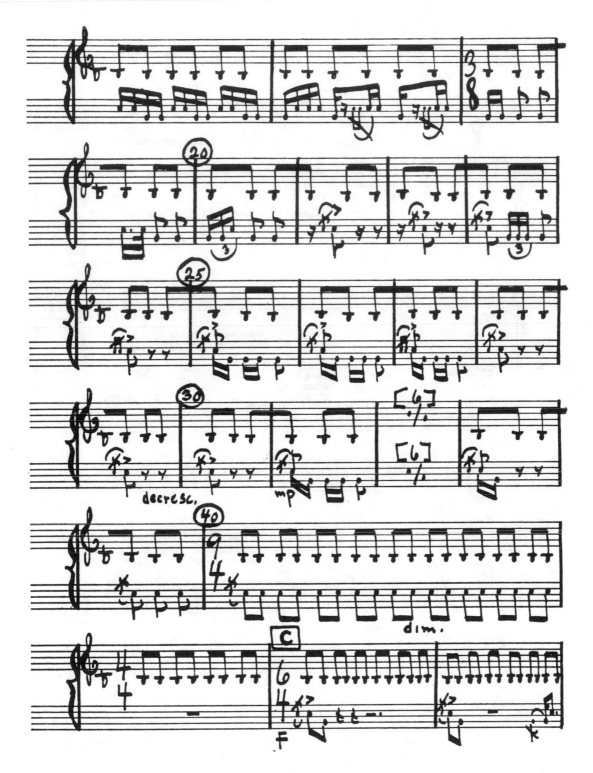

153

154

155

RUANDA
(Kigali)
*Played by King
Rudahigwa and
Chiefs*

19. WATUTSI *
ROYAL DRUMS

Denis-Roosevelt
Reeves Sound Studios
Side 9 – Band 1

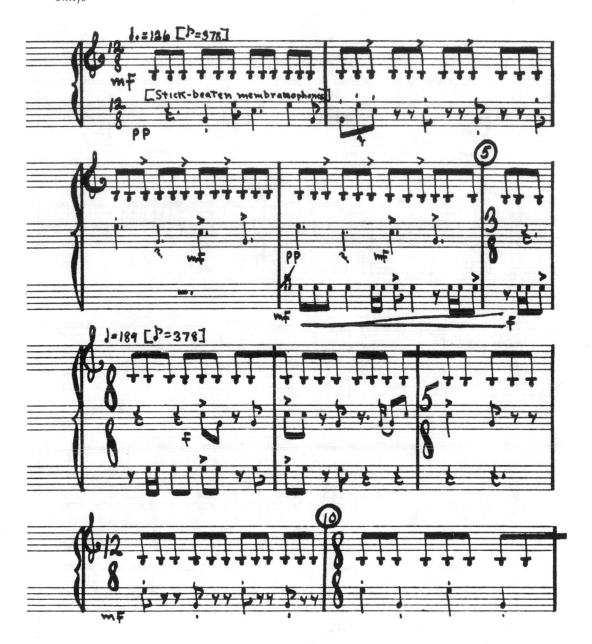

* Transcription published in *Journal of the American Musicological Society*, V (1952), p. 20.

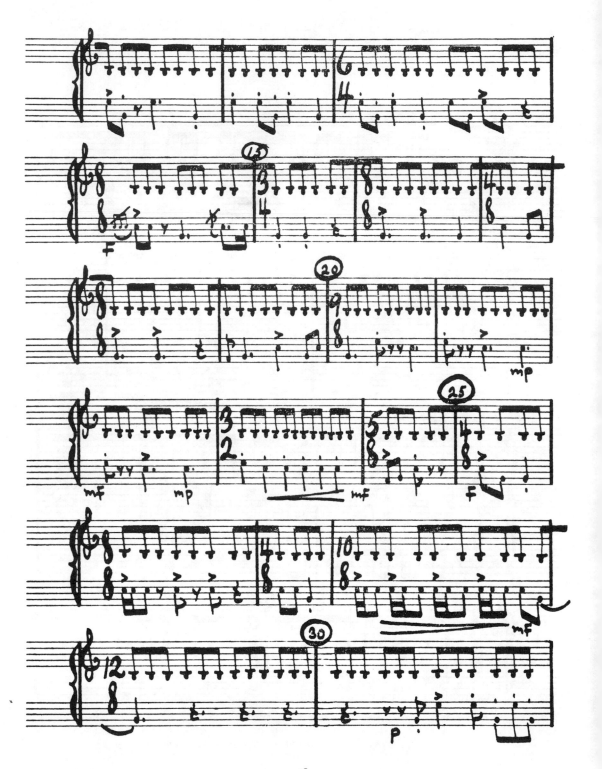

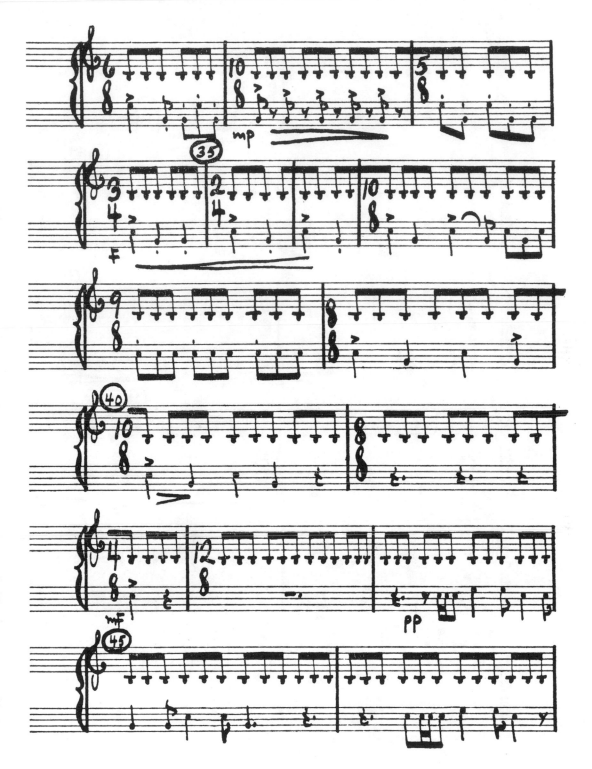

159

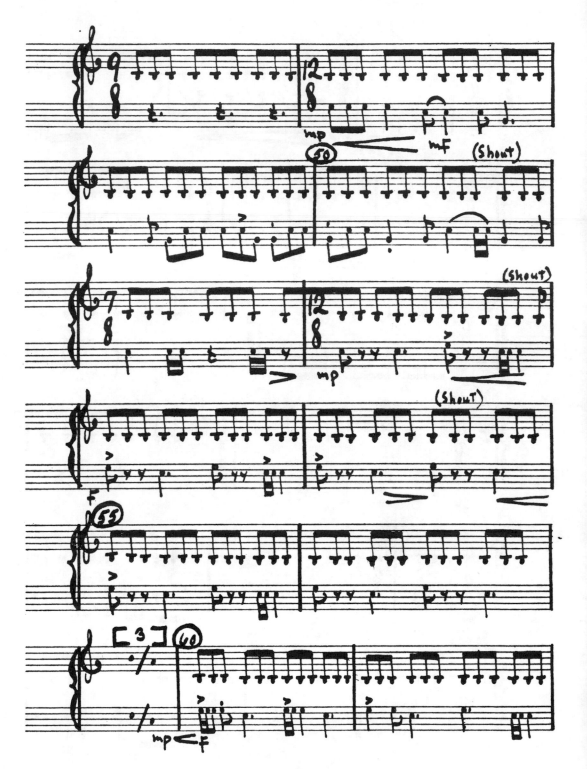

160

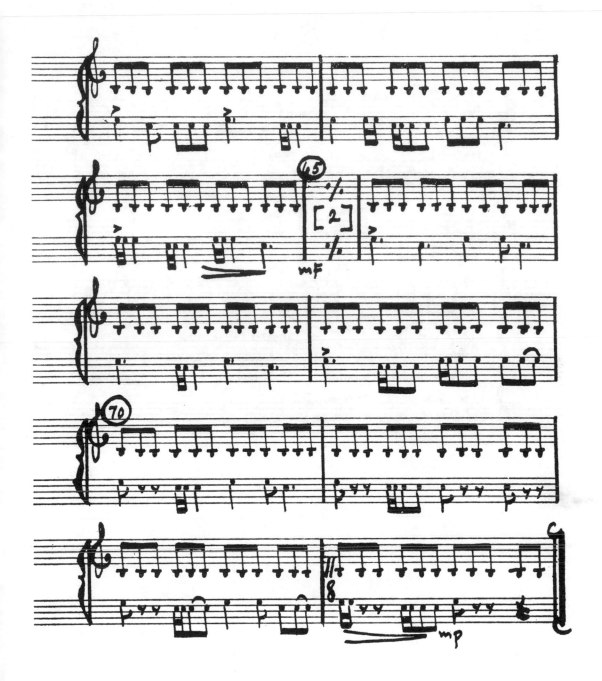

20. WATUTSI
EPIC SONG OF WAR *

Folkways P428
Side 1 – Band 3

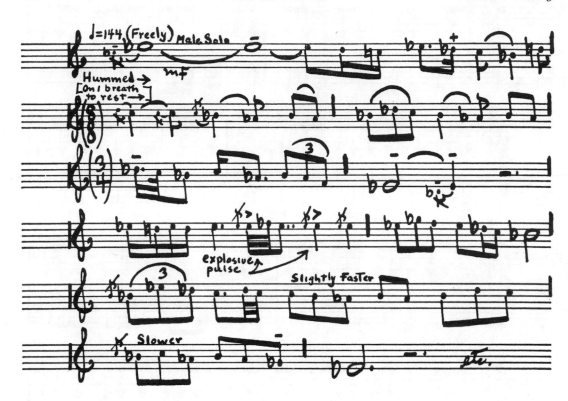

* The singer, Muyunzwe, tells of the exploits of the Urwintwali, a warrior group to which he belongs. This group was formed in the 1920's during King Musinga's reign.

21. WATUTSI
EPIC SONG OF WAR*

Folkways P428
Side 1 – Band 4

* "Heroes are called to arms . . ." The singer, Muyunzwe, tells about a warrior group, the Ibabazabahizi, which was formed c. 1880 and which fought in the provinces of Kigesi and Nkore.

BELGIAN CONGO
(Southwest)
(bet. Kasai +
Kwilu Rivers)
*Transposed
down major 2nd*

22. BABUNDA
NEW YEAR SONG

Folkways P427
Side 1 – Band 1

de ko to pa ne wa

165

BELGIAN CONGO
(Southwest)
(-between Kwilu
and Kwango
Rivers)

23. BAMBALA
DRUM TELEGRAPHY *

Folkways P427
Side 1 – Band 6

* A message announcing the close of an official litigation is sent by the Bambala chief upon a small slit-log drum. Pitch levels and rhythms of actual words are reproduced.

* The music accompanies a circle dance by men and women.

FRENCH EQUATORIAL
(Ouessa)

25. MBOKO
MOUTH BOW *

Folkways P402
Side 1 – Band 5

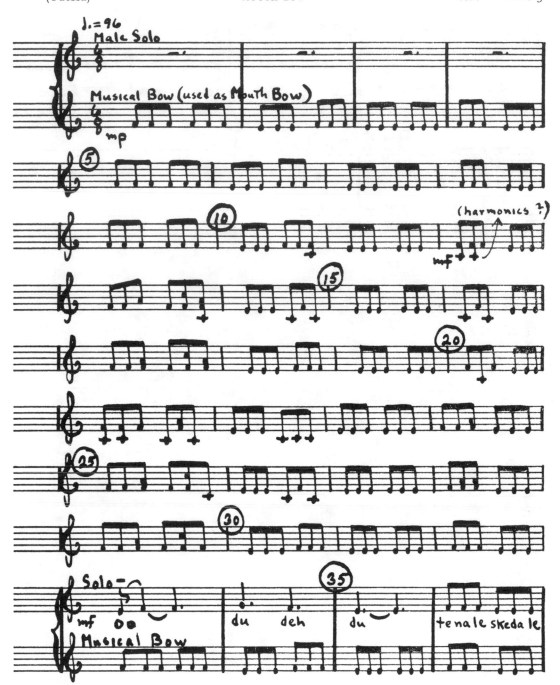

* CF 4. The player uses his mouth as a resonator for the bow. At his vocal interlude (an almost literal duplication of the bow's four-measure phrase), he uses the bow in its original capacity (non-orally).

[end of singer's interlude]

etc.

FRENCH EQUATORIAL
(Ouessa)

26. MBOKO
RIDDLE SONG *

Folkways P402
Side 1 – Band 6

* CF 5. The song contains a riddle about the antelope (*djombi*). The singer is also the instrumentalist.

[rattle: becomes apparent from here on — somewhat obscures stick pattern]

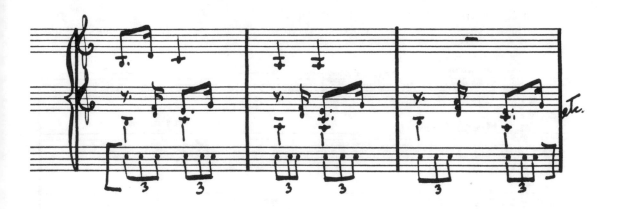

FRENCH EQUATORIAL
(Ouessa)

27. POMO
PERAMBULATING SONG *

Folkways P402
Side 2 – Band 3

* The soloist sings an exhortation as he leads a procession through the village.

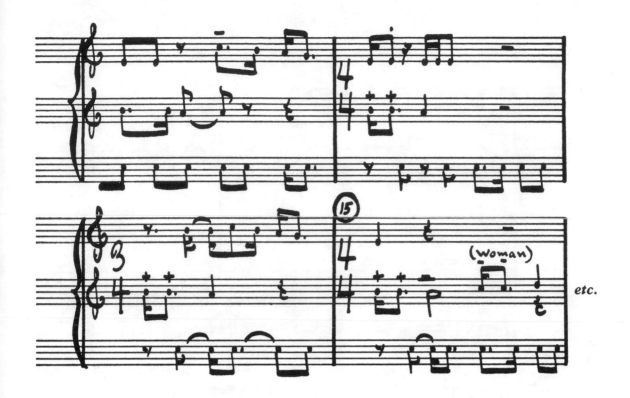

FRENCH EQUATORIAL
*Transposed down
minor 2nd*

28. N'GUNDI
HUMOROUS LOVE SONG **

Folkways P402
Side 1 – Band 3

* CF 6.

** The song belongs to "The Sons of Sô," a secret society, and tells of a woman who complains that too much eating has reduced her husband's lovemaking capacity.

178

179

* In this song, the girls "scoff at a young boy who has bragged too much about his capabilities."

FRENCH EQUATORIAL
(Forest near Ouessa)

30. BABINGA PYGMIES
ELEPHANT-HUNT RITUAL
"Yeli" *

Folkways P402
Side 2 – Band 5

* *Yeli* is called upon to insure a successful hunt, in this religious yodel-song of the women.

31. BABINGA PYGMIES

SOCIAL DANCE

"Djoboko"

185

etc.

FRENCH EQUATORIAL
(Ouessa)

32. YASWA
XYLOPHONES *

Folkways P402
Side 1 – Band 8

* CF 7. Calabash-resonated xylophones (with film covering on each calabash). Played by professional musicians.

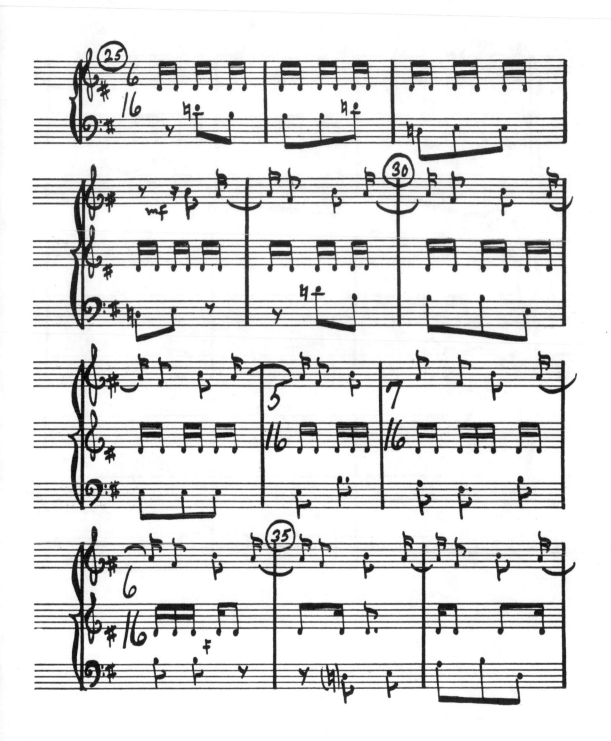

189

190

33. KUKUYA
IVORY HORNS *

Folkways P402
Side 2 – Band 4

* CF 8. The five ivory horns play one note each in hocket style. The singer is also the drummer. This is a professional band.

etc.

FRENCH EQUATORIAL
(Fort Rousset)

34. KUYU
SHAMAN'S ALLIGATOR-SONG
"Kabe"

Folkways P402
Side 2 – Band 7

* CF 9. This is a magical shaman's song to attract alligators.

194

196

FRENCH EQUATORIAL
(Fort Rousset)
*Transposed
down min. 2nd*

35. KUYU
WOMEN'S DANCE *
Birth of Twins

Folkways P402
Side 2 – Band 8

* This song, *Kano*, accompanies a women's circle dance on the occasion of the birth of twins.

FRENCH EQUATORIAL
(Pikounda)

36. BONGILI
GIRLS' BANANA WORK SONG *

Folkways P402
Side 2 – Band 1

* In time to the pounding of the pestle, the women sing of the tempting banana paste they are preparing.

FRENCH EQUATORIAL
(Ogooué River
near Franceville)
*Transposed
down minor 2nd*

37. BADUMA
PADDLERS' SONG *

Folkways P402
Side 1 – Band 1

* The paddlers sing of their difficult work as they row with precision in their dugout. A non-Bantu word, *miseria*, has been adapted to the song.

FRENCH EQUATORIAL
(Ogooué River
near Franceville)

38. BADUMA

PADDLERS' SONG WITH SANZA *

Folkways P402
Side 1 – Band 2

* CF 10.   The almost "tempered" tuning of the sanza suggests Western influences, as does also the jazz-like figure at the end of each measure. This is a dance-song about emulating white men.

203

204

FRENCH EQUATORIAL
(Area of Ogooué
River)
*Transposed
down minor 2nd*

39. OKANDI
WOMEN'S DANCE *

Folkways P402
Side 1 – Band 7

* To the soloist's question, "With whom (with which wife) will my husband spend the night?" the chorus responds with a different answer each time.

* CF 11. This dance melody "Musingasinga yakora egali" is played by four men on one xylophone (the loose-log *ntara*). The "mixer" faces the other three.

209

UGANDA
(Hoima)
*Transposed
down min. 2nd*

41. BANYORO
ROYAL GOURD-HORN ENSEMBLE *
"Irambi"

London LB 832
Side 2 – Band 1

* CF 12. The *makondere* gourd horns (transverse) of the Mukama are played on the first day of each new moon.

etc.

UGANDA
(Toro District, near
Ruwenzori Mts.)
*Transposed
down maj. 2nd*

42. BATORO

DANCE SONG
"Mutitira" *

London LB 832
Side 1 – Band 1

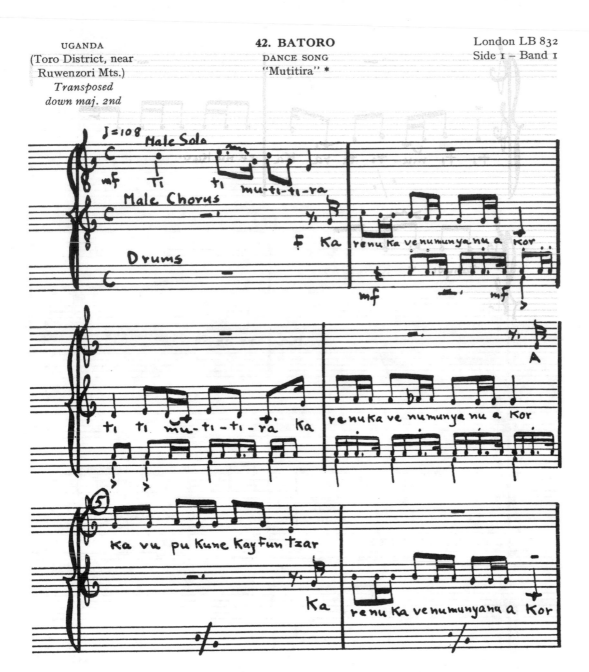

* The men sing of *Mutitira* (happiness).

UGANDA
(Ruwenzori Mts.)
(Bundibugyo Village)

43. BAMBA
FLUTES *

London LB 832
Side 1 – Band 5

* CF 13. These *luma* flutes (made of bamboo) are vertical, stopped, and play one note each.

217

UGANDA
(probably near
Kampala)

44. BAGANDA
HISTORIC SONG WITH HARP *

London LB 832
Side 2 – Band 3

* CF 14. A song about "The Executioner" is sung and played by Timuso Mukasa on an arched *enonga* harp.

* A song about an eccentric person is sung by Muliama Namale and women's chorus.

UGANDA
(Kampala)
*Transposed
down major 2nd*

46. BAGANDA
ROYAL XYLOPHONES *
"Katego"

London LB 832
Side 2 – Band 5

* CF 15. Royal *madinda* xylophones of the Kabaka. Xylophone tune based on song about king and certain war.

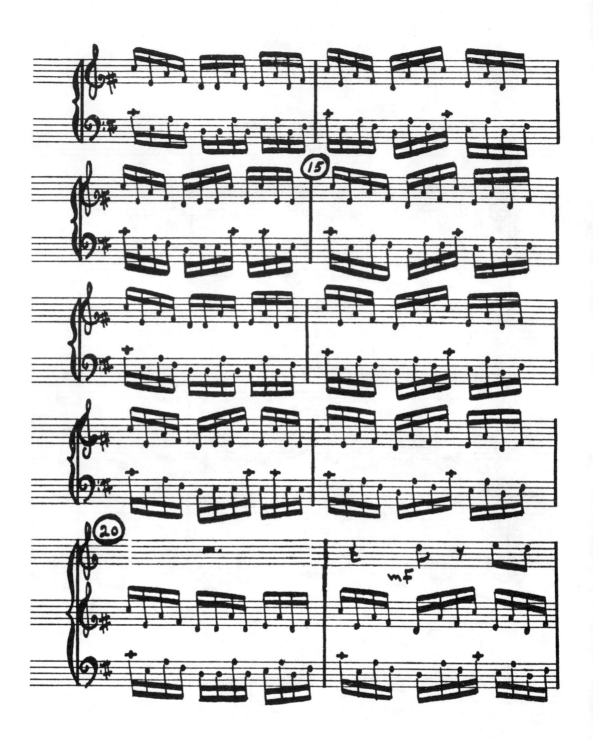

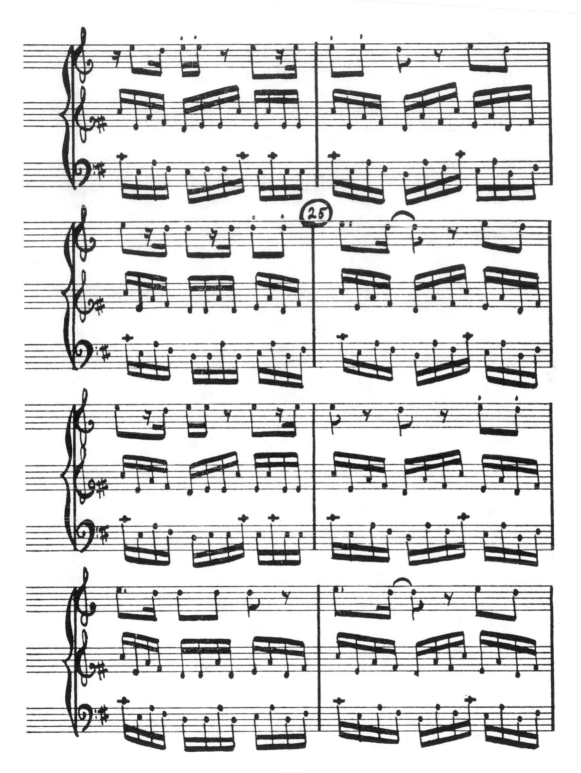

223

etc.

TANGANYIKA
(Shinyanga)
*Transposed
down minor 2nd*

47. WASUKUMA
WEDDING SONG *
"Kabunga"

African
Music Society
Trek DC 158
Side B

* "Come and see me. I am the chief's important man."

226

TANGANYIKA
(Itetemia,
Tabora District)

48. WANYAMWEZI
CHIEF INSTALLATION *

African
Music Society
GB 1311 – Side A

* "The new chief has come." Sung at installation of Chief N. S. Fundikira II, March 3, 1948.

230

231

233

TANGANYIKA
(Tabora district)
*Transposed
down min. 2nd*

49. WANYAMWEZI
WEDDING TUNE ON SANZA *

African Music Soc.
GB 1315 – Side A

* CF 16. *Mbira* is the local name of the sanza. The *harusi* (wedding) tune is played by Ngayamiso Kitunga.

236

TANGANYIKA
(Marangu, near
Kilimanjaro)
*Transposed
up major 2nd*

50. WACHAGA
CHIEF-PRAISE SONG *
"O Cheye"

African Music Soc.
GB 1553 – Side A

* "The Mangi (chief) is visiting his people. The one who has passed through your garden is the chief of this country." The soloist is Lengare Sakarani.

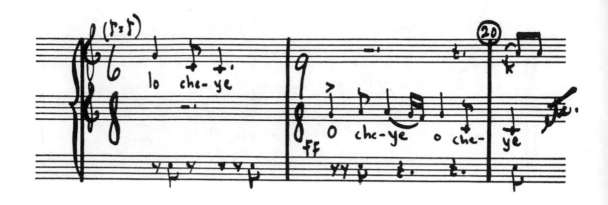

TANGANYIKA
(Arusha, near
Mt. Meru)

51. WAMERU
SPELL-BREAKING PARTY SONG *
"Nabobo"

African Music Soc.
GB 1561 – Side B

* "Sleep well you girls, sleep well, my love." Last dance-song at a party; soloist is Melany Mewarali.

TANGANYIKA
(Iringa)
*Transposed
up major 3rd*

52. WAHEHE
ELEPHANT HUNTING SONG *
"Chigoma"

African Music Soc.
GB 1331 – Side A: 1

* "I am glad to have the chance of looking at a dead elephant." Sung after the elephant hunt by Mugabe and chorus.

MELODY TYPE CHART *

1) *One- or Two-Step*

   Bapere Circumcision Bird (8); compass of third
   Mangbetu (1, Section E); compass of third
   Babinga Pygmies Ritual-Hunt (30); nucleus of third
   N'Gundi Girls (29); nucleus of third (solo part)
   Kuyu Medicine Song (34): compass of second (chorus)
   Mboko (25); compass of second (mouth bow); third (solo)
   Baganda Historic Song (45); compass of second (chorus)
   Wameru Spell-Breaking Song (51); open-fourth ostinato (chorus)
   Kukuya Horns (33); ostinato of third (two bottom horns)
   Bapere Xylophone (11); ostinato of second (lowest line)
   Baganda Royal Xylophones (46); ostinato of second (top line)

2) *Descending Tetrachord*

   Mambuti Pygmies (14); chorus; chasmatonic, non-hemitonic
   Mangbetu (1, Sections B, I); solo; diatonic
   N'Gundi Girls (29); chorus; chasmatonic, non-hemitonic
   Yaswa Xylophones (32); top line; chasmatonic, non-hemitonic
   Wameru Spell-Breaking Song (51); chorus; chasmatonic, 1-step

3) *Rising Pentachord Fanfare*

   Bapere Circumcision (7); solo; chasmatonic
   Bapere Flagellation (9); solo-chorus; chasmatonic
   Babira Circumcision (8); chorus; chasmatonic
   Babira (3); chorus; chasmatonic
   Batwa Pygmies (15); chorus; chasmatonic
   Wanyamwezi Sanza (49); chasmatonic

4) *Hexachord*

   Mangbetu (1, Sections G, I); chorus; diatonic
   Wachaga Chief-Praise Song (50); solo-chorus; chasmatonic

* Transcription numbers in parentheses.

Baganda Historic Song (44); harp, chasmatonic; solo, diatonic
Babinga Pygmies (31); male chor. 1; chasmatonic
Mboko Riddle Song (26); solo; chasmatonic
Wameru Spell-Breaking Song (51); solo; chasmatonic

5) *Minor Seventh With Tritone Effect*

Bapere Horns (10); chasmatonic
Mambuti Pygmies: Flutes (13); chasmatonic
Mambuti Pygmies Feast Song (12); diatonic
Kukuya Horns (33); chasmatonic-diatonic
Baganda Xylophones (46); chasmatonic

6A) *Octave Descent*

Mangbetu (1, Sections A, C); diatonic-chasmatonic; zig-zag thirds
Babunda New Year (22); chasmatonic
Batwa Pygmies (16); chasmatonic; hemitonic
Watutsi Historic Songs (20, 21); diatonic
Bahutu (17); chasmatonic; hemitonic
Bongili Girls Banana Song (36); diatonic
Baya (24); chasmatonic
Pomo (27); chasmatonic
Baduma Paddlers (38); diatonic; zig-zag thirds
N'Gundi (28); solo, diatonic; sanza, chasmatonic
Okandi (39); diatonic
Banyoro Xylophone (40); chasmatonic
Banyoro Horns (41); chasmatonic
Batoro (42); diatonic-chasmatonic
Bamba Flutes (43); chasmatonic
Baganda Historic Song (45); chasmatonic
Wahehe Elephant Hunt (52); diatonic
Wasukuma Wedding (47); chasmatonic

6B) *Octave Ascent*

Kuyu Medicine Song (34); chasmatonic
Kuyu Women: Birth of Twins (35); chasmatonic
Baduma Paddlers (37); diatonic
Wanyamwezi Chief Installation (48); diatonic; zig-zag thirds

7) *Supra-Octave Ladder of Thirds*

Batwa Pygmies (15)
[Wachaga Chief-Praise (50, middle section); partly diatonic]
[Mangbetu (1, Section J); ladder within octave]

CENT-FREQUENCY CHARTS

(Cent numbers are given for every melodic or harmonic interval actually appearing in a piece; some additional cent numbers are also given.)

1. *Bapere Horns (Transcr. 10)*

(Aerophone; made of reed; one note each)

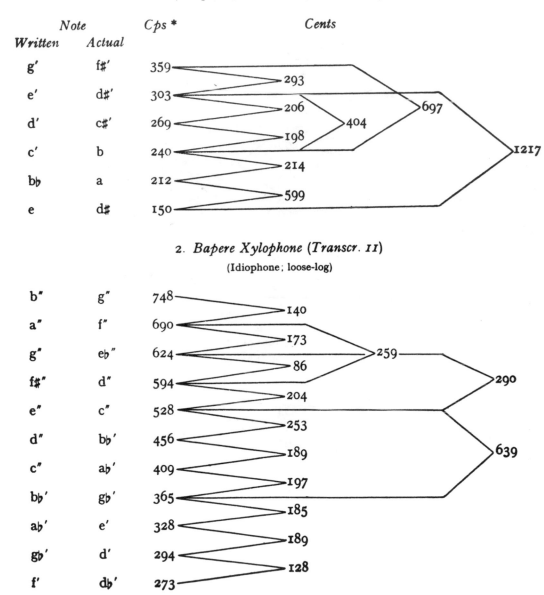

2. *Bapere Xylophone (Transcr. 11)*

(Idiophone; loose-log)

* Cps: Cycles per second.

3. *Mambuti Flutes (Transcr. 13)*

(Aerophone; vertical; wooden; one note each)

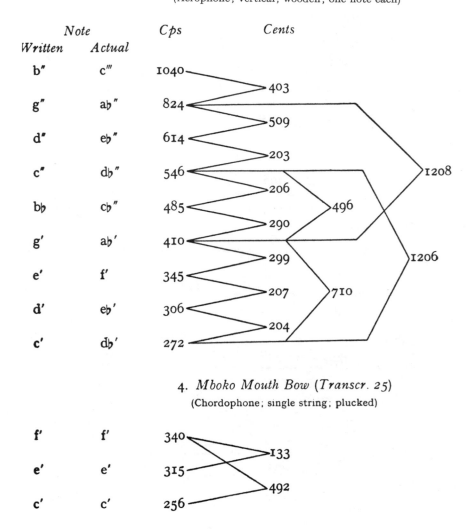

4. *Mboko Mouth Bow (Transcr. 25)*

(Chordophone; single string; plucked)

5. *Mboko Zither (Transcr. 26)*

(Chordophone; idiochordic palm fiber; plucked)

Note		Cps	Cents
Written	Actual		
a′	a′	418	
			142
g′	g′	385	352
			210
f′	f′	341	
			94
e′	e′	323	
			192
d′	d′	289	
			183
c′	c′	260	
			139
b	b	240	345
			206
a	a	213	

6. *N'Gundi Sanza (Transcr. 28)*

(idiophone; set of lamellas; thumb-plucked)

Note		Cps	Cents
c″	d♭″	550	
			71
b′	c″	528	508
			219
a′	b♭′	465	
			218
g′	a♭′	410	
			294
e′	f′	346	
			207
d′	e♭′	307	
			197
c′	d♭′	274	
			91
b	c′	260	
			197
a	b♭	232	

7. Yaswa Xylophones (Transcr. 32)
(Idiophone; calabash resonators with membrane)

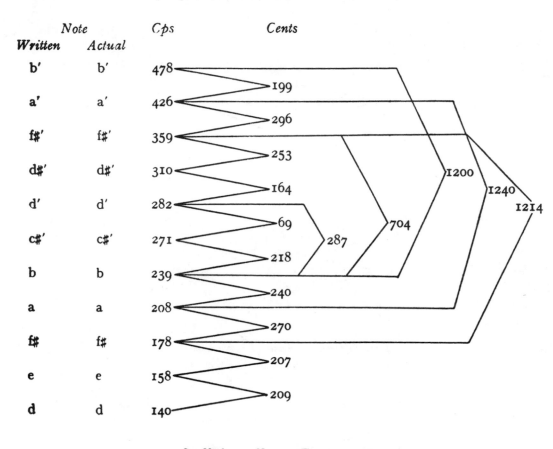

Note		Cps	Cents
Written	Actual		
b′	b′	478	
			199
a′	a′	426	
			296
f♯′	f♯′	359	
			253
d♯′	d♯′	310	
			164
d′	d′	282	
			69
c♯′	c♯′	271	
			218
b	b	239	
			240
a	a	208	
			270
f♯	f♯	178	
			207
e	e	158	
			209
d	d	140	

(1200, 1240, 1214, 287, 704)

8. Kukuya Horns (Transcr. 33)
(Aerophone; ivory, one note each)

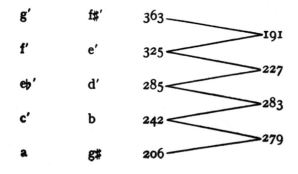

Written	Actual	Cps	Cents
g′	f♯′	363	
			191
f′	e′	325	
			227
e♭′	d′	285	
			283
c′	b	242	
			279
a	g♯	206	

9. *Kuyu Horn (Transcr. 34)*
(Aerophone; antelope; transverse)

10. *Baduma Sanza (Transcr. 38)*
(Idiophone; set of lamellas; thumb-plucked)

11. *Banyoro Xylophone (Transcr. 40)*
(Idiophone; loose-log)

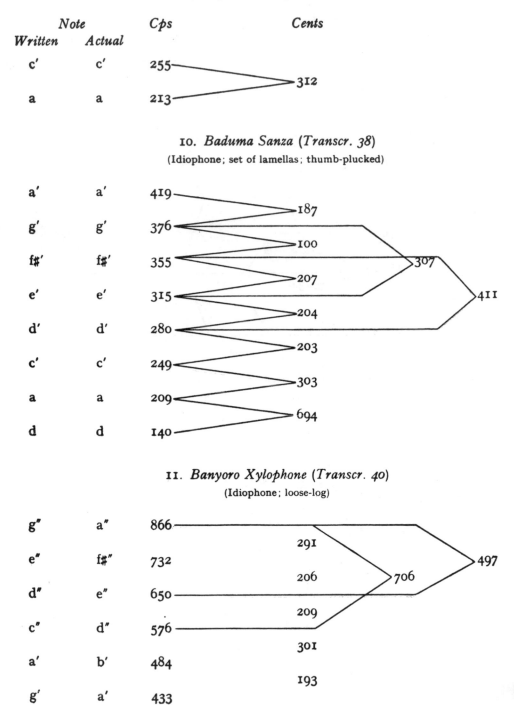

12. *Banyoro Royal Horns* (*Transcr. 41*)
(Aerophone; multi-gourd; transverse)

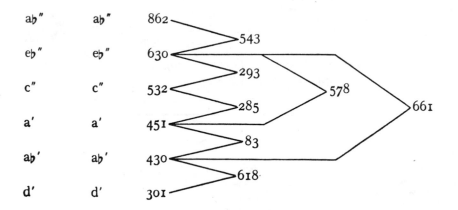

Note			
Written	*Actual*	*Cps*	*Cents*
e♭′	e′	320	
d′	d♯′	305	83
c′	c♯′	270	211
b♭	b	240	204
g	g♯	200	315
f	f♯	178	202
e♭	e	156	228
d	d♯	153	34
c	c♯	138	179

294   519   643   433   1162   1243

13. *Bamba Flutes* (*Transcr. 43*)
(Aerophone; bamboo; vertical; stopped; one note each)

a♭″	a♭″	862	
e♭″	e♭″	630	543
c″	c″	532	293
a′	a′	451	285
a♭′	a♭′	430	83
d′	d′	301	618

578   661

14. *Baganda Harp* (*Transcr. 44*)
(Chordophone; arched)

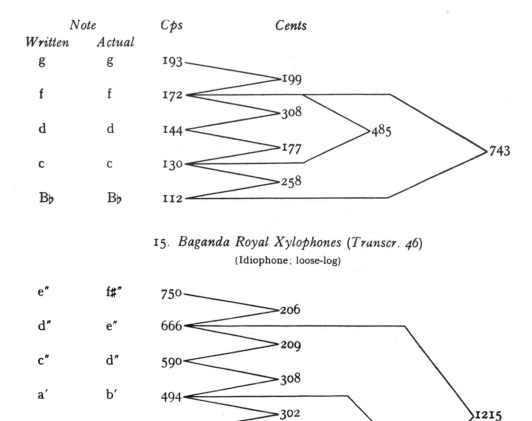

	Note		Cps	Cents
Written	*Actual*			

15. *Baganda Royal Xylophones* (*Transcr. 46*)
(Idiophone; loose-log)

16. *Wanyamwezi Sanza (Transcr. 49)*

(Idiophone; set of lamellas; thumb-plucked)

	Note		Cps	Cents

Written	Actual			
b♭′	b′		481	
a♭′	a′		430	194
g′	g♯′		406	100 294
f′	f♯′		362	198
e♭′	e′		322	203 401 695
d′	d♯′		303	105
c′	c♯′		271	193 298 699
b♭	b		241	203
g	g♯		203	298
e♭	e		161	401

NUMERICAL-TERRITORIAL INDEX OF TRANSCRIPTIONS *

BELGIAN CONGO AND RUANDA-URUNDI

Transcr.	Tribe	Recording	Description
1	Mangbetu	DR–1	Male Choral Song
2	Babira	,, 2:1	Male Choral Song
3	Babira	,, 2:4	Male Choral Song
4	Babira	,, 11:1	Circumcision Drums
5	Babira	,, 11:2	Circumcision Dance
6	Babira	,, 11:3	Circumcision Dance (Male chorus, drums)
7	Bapere	,, 12:1	Circumcision Dance (Male solo, male choruses, drums)
8	Bapere	,, 12:2	Circumcision Bird (Male solo, male chorus, bull roarer)
9	Bapere	,, 12:3	Circumcision Flagellation (Male solo, male chorus, drums)
10	Bapere	,, 3:2	Horns of reed (one-note each), drum, bells
11	Bapere	,, 4	Xylophone
12	Mambuti Pygmies	,, 5:1	Elephant Feast (Male solos, male chorus)
13	Mambuti Pygmies	,, 5:2	Dance (Wooden, one-note flutes; drum)
14	Mambuti Pygmies	,, 5:3	Hunting Song (Male solo, male chorus)
15	Batwa Pygmies	,, 6:1	Dance (Female solo, male choruses)
16	Batwa Pygmies	,, 6:2	Dance (Male choruses)
17	Bahutu	,, 10:3	Dance (Male solo, mixed chorus)
18	Watutsi	,, 7	Royal Drums
19	Watutsi	,, 9:1	Royal Drums
20	Watutsi	F–P428–1:3	Epic War Song (Male solo)

* The transcriptions are listed according to the geographical proximity of the tribes to one another.

Transcr.	Tribe	Recording	Description
21	Watutsi	,, 1:4	Epic War Song (M. solo)
22	Babunda	F–P427–1:1	New Year (M. solo, mixed chorus)
23	Bambala	,, 1:6	Drum Telegraphy

DR: Denis-Roosevelt Expedition (1935–36); Reeves Sound Studios
F: Folkways P402, P427, P428 (recorded in 1946, 1951, 1952, respectively)
L: London LB 832
AMS: African Music Society (International Library African Music)

FRENCH EQUATORIAL AFRICA

24	Baya	F–P402–2:2	Dance (Male solo, mixed chorus, drums)
25	Mboko	,, 1:5	Mouth bow (musical bow), male solo
26	Mboko	,, 1:6	Riddle Song (Male solos, idiochordic zither, sticks)
27	Pomo	,, 2:3	Perambulating chant (Male solo, mixed chorus, iron bell)
28	N'Gundi	,, 1:3	Humorous Love Song: Secret Society (Male solo, sanza, sticks)
29	N'Gundi	,, 1:4	Female solo, female chorus, hand-clapping (some yodelling)
30	Babinga Pygmies	,, 2:5	Elephant-hunt Ritual (Female yodeller, female chorus, hand-clapping)
31	Babinga Pygmies	,, 2:6	Dance (Mixed chorus, drums)
32	Yaswa	,, 1:8	Xylophones
33	Kukuya	,, 2:4	Ivory horns (one note each), drum, male solo
34	Kuyu	,, 2:7	Shaman's alligator song (Male solo, male chorus, transverse antelope horn, sticks, hand clapping)
35	Kuyu	,, 2:8	Birth of twins, dance song (Female chorus, female solo, iron bell, drums)
36	Bongili	,, 2:1	Banana work song (Female solo, female chorus, pestle)
37	Baduma	,, 1:1	Paddlers (Male solo, male chorus)
38	Baduma	,, 1:2	Paddlers (Male solos, sanza, rattles, horn)
39	Okandi	,, 1:7	Dance (Female solo, female chorus, drums)

UGANDA

Transcr.	Tribe	Recording		Description
40	Banyoro	L–LB 832–1:4		Dance melody on xylophone (four players)
41	Banyoro	,,	2:1	New moon celebration; royal gourd-horns (transverse)
42	Batoro	,,	1:1	Dance song (Male solo, male chorus, drums)
43	Bamba	,,	1:5	Bamboo flutes (stopped, vertical), drum
44	Baganda	,,	2:3	Historic song (Male solo, arched harp)
45	Baganda	,,	2:4	Historic song (Female solo, female chorus, hand clapping, drums)
46	Baganda	,,	2:5	Historic war melody on royal xylophones

TANGANYIKA

Transcr.	Tribe	Recording		Description
47	Wasukuma	AMS–DC 159–B		Wedding song (Male solo, mixed chorus)
48	Wanyamwezi	,,	GB 1311–A	Chief installation (Male solo, female chorus, drums)
49	Wanyamwezi	,,	GB 1315–A	Wedding tune on sanza
50	Wachaga	,,	GB 1553–A	Chief praise song (Male solo, male chorus, leg bells)
51	Wameru	,,	GB 1561–B	Spell-breaking party song (Male solo, mixed chorus)
52	Wahehe	,,	GB 1331–A:1	Elephant hunting song (Male solo, male chorus, hand clapping)

TRIBAL INDEX

Tribe	Territory	Language	Transcription
Babinga Pygmies	French Equatorial	Bantu	30, 31
Babira	Belgian Congo	Bantu	2–6
Babunda	Belgian Congo	Bantu	22
Baduma	French Equatorial	Bantu	37, 38
Baganda	Uganda	Bantu	44–46
Bahutu	Ruanda-Urundi	Bantu	17
Bamba	Uganda	Bantu	43
Bambala	Belgian Congo	Bantu	23
Banyoro	Uganda	Bantu	40, 41
Bapere	Belgian Congo	Bantu	7–11
Batoro	Uganda	Bantu	42
Batwa Pygmies	Ruanda-Urundi	Bantu	15, 16
Baya	French Equatorial	Sudanic (N)*	24
Bongili	French Equatorial	Bantu	36
Kukuya	French Equatorial	Bantu	33
Kuyu	French Equatorial	Bantu	34, 35
Mambuti Pygmies	Belgian Congo	Bantu	12–14
Mangbetu	Belgian Congo	Sudanic (N)*	1
Mboko	French Equatorial	Cameroon Bantu	25, 26
N'Gundi	French Equatorial	Bantu	28, 29
Okandi	French Equatorial	Bantu	39
Pomo	French Equatorial	Bantu	27
Wachaga	Tanganyika	Bantu	50
Wahehe	Tanganyika	Bantu	52
Wameru	Tanganyika	Bantu & NH*	51
Wanyamwezi	Tanganyika	Bantu	48, 49
Wasukuma	Tanganyika	Bantu	47
Watutsi	Ruanda-Urundi	Bantu	18–21
Yaswa	French Equatorial	Bantu	32

* N: Nigritique (a sub-group of the Sudanic languages).
* NH: Nilo-Hamitic language (some of the Wameru speak a Bantu and some a Nilo-Hamitic language).

BIBLIOGRAPHY

Included in this bibliography are all the sources referred to in the footnotes as well as several additional sources. Asterisks * indicate works on African music or instruments of special relation to the present study.

*ANKERMANN, BERNHARD. *Die afrikanischen Musikinstrumente*. Berlin, 1901. 132 pp.

BABAULT, GUY. "Les Batwa pygmées du Kivu (Nord-Ouest)," *L'Anthropologie*, XL (1930), 539–540.

BAUMANN, HERMANN. "Die materielle Kultur der Azande und Mangbetu," *Baessler-Archiv*, XI (1927), 3–129.

BAUMANN, HERMANN, and D. WESTERMANN. *Les Peuples et les civilisations de l'Afrique*. Paris, 1948. 605 pp.

Les Beaux-Arts. Belgian Congo issue. Brussels, 1955. 38 pp.

BIRNBAUM, M. "The Long-Headed Mangbetus," *Natural History*, XLIII (1939), 73–83.

*BLACKING, JOHN. "Eight Flute Tunes from Butembo, East Belgian Congo," *African Music*, I, 2 (1955), 24–52. (Transcr.)

— —. "Some Notes on a Theory of African Rhythm Advanced by Erich von Hornbostel," *African Music*, I, 2 (1955), 12–20.

BÖSCH, P. FR. *Les Banyamwezi*. Münster, 1930. 552 pp.

*BOONE, OLGA. *Les Xylophones du Congo Belge*. Tervuren: Annales du Musée du Congo Belge, Série III, Ethnographie, III, fasc. 2. 1936. 144 pp.

BORGONJON, FR. P. J. "De Besnijdenis bij de Tutshiokwe," *Aequatoria*, VIII (1945), 59–74.

BOSE, FRITZ. "Musikpolitische Aufgaben in Afrika," *Koloniale Rundschau*, XXXII (1941), 236–244

— —. *Musikalische Völkerkunde*. Freiburg, 1953. 197 pp.

BOURGEOIS, R. *Banyarwanda et Barundi*. II, "La Coutume." Brussels, 1954. 472 pp.

*BRANDEL, ROSE. "Music of the Giants and the Pygmies of the Belgian Congo," *Journal of the American Musicological Society*, V (1952), 16–28. (Transcriptions)

*— —. "The Music of African Circumcision Rituals," *Journal of the American Musicological Society*, VII (1954), 52–62. (Transcriptions)

— —. Review of Sukehiro Shiba, *Score of Gagaku*, in *Journal of the American Musicological Society*, X (1957), 39–44.

BROWN, J. T. "Circumcision Rites of the Becwana Tribes," *Journal of the Royal Anthropological Institute*, LI (1921), 419–427.

BRUEL, G. "Notes ethnographiques sur quelques tribus de l'Afrique Équatoriale Française," *La Revue d'Ethnographie et de Sociologie*, IV (1910), 3–32; 111–125.

BURSSENS, AMAAT. *Introduction à l'étude des langues bantoues du Congo Belge*. Antwerp, 1954. 152 pp.

CALDWELL, MORRIS. "The Culture of the Baya Tribe of West Africa," *Scientific Monthly* (April, 1930), 320–325.

*CARRINGTON, JOHN F. *A Comparative Study of Some Central African Gong-Languages*. Brussels, 1949. 119 pp.

— —. "Drum Language of the Lokele Tribe," *African Studies*, III (1944), 75–88.

— —. "Notes on an Idiophone Used in *Kabile* Initiation Rites by the Mbae," *African Music*, I, 1 (1954), 27–28.

*— —. *Talking Drums of Africa*. London, 1949, 96 pp.

CAUVIN, A. Photographs of Watutsi ceremony, in *Pageant*, (April, 1949), 94–100.

COLLAER, PAUL. "Notes sur la musique d'Afrique centrale," *Problèmes d'Afrique Centrale*, XXVI (Quatrième Trimestre, 1954), 267–271. (Transcriptions)

CZEKANOWSKI, JAN. *Wissenschaftliche Ergebnisse der deutschen Zentral-Afrika-Expedition, 1907–08*. VI, parts 1–3. Leipzig, 1917.

DECKER, J. M. DE. *Les Clans Ambuun (Bambunda)*. Brussels, 1950. 146 pp.

DOKE, CLEMENT M. *Bantu; Modern Grammatical, Phonetical, and Lexicographical Studies since 1860*. London, 1945. 119 pp.

DOUET, L. "Les Babingas," *Société d'ethnographie de Paris*. Bull. N.S. IV, 2 (1914), 15–32.

DREXEL, ALBERTO. "Razze, popoli e lingue dell'Africa," *Bibliotheca Ethnologica-linguistica Africana*, V(1933), 74–79.

EBERLE, OSKAR. *Cenalora (Leben, Glaube, Tanz und Theater der Urvölker)*. n.p. (Switzerland), 1955. 575 pp.

FARIS, E. "Culture and Personality among the Forest Bantu," *American Sociological Society*, XXVIII (May, 1934), 3–11.

FREUD, SIGMUND. *Totem and Taboo*. Translated by James Strachey. New York, 1952. 171 pp.

GBEHO, PHILLIP. "Cross Rhythm in African Music," *West African Review*, XXIII (1952), 11–13.

GIORGETTI, P. FILIBERTO. *Note di musica Zande*. Missione Africane. Verona, 1951. 34 pp. (Music)

GRAUWET, R. "An Egyptian Statuette in Katanga," synopsis in *The Belgian Congo Today*, XIV (Apr. 1955), 69–70.

GREENBERG, JOSEPH H. "The Classification of African Languages," *American Anthropologist*, L (1948), 24–30.

GUSINDE, M. *Urwaldmenschen am Ituri*. Vienna, 1948. 419 pp.

HAARDT, G. M. and L. ANDOUIN-DUBREUIL. "Expédition Citroën centre-afrique," *La Géographie*, XLV (1926), 295–331.

HABIG, J. M. "La Valeur du rythme dans la musique Bantoue," *Problèmes d'Afrique Centrale*, XXVI (Quatrième Trimestre, 1954), 278–285.

HAMBLY, WILFRID D. *Source Book for African Anthropology*. Parts 1 and 2. Chicago: Field Museum of Natural History, Publications. Anthropological Series, No. 26. 1937. 953 pp.

— —. *Tribal Dancing and Social Development*. New York, 1927. 296 pp.

*HARTMANN, HERMANN. "Ethnographische Studie über die Baja," *Zeitschrift für Ethnologie*, LIX (1930), 1–61. (Music, dance)

— —. "Die Sprache der Baja," *Zeitschrift für Ethnologie*, LXII (1930), 302–310.

HEINITZ, W. "Zwei Phonogramme aus Rutenganyo," *Vox*, XXII (1936), 50–56. (Transcriptions)

HERSKOVITS, MELVILLE J. *Patterns of Negro Music*. n.p., 194–†††. 5 pp.

— —. "Peoples and Cultures. Belgian Congo," in J. A. Goris. *Belgium*. U.N. Series, 1945. 353–365.

— —. "A Preliminary Consideration of the Culture Areas of Africa," *American Anthropologist*, XXVI (1924), 50–63.

*HERZOG, GEORGE. Transcriptions and discussion in Wilfrid Hambly. *The Ovimbundu of Angola*. Chicago: Field Museum of Natural History. Anthropological Series, XXI, 1934. 217–223.

— —. "Speech Melody and Primitive Music," *Musical Quarterly*, XX (1934), 452–466.

HICKMANN, HANS. "Afrikanische Musik," *Die Musik in Geschichte und Gegenwart*. Edited by Friedrich Blume. I, 1949–1951, col. 123–132.

HODGSON, A. G. O. "Some Notes on the Wahehe of Mahenge District, Tanganyika Territory," *Journal of the Royal Anthropological Institute of Great Britain and Ireland*, LVI (1926), 37–58.

*HORNBOSTEL, ERICH M. VON. *African Negro Music*. International Institute of African Languages and Cultures, Memorandum 4. 1928. 35 pp.

*— —. Transcriptions and discussion in Jan Czekanowski. *Wissenschaftliche Ergebnisse der deutschen Zentral-Afrika-Expedition 1907–08*. VI, Part 1. Leipzig, 1917. 379–412. (Watutsi, Bahutu, Batwa of Ruanda; 44 exx.)

*— —. "The Ethnology of African Sound-Instruments," *Africa*, VI (1933), 129–157; 277–311.

*— —. "Wanyamwezi-Gesänge," *Anthropos*, IV (1909), 781–800; 1033–1052. (Transcriptions)

HOWELL, J. "The Bantu Tribes of the Congo Watershed," *Birmingham Natural History and Philosophical Society Proceedings*, XV (1927), 107–116.

HULSTAERT, G. "Chants de Portage," *Aequatoria*, XIX (1956), 53–64. (Mongo tribe, Belgian Congo.)

*— —. "Note sur les instruments de musique à l'Équateur," *Congo*, II, Année 16 (1935), 185–200; 354–375. (Belgian Congo.)

— —. "Les Tons en Lonkundo (Congo Belge)," *Anthropos*, XXIX (1934), 75–97.

HUNTINGFORD, G. W. B. *East African Background*. London, 1950. 124 pp. (Language-map appendix)

HUSMANN, H. "Sieben afrikanische Tonleitern," *Jahrbuch der Musikbibliothek Peter, für 1939*, 44–49.

HUTCHINSON. Ann. *Labanotation*. New York, 1954. 274 pp.

JACOBS, J. "Signaaltrommeltaal bij de Tetela," *Kongo-Overzee*, XX (1954), 409–422.

*JONES, ARTHUR M. *African Music in Northern Rhodesia and Some Other Places*. Northern Rhodesia: Rhodes-Livingstone Museum, Occasional Papers, No. 4. 1949. 78 pp.

*— —. "African Rhythm," *Africa*, XXIV (1954), 26–47.

— —. "East and West, North and South," *African Music*, I, 1 (1954), 57–62.

JULIEN, PAUL. *Pygmeeën*. Amsterdam, 1953. 254 pp.

KAGAME, FR. ALEXIS. "Le Rwanda et son roi," *Aequatoria*, VIII (1945), 41–58.

KIRBY, PERCIVAL R. "Bantu," *Die Musik in Geschichte und Gegenwart*. Edited by Friedrich Blume. I, 1949–1951, col. 1219–1228.

*— —. *The Musical Instruments of the Native Races of South Africa*. Johannesburg, 1953 (first edition, 1934). 285 pp.

KOLINSKI, MIECZYSLAW. "La Música del Oeste Africano," *Rivista de Estudios Musicales*, I (1949), 191–215.

*KUNST, JAAP. *Ethno-Musicology*. The Hague, 1955. 158 pp.

— —. *Music in Flores*. Leyden, 1942. 167 pp.

*— —. "A Musicological Argument for Cultural Relationship between Indonesia – probably the Isle of Java – and Central Africa." *Proceedings of the Musical Association*, Session LXII (1936), 57–76.

KYAGAMBIDDWA, JOSEPH. *African Music from the Source of the Nile*. New York, 1955. 255 pp.

LAGERCRANTZ, STURE. *Contribution to the Ethnography of Africa*. Sweden, 1950.

LAMAN, KARL. *The Kongo*. Studia Ethnographica Upsaliensia, No. 4. Stockholm, 1953. 155 pp.

— —. *Musical Accent, or Intonation in the Kongo Language*. Stockholm, 1922. 153 pp. (Transcriptions by W. Heinitz)

LANG, H. "Nomad Dwarfs and Civilization," *Natural History*, XIX (1919), 697–713.

LAUBSCHER, B. J. F. *Sex, Custom and Psychopathology*. London, 1937. 347 pp.

LAWRENCE, J. C. D. *The Iteso*. London, 1957. 280 pp. (Music, dance)

LINTON, RALPH. *The Tree of Culture*. New York, 1957. 692 pp.

LOUPIAS, P. "Tradition et légende des Batutsi," *Anthropos*, III (1908), 1–13.

MacCURDY, GEORGE G. "The Field of Paleolithic Art," *American Anthropologist*, XXVI (1924), 27–49.

MAES, JOSEPH. *Aniota-Kifwebe*. Antwerp, 1924. 63 pp. (Circumcision masks)

*— —. "Les Lukombe ou instruments de musique à cordes des populations du Kasai – Lac Léopold II-Lukenie," *Zeitschrift für Ethnologie*, LXX (1939), 240–254. (Multiple-bow lute)

— —. *Les Peuplades du Congo Belge*. Tervuren: Musée du Congo Belge, Publications du Bureau de Documentation Ethnographique, Série 2. I, 1935. 379 pp.

*MAEYENS, L. "Het inlandsch Lied en het musikaal Accent met semantische Functie bij de Babira," *Kongo-Overzee*, IV (1938), 250–259. (Music)

MALINOWSKI, B. *The Dynamics of Culture Change*. New Haven, 1945. 171 pp. (Africa)

MAQUET, JEAN-NOËL. *Note sur les instruments de musique congolais*. Brussels: Académie Royale

des Sciences Coloniales, Classe des Sciences Morales et Politiques. Mémoires in-8°, Nouvelle
série. VI, 4, 1956. 71 pp. (Transcriptions)

MERRIAM, ALAN P. "An Annotated Bibliography of African and African-Derived Music Since
1936," *Africa*, XXI (1951), 319–329. (Extension of Varley's bibliography)

——. "Song Texts of the Bashi," *African Music*, I, 1 (1954), 44–52.

MOELLER, ALFRED. *Les Grandes Lignes des migrations des Bantous de la province orientale du Congo
Belge.* Brussels, 1936. 578 pp.

MOL, O. P. VAN. "Het huwelijk bij de Mambutu's," *Congo*, Année 13, II (1932), 204–224.

——. "Puberteitsviering en besnijdenis bij de Mambutu's," *Congo*, I (1924), 358–376.

MOLITOR, MARTHE. *Danseurs du Ruanda.* Brussels, 1952. 19 pp.

MOLITOR, P. H. "La Musique chez les Nègres de Tanganyika," *Anthropos*, VIII (1913), 714–735.

MUKADY, ALPHONSE-MARIE. "L'Art musical au Congo," *La Voix du Congolais*, XI (1955), 956–957.

NETTL, BRUNO. "Unifying Factors in Folk and Primitive Music," *Journal American Musicological
Society*, IX (1956), 196–201.

NICOLAS, FRANÇOIS-J. "Origine et valeur du vocabulaire désignant les xylophones africains,"
Zaïre, XI (1957), 69–89.

OBERG, KALERVO. "Kinship Organization of the Banyankole," *Africa*, XI (1938), 129–159.

OLBRECHTS, FRANS M. "De Studie van de inheemse Muziek van Belgisch-Congo," *Miscellanea
Musicologica Floris van der Mueren*, (1950), 147–150.

OSCHINSKY, L. *The Racial Affinities of the Baganda and Other Bantu Tribes of British East Africa.*
Cambridge, 1954. 188 pp.

PAGES, A. "Cérémonies du mariage au Ruanda," *Congo*, II (1932), 42–68.

*PEPPER, HERBERT. "Essai de définition d'un grammaire musicale noire," *Problèmes d'Afrique
Centrale*, XXVI (Quatrième Trimestre, 1954), 229–298. (Transcriptions)

——. "Réflexion sur l'art musical en Afrique Équatoriale," *L'Afrique Française*, XXVIII
(Quatrième Trimestre, 1952), 82–85.

PIERPONT, J. DE. "Les Bambala," *Congo*, Année 13, I (1932), 22–37; 185–205.

POUPON, M. A. "Étude ethnographique de la tribu Kouyou," *Anthropologie*, XXIX (1918–19),
53–88; 297–335. (Dance, music)

REESE, GUSTAVE. *Music in the Middle Ages.* New York, 1940, 502 pp.

——. *Music in the Renaissance.* New York, 1954. 1022 pp.

REIK, THEODOR. "The Puberty Ritual of the Primitives," *International Psycho-Analytical Library*,
No. 19. London, 1931. 91–166.

REINHARD, KURT. "Tonmessungen an fünf ostafrikanischen Klimpern," *Die Musikforschung*, IV
(1951), 366–370.

ROUGET, GILBERT. "Note sur les travaux d'ethnographie musicale de la mission Ogooué-Congo,"
Conferência Internacional dos Africanistas Ocidentais, 2, *Bissau*. Actas, V, No. 2 (1947), 195–204.

RYCKMANS, A. "Étude sur les signaux de 'Mondo' (tambour-téléphone) chez les Bayaka et Bankanu
du territoire de Popokabaka," *Zaïre*, X (1956), 493–515.

*RYCROFT, DAVID R. "Tribal Style and Free Expression," *African Music*, I, 1 (1954), 16–27.
(Transcriptions; N. Rhodesia)

SACHS, CURT. "Anfänge der Musik," *Bulletin de la Société Union Musicologique*, VI, fasc. 2 (1926),
136–149.

——. *The Commonwealth of Art: Style in the Fine Arts, Music, and the Dance.* New York, 1946.
404 pp.

——. *Geist und Werden der Musikinstrumente.* Berlin, 1929. 282 pp.

——. *Handbuch der Musikinstrumentenkunde.* Leipzig, 1920. 412 pp.

——. "Heterophonie," *Die Musik in Geschichte und Gegenwart.* Edited by Friedrich Blume. VI,
1 (1957), col. 327–330.

*——. *The History of Musical Instruments.* New York, 1940. 505 pp.

*——. *Les Instruments de musique de Madagascar.* Paris, 1938. 96 pp.

*— —. *Man's Early Musical Instruments*. Album notes. Folkways P525. 1956.

*— —. *Real-Lexikon der Musikinstrumente*. Berlin, 1913. 442 pp.

*— —. *Rhythm and Tempo: A Study in Music History*. New York, 1953. 391 pp.

*— —. *The Rise of Music in the Ancient World East and West*. New York, 1943. 324 pp.

— —. "Towards a Prehistory of Occidental Music," *Musical Quarterly*, XXIV (1938), 147–152.

*— —. *Vergleichende Musikwissenschaft in ihren Grundzügen*. Leipzig, 1930. 87 pp. (Revised edition, 1958)

*— —. *The Wellsprings of Music: An Introduction to Ethnomusicology*, MS. 1958.

*— —. *World History of the Dance*. New York, 1937. 469 pp.

SCHAEFFNER, ANDRÉ. *Origine des instruments de musique*. Paris, 1936. 405 pp.

*— —. "Les Rites de circoncision en pays Kissi (Haute-Guinée française)," *Études Guinéennes*, No. 12 (1953). Paris, 1954. 56 pp.

SCHEBESTA, PAUL. *Among Congo Pygmies*. London, 1933. 287 pp.

*SCHNEIDER, MARIUS. "Gesänge aus Uganda," *Archiv für Musikforschung*, II (1937), 185–242. (76 examples)

— —. *Geschichte der Mehrstimmigkeit*, I. Berlin, 1934. 107 pp.

— —. "Der Hochetus," *Zeitschrift für Musikwissenschaft*, XI (1927), 390–396.

SCHWEINFURTH, G. *Heart of Africa*. 2 volumes. London, 1873. 189 pp.

SICARD, HARALD VON. *Ngoma Lungundu*. Uppsala, 1952. 192 pp.

*SÖDERBERG, BERTIL. *Les Instruments de musique au Bas-Congo et dans les régions avoisinantes*. Ethnographical Museum of Sweden, Monographs, No. 3. Stockholm, 1956. 284 pp., 25 plates.

SPELLIG, FRITZ, "Über Geheimbünde bei den Wanyamwezi," *Zeitschrift für Ethnologie*, LIX (1927), 62–66; 201–252.

STANLEY, DOUGLAS. *The Science of Voice*. Third edition. New York, 1939. 384 pp.

— —. *Your Voice*. New York, 1945. 306 pp.

STANLEY, DOUGLAS and J. P. MAXFIELD. *The Voice, its Production and Reproduction*. New York, 1933. 287 pp.

SULLIVAN, L. R. "Pygmy Races of Man," *Natural History*, XIX (1919), 687–695.

SWANTON, JOHN R. "Three factors in Primitive Religion," *American Anthropologist*, XXVI (1924), 358–365.

TANGHE, J. "Chansons de Pagayeurs," *School of Oriental Studies*, London Bull. IV (1928), 827–838.

— —. "La Musique Nègre," *Congo*, Année 15, I, Mélanges (1934), 397.

Tervuren: Annales du Musée du Congo Belge. Série III, Ethnographie et Anthropologie. I, fasc. 1, "La Musique." 1902. 144 pp.

TORDAY, E. and T. A. JOYCE. "Notes ethnographiques sur des populations habitant les bassins du Kasai et du Kwango oriental," *Tervuren: Annales du Musée du Congo Belge*. Série IV, Tome III. 1922. 359 pp. (Instruments)

TRACEY, HUGH. "Bantu Music," *Theoria*, V (1953), 55–62.

— —. "African Winds," *Woodwind Magazine*, V, No. 7 (Mar. 1953), 4–5.

— —. *Ngoma: An Introduction to Music for South Africans*. London, 1948. 91 pp.

TRILLES, R. P. *Les Pygmées de la forêt équatoriale*. Paris, 1932. 530 pp. (Music)

*TROWELL, MARGARET and K. P. WACHSMANN. *Tribal Crafts of Uganda*. London, 1953. 423 pp. (Instruments; plates 97–115)

TURNBULL, COLIN. "Pygmy Music and Ceremonial," *Man*, LV (1955), 23–24.

VANCOILLIE, G. "Recueil de signaux claniques ou Kumbu des tribus Mbagani et du Kasai," *African Studies*, VIII (1949), 35–45; 80–99. (Instruments)

VARLEY, D. H. *African Native Music: An Annotated Bibliography*. London, 1936. 116 pp.

VEKENS, A. "La Langue des Makere, Madje et Mangbetu," *Bibliothèque Congo*, No. 25 (1928). 223 pp.

*WACHSMANN, K. P. "Approach to African Music," *Uganda Journal*, VI, 3 (1931), 148–163.

— —. "An Equal Stepped Tuning in a Ganda Harp," *Nature*, CLXV (1950), 40–41.

— —. "Harp Songs from Uganda," *Journal of the International Folk Music Council*, VIII (1956), 23–25.

*— —. "Sound Instruments of Uganda," in Margaret Trowell and K. P. Wachsmann. *Tribal Crafts of Uganda*. London, 1953. 311–415. plates 97–115.

*— —. "A Study of Norms in the Tribal Music of Uganda," *Ethnomusicology*, Newsletter 11 (1957), 9–16.

— —. "The Transplantation of Folk Music from One Social Environment to Another," *Journal of the International Folk Music Council*, VI (1954), 41–44.

WALTON, JAMES. "Iron Gongs from the Congo and Southern Rhodesia," *Man*, LV (1955), 20–23.

WANGER, W. "Gemeinschaftliches Sprachgut in Sumer und Ntu," *P. Wilhelm Schmidt Festschrift*, 1928, 157–164.

— —. "Linguistics and Dogma," *Bibliotheca Ethnologica-Linguistica Africana*, IV, No. 2 (1930–1931), 54–66.

WATERMAN, RICHARD A. "African Influence on the Music of the Americas," in Sol Tax. *Acculturation in the Americas*, II. Chicago, 1952. 207–218.

WIESCHHOFF, HEINZ. *Anthropological Bibliography of Negro Africa*. New Haven, 1948. 461 pp.

— —. *Die afrikanischen Trommeln und ihre aussereuropäischen Beziehungen*. Stuttgart, 1933. 148 pp. (Maps)

WINTER, EDWARD H. *Bwamba*. Cambridge, 1956. 264 pp.

ZUURE, B. D. *L'Âme du Murundi*. Paris, 1931. 506 pp.

Addendum:

* JONES, ARTHUR M. *Studies in African Music*. London, 1959. Vol. I, 295 pp.; Vol. II, 238 pp. (Transcriptions)

INDEX-GLOSSARY

Page numbers in italics refer to entire transcriptions

abacumbi (Watutsi exorcisers), 21
abagare (Watutsi prophets), 22
abajiji (Watutsi healers), 22
abasizi (Watutsi court bards), 38
abstraction, 43ff, 102
a cappella, 72
accent: dynamic, 16, 73, 79, 98; length, 73f; pitch, 16, 73f; timbre, 16, 74, 79, 98
acculturation, 21, 33
additive rhythm, see rhythm
adenden (Teso harpist), 37
Adonis, 25
aerophones, 18, 27, 31f, 36f, 45f, 48, 54, 64f, 72; also see Cent-Frequency Charts
agricultural area, see culture area
Aka Pygmies, 4f
ālāpa, 66, 83
alligator song, 53f, 69, *193*
Alur, 36
American Negro, 59
andpeira, 83
Angola, 84, 87
Ankole, 30
antiphonal style, see choral style
Apel, Willi, 98
Arabic influence, 66, 72, 99ff; also see Islam
Aristotle, 36, 66
Aron, Pietro, 83
arytenoid muscles, 94ff
Ashanti, 50
asymmetry, 74, 83, 101f
atuamba (Bapere bull-roarer), 26
"authentic" octave, 60, 68
Azande, 36
Babenzele, see Babinga Pygmies
Babinga Pygmies: ceremonial, 31; culture area, 4; language, 5, 260; music, 9, 31, 56, 77, 81f, 87ff, 100, *182ff;* musical ethnology, 31, 96, 99; race, 4, 6; territory, 4, 260
Babira: ceremonial, 25ff; culture area, see agricultural; language, see Kibira and 48; music, 16, 25f, 61f, 63f, 75ff, 84, 89f, *119ff;* musical ethnology, 25ff, 48, 98; territory, 5, 260
Babunda: ceremonial, 32; culture area, see agricultural area; language, 260; music, 32, 75f, *164ff;* musical ethnology, 32; territory, 260
Babylonia, 83
Baduma: culture area, see agricultural area; lan-
guage, 260; music, 33f, 65, 67ff, 72, 84f, *200ff*, 253; musical ethnology, 33f; territory, 260
Baganda: culture area, see agricultural area; language, see Luganda; music, 38, 53, 63, 71, 88, 99, 101f, *218ff*, 255; musical ethnology, 37f, 71; territory, 6, 260
baganja (Ituri Forest circumcision subjects), 26
Bahima, 7, 22, 35
Bahutu: ceremonial, 22; culture area, 7, 35, and see agricultural area; language, 260; music, 18, 59, 83, 88, 99, *150f;* territory, 260
Baila, 27
Bairu, 7, 35
Bakongo, 5
Bakuba, 38, 103
Bakumu, 21, 29
Baluba-Hemba, 5
Bamba: culture area, see agricultural area; language, 260; music, 72, *216f*, 254; territory, 260
Bambala: ceremonial 39f; culture area, see agricultural area; language, 260; music, 166; musical ethnology, 39f, 50; territory, 260
Bangombe, see Babinga Pygmies
Bantu: ceremonial 24ff; language, 5ff, 47f, 109; Sumerian language similarities, 6; music, 25ff, 61f, and *passim;* territory, 5; tribes, 260; and *passim*
Banyankole, 24
Banyoro: ceremonial, 32, 37; culture area, see agricultural area; language, 260; music, 32, 60, 71f, 83, 89, *208ff*, 253f; musical ethnology, 32, 37; territory, 260
Bapere: ceremonial, 21, 26, 51; culture area, see agricultural area; language, 260; music, 18, 26f, 51f, 54, 60f, 63f, 70, 72, 84f, 91, 100, *125ff*, 249; musical ethnology, 26f, 51f, 72, 98; territory, 260
bapfumu (Watutsi healer-prophets), 21f
barring, 73ff, 78
Bashi, 40
Bashongo, 5, 29
bass, 96
Basuto, 18
Batetela, 49f
Batoro: language, 260; music, 91f, *213ff;* territory, 260
Batwa Pygmies: culture area, 4, 35; language, 260; music, 13, 18, 48, 59, 68, 70, 88f, 91f, 101f,

145ff; musical ethnology, 4, 42, 46; race, 4, 6; territory, 4, 260

Baumann, Hermann, 4ff, 47

Baya: ceremonial, 32; culture area, see agricultural area; language, 5; music, 167f; musical ethnology, 32; territory, 5, 260

beat: equal (divisive), see rhythm; long and short (additive), see hemiola style; also see conductor's beat, downbeat, upbeat

bebuka, 66, 83

Becwana, 27

Beku Pygmies, 4

Belgian Congo: ceremonial, 25ff, 31f; culture area, 3f; language, 5f; music, 18, 26f, 31f, 51ff, 54, 57f, 61ff, 67, 70, 72, 74ff, 77, 83ff, 87f, 90ff; musical ethnology, 25ff, 31f, 36ff, 71f; race, 6; territory, 3 (also see Republic of the Congo: Léopoldville); tribes, 260; and *passim*

bell, 27, 36, 48, 174

Bell, C.R.V., 5ff, 24

Bemba, 84

birth, 30, 197

Bongili: culture area, see agricultural area; language, 260; music, 9, 13, 17, 34, 67, 83, 87, 91, 101, *199;* musical ethnology, 34; territory, 9, 260

Bongo Pygmies, 4

Boone, Olga, 71

Borgonjon, P. J., 25

Bösch, P., 28

Bourgeois, R., 21f, 29, 31, 39

bow-lute, multiple, 50

bow, musical, 18, 54, 56, 169; Cent-Frequency Chart, 260

Brandel, Rose, 9, 73, 76, 92

breathiness, 98

Brown, J. T., 27

Buganda, 6

bull-roarer, 26, 127

Burssens, Amaat, 7

Bushmen, 4

cadence, 55f, 87f, 91, 102

cannibalism, 24, 28

canon, 9, 34, 56, 65, 87; at the unison, 87; at the fifth, 87; at the octave, 87

cantillation, 54f

Carrington, John F., 18, 31, 48ff

cattle area, see culture area

cent-frequency charts, 71f, 107f, 249ff; method of computing, 107f

cents, 17, 70ff, 107f, 249ff

ceremonial: music, 20ff, 51f, 61, 100f; also see birth, dance, healing, hunting, initiation, litigation, marriage, New Year and New Moon, secret society

changing style (musical), 33

chasmatonic: see scale; melody, 58ff, 64f, 67ff, 70f, 93, 100; also see melody type chart

chief installation song, 69, 82, 91f, 229

chief praise song, 63, 70, 90, 238

China, 17, 47, 65

choral style: antiphonal, 18, 87f, 90f, 100, 102; responsorial, 18, 32, 34, 87, 91f, 100, 102; drone, 18; ostinato, 18, 31, 34, 44, 53, 56f, 60, 87; refrain, 34, 53, 56

chord, 83, 90

chordophones, 6, 18, 36ff, 48, 50, 54, 56, 63

circumcision: instruments, 18, 26f; music, 25ff, 51f, 56, 61, 63f, 76f, 90, 121ff; ritual, 24ff, 76

circumcision birds, (*ebebe, mukumo*), 26, 51f, 127

class system (social), 35f

clitoridectomy, 24

coloratura, 38, 66, 93

conductor's beat, 15f, 52, 73ff, 78, 82

constrictor muscles, 97

counterpoint, 87, 89ff

Coussemaker, Charles E. H., 14

cultural temperament, 47, 58

culture area: agricultural, 3, 43; cattle, 3f, 43, 101; Pygmy, 4f

Czekanowski, Jan, 7

dance, 22f, 25f, 32, 40ff, 52, 102, 140, 150, 167, 197

death and rebirth, theme of, 25

Denis, Armand, 107

development (musical), 92, 100ff

diaphragm breathing, 98

diatonic: see scale; melody, 58f, 64, 66f, 100; also see melody type chart

Didier, André, 107

diminished fifth, 61, 70

Dionysus, 25

discant, 13

divisive rhythm, see rhythm

dochmiac, 76

Doke, Clement M., 6f, 47

Dorian, 17, 59

downbeat, 17, 52f, 73f; overlapping, 78f

drone-ostinato, 18, 55, 87, 91

drone, vocal, 18

drum, ceremonial, 7, 22f, 26ff, 31, 38f, 45f, 152ff, and *passim*

drum: conical, 29; cylindrical, 30, 50; friction (*amahoto, mabilango*), 27; goblet-shape, 7; hand-beaten, 22, 45; rattle, 23; stick-beaten, 23, 45, 50; and *passim;* also see slit drum

drum, leader, 79

drum music, 77, 79f, 152ff, and *passim*

drum pitch, 49f

drum telegraphy (talking drum), 6, 31, 39f, 47ff, 166

dynamics, see intensity

East Africa, 6

East Horn, 7

Eberle, Oskar, 42

Efé Pygmies, 4f

Egypt, 6f, 25, 30, 37f, 42

elephant song, 64, 65, 69, 72, 85, 88ff, 135ff, 182ff, 243

Ellis, Alexander J., 70, 107

enanga, (Baganda arched harp), 6, 18, 38, 218

enharmonion, 17

ensemble, instrumental, 36f, 46, 54, 64f, 72, 79f, 211, and *passim;* vocal-instrumental, 81f, 90, and *passim*

entertainment, music for, 35ff

epic song, 66, 162f; also see historic song

erotic dance, 44, 46

ethnology, musical, see ceremonial, work song, entertainment, litigation, dance, speech melody

ethnomusicology, 8, 21; Journal of Society for, 71

etida (Iteso medicinal dance and membrane drum), 23

Europe: early harmony, 13, 83f; folk music, 14; rhythm, 73, 76, 78

Ewe, 50

extrovert, 41f, 44, 46f, 64, 103

falsetto, see register, upper vocal

Far East, 10f, 30, 37, 41, 44, 47, 58, 65, 93

female musician, 37f

fetishism, 43

fifth (interval of): chronology of, 14; melodic, 60, 65, 72; parallel, 86f, 100f; size of, 70ff; vertical, 87ff

flagellation, 24, 27, 61, 70, 85, 129

Flores, 65

flute, 27, 36, 45; bamboo, 72, 216, 254; bowl, 48; cent-frequency chart, 250, 254; wooden, 64, 140f, 250

form, musical, 33, 46, 55f, 68, 83, 91f, 100ff

Fôte Pygmies, 4

fourth (interval of): chronology of, 14; melodic, 57ff, 72; parallel, 86f, 100f; raised, see tritone; size of, 70ff; vertical, 88f

French Equatorial Africa: ceremonial, 29ff; culture area, 3f; language, 5f; music, 9, 30f, 33f, 53f, 57, 60, 65, 67ff, 72, 75ff, 80ff, 84ff, 87ff; musical ethnology, 28, 30ff, 33f, 71f; race, 6; territory, 3 (also see Republic of the Congo: Brazzaville); tribes, 258, 260; and *passim*

frequency, 95, 97, 107f, 249ff

Freud, S., 30

funeral dance, 43ff

Gabon, 4

Galla, 6f

gapimbi (Kasai membrane drum), 50

Gatsindamikiko (Watutsi royal drum), 39

Gauvin, André, 29

Gagaku, 49

geisha, 93

Gilbert, Dorothy R., 50

glissando, 99

glottis, 98f

gong, 48

Goris, J. A., 4

grace note, 93, 99

Grawet, R., 6

Greece, 17, 20f, 25, 50, 59, 66, 73, 83

Greenberg, Joseph H., 6, 48

gutturalness, 96ff, 102

gymel, 13

Hambly, Wilfrid D., 6, 84

Hamite, 5ff, 35

handclapping, 31, 45

harmony: chronology of the third, 14, 84; comparison of Africa and Europe, 13f, 83f; importance of the third, 13f, 84ff; "leading" tone, 13, 65, 91; parallel intervals, 84ff, and see under individual interval names; preharmony, 13f, 83f; also see polyphony

harp: arched, 6, 18, 38, 218, 255; cent-frequency chart, 255; performance, 37, 63, 88

Hartmann, Hermann, 32

healing, 21ff

Hebrew, 50

Heinitz, W., 84

hemiola style: African, 15ff, 45, 53, 73ff, 83, 100; European, 15ff, 74, 76; Greek, 15, 74; horizontal, 16, 74ff, 78; immediate, 16, 74, 76; sectional, 16, 76f; vertical, 16, 77ff; also see rhythm

Herskovits, Melville J., 3f, 6

Herzog, George, 84

heterophony, 86

hexachord, 62f, 247f

high civilization, 8ff, 21, 35f, 37

historic song, 37f, 53, 63, 66, 83, 88, 218ff

hoarseness, 96f, 99

hocket, 32, 64f, 99, 191, 216

Hodgson, A. G. O., 24

horn: antelope, 31, 48, 54, 89, 193, 253; cent-frequency chart, 249, 252ff; cow, 46; gourd, 32, 37, 72, 89, 211, 254; ivory, 65, 72, 191, 252; reed, 64, 72, 131, 249

Hornbostel, Erich M. von, 14, 52f, 87, 107f

Hottentots, 5

Hulstaert, G., 18, 48, 50

humming, 38, 66, 83, 99

humorous song, 75

hunting (music and ceremonial), 31f, 65, 69, 85, 88, 142ff, 182ff, 243

Huntingford, G. W. B., 5ff, 24

Hutchinson, Ann, 41

hyoid muscle, 97

idiophones, 6, 27f, 31f, 36, 40, 48ff, 54, 57, 60, 62, 67f, 71f, and *passim*

impara (Watutsi priest class), 21

incest, 30

India, 6, 66, 73, 76, 83

Indonesia, 6, 17, 66, 71, 83

ingonga (musical bow of west central Belgian Congo), 18

initiation: puberty, 23ff, and also see circumcision; royal, 29; secret society, 3f, 28f

instruction, musical, see music school

instruments, 18, 22f, 26f; tuning, 23, 70ff, 100; also see under individual types, and cent-frequency charts

intensity (dynamics), 46, 53, 66, 74, 79, 93ff, 100

interlocking style, 32; also see hocket

interval ratio, 107f

intervals, see under individual names, and also tuning

introduction (musical), 66, 83

introvert, 41f, 44, 47

inversion, 55f

Islam, 6, 24, 29, 50

isorhythm, see rhythm

isotonic, see scale

Iteso, 23, 30, 37

Ituri Forest, 3f, 26f, and *passim*; also see Babira, Bapere, Mambuti

Ives, Charles, 79

Jacobs, J., 48ff

jazz, 202

Johnston, Harry, 42

Jones, Arthur M., 14, 18, 78, 84

kabile (Mbae circumcision ritual), 18

Kagame, Alexis, 38

kanbile (Ituri Forest circumcision mirliton), 18, 27

Karinga (Watutsi royal drum), 39
Kasai, 48, 50
Katanga, 6
Kibira (Babira-Bakumu language), 5
kiendú (Kasai slit drum), 50
kinguvú (Kasai slit drum), 50
Kissi, 25
Koa Pygmies, 4
Kongo, 47
Kukuya: culture area, see agricultural area; language, 260; music, 65, 72, *191f*, 252; territory, 260
Kunst, Jaap, 17, 65, 70f, 107f
kutu (Kuyu funeral dance), 43ff
Kuyu: ceremonial, 29ff, 44f; culture area, see agricultural area; language, 260; music, 30, 31, 53, 68f, 83, 89, 91, *193ff*; musical ethnology, 29ff, 44f, 95f, 98f; territory, 260
labanotation, 41
ladder of thirds, 13, 69f
lai, 92
Laman, Karl E., 47
Lang, H., 42
language: Bantu, 5ff, 47ff; Hamitic, 5f; and music, see speech melody; Nigritique, 5; Nilo-Hamitic, 5; Nilotic, 5; Sudanic, 5ff, 47f; tonemes (pitch levels), 5f, 45, 47ff, 166; written, 12f
larynx, 93ff, 97f, 99
Lawrence, J. C. D., 23, 30, 37
leading tone, 65, 91, 100f
lilis, 7
Linton, Ralph, 3f, 6, 9f, 35, 43
litany form, 91f, 101f
litigation, music for, 39f, 166
Loeb, E. M., 24
logogenic style, 48, 54f, 66
Lokele, 48f
longombé (Kasai multiple bow-lute), 50
Luganda, 6
lukembe (Ituri Forest thumb-plucked idiophone), 72; also see sanza
lukumbi (Batetela slit drum), 50
luma (Bamba flute), 216
Lusumba (Mambuti men's secret society), 21
lute, 36
Lyangombe (Wanyamwezi secret society demon), 22
lyre, 18
Madagascar (Malagasy Republic), 6
madinda (Baganda xylophone), 71, 221
Maes-Tervueren, Joseph, 50
Maeyens, L., 48
magic, see religion
major, 83, 86
makondere (Banyoro gourd-horn ensemble), 32, 37, 72, 189, 211
malimba (Belgian Congo fixed-log xylophone), 71
Mambuti Pygmies: ceremonial, 21, 24, 31; culture area, 4, 11; language, 5; music, 11, 17, 31f, 46, 57, 60f, 64, 72, 83, 87ff, 99, *135ff*, 250; musical ethnology, 21, 31f, 37, 42, 45f; race, 4, 6; territory, 4, 260
Mamvu-Walese, 5
Mangbetu: culture area, 7; language, 5, 7; music, 13, 56, 58f, 61, 63, 67f, 70, 74, 84, 92, 100, *111ff*; musical ethnology, 37, 50, 97f; territory, 5, 7, 260

march, 29, 36
marriage, 30f, 37, 62
mask, 4, 25f, 43
mbira (African thumb-plucked idiophone), 72; also see sanza
Mboko, 54, 75f, 84f, 101, *169ff*, 250f
Mead, Margaret, 24
measure, 73ff, and *passim*
melisma, 66, 99ff
melodic shape: ascending, 52, 60f, 65f, 68f; curving 67f; descending, 57f, 65ff, 100; fanfare, 60ff; ladder of thirds, 69f; zig-zag, 67ff; also see chasmatonic and diatonic
melody, double, 89ff; triple, 89
melody, large-ranged, 59, 62ff, 92
melody types, 48, 51ff, 70, 91; chart, 247f; also see under individual types
membranophones, 22, 48, 50, and *passim*
Merriam, Alan P., 40, 42
Middle East, 6, 24, 29, 37f, 50, 58, 66, 73, 83
migration (to Africa): southwest Asian, 6; Malayo-Polynesian, 6
mimesis, animal, 25f, 28f, 32, 41ff, 102
minor, 83, 86
minor seventh melody, 63ff, 70, 248
mirliton, 18, 27
Moeller, Alfred, 18, 21, 25ff
Molitor, Marthe, 38, 46
Molitor, P. H., 36, 38, 87
monochord, 107
monotheism, 31, 43; also see religion
mordent, 99; double, 99
Moslem, see Islam
Muganda, 6
music school, 37, 93
Mutara III, Charles Rudahigwa, 38, 152
mutwale (Wanyamwezi secret-cult priest), 22
mwami (Ruanda-Urundi king), 29, 80
nanga (Tanganyika trough zither), 18
nasality, 47, 98, 102
New Year and New Moon, 32, 75f, 164f, 211
ngoma (tubular membrane-drum of Central Africa), 22f, 28, 45f, 48, 50
N'Gundi: culture area, see agricultural area; language, 5, 260; music, 16, 48, 57, 60, 72, 75, 81, 88f, 92, 100f, *176ff*, 251; musical ethnology, 28, 36, 96ff; territory, 5, 260
Nilo-Hamite, 5
Nilotic, 5
ninth (interval of), 70
nkumbi (Mambuti circumcision), 24
Nkundo-Mongo, 48
non-literate music, 12, 14, 33, 71, 87
norm (musical), 71
notation, musical, 12, 14, 74, 82
ntara (Banyoro xylophone), 208
Oberg, Kalervo, 24
ocarina, 48
Occident, 83
octave: ascending, 58, 65f, 68f, 248; chasmatonic, 17f, 60, 65, 67f, 71; curving, 67ff; descending, 46, 65ff, 69, 248; diatonic, 17, 66, 69f; isotonic, 17, 71; leap, 46, 66; parallel, 86; pentatonic, 17,

65, 67f, 71; supra, 69f, 248
octave melody, 65ff
offbeat, see upbeat
Okandi: culture area, see agricultural area; language, 260; music, 67, 84f, 86, 99, 206f; territory, 260
one- or two-step melody, 51ff, 54ff, 100, 247
organum, 86
ornaments (musical), 66, 93, 99ff
Osiris, 25
ostinato, 100, 102; instrumental, 54ff, 79f, 87, 88ff; vocal, 18, 31, 53, 55ff, 60, 87f, 91f
paddler's song, 33, 68f, 85, 200ff
padingbwa (north Belgian Congo loose-log xylophone), 71
paeonic rhythm, 15; also see hemiola
Pages, A., 30
Paleolithic culture, 4, 9f
partials, 95f, 97f
passing note, 65
pathogenic style, 46, 48, 66, 70
pelog, 6, 71
pentachord fanfare, 52, 58, 60ff, 65, 67f, 84, 90, 247
pentatonic, see chasmatonic and octave
percussion sticks, 27, 81, 171, 176
pharynx, 93ff, 97
phrasing, vocal, 99
Phrygian, 59, 66
pièn, 17, 65, 68f
pitch, 74, 79, 94ff; also see tuning
"plagal" octave, 60
Plato, 20, 22
polygamy, 3f, 30
polyphony, 56, 73, 77, 83ff, 90f, 100; also see chord, counterpoint, harmony, and melody (double)
polyrhythm, see rhythm
Pomo: culture area, see agricultural area; language, 5, 260; music, 174f; territory, 5, 260
Poupon, M. A., 29, 44, 99
primal music, 13, 52, 55ff, 101
primeval music, 12, 66
primitive: music, 8ff, 54f; society, 8ff, 35ff, 71, 93, 101; and *passim*
professional musician, 35ff, 191
Pygmy: ceremonial, 24, 31; culture area, 4, 9; language, 5; music, 11, 31f, 56f, 59, 64, 68, 72, 77, 81f, 87ff; musical ethnology, 21, 31f, 41ff, 56; race, 6; territory, 4f; tribes, 4f, 260; also see Babinga, Batwa, Mambuti; and *passim*
race, 4, 6f, 93
range, vocal, 93ff; also see melodic range
rattle, 27, 36, 131
realism, 43ff, 103
recordings, list of, 107
Reese, Gustave, 13f, 73, 78, 83f
refrain, 53, 56f, 92, 102
register, vocal: lower, 94ff, 99f; upper, 94ff, 99f; combined, 94ff, 100; isolated, 94ff
registration, vocal, 94ff, 99f
religion, 21ff, 26, 31, 43, 103; also see ceremonial
Renaissance, 73, 78
repetition, musical, 55f, 62, 76, 91f, 101f
Republic of the Congo: Brazzaville, see French Equatorial Africa, and preliminary note; Léo-

poldville, see Belgian Congo, and preliminary note
resonance, 53, 95, 97
responsorial style, see choral style
Rhodesia, Northern, 84, 87
rhythm: additive (non-symmetric), 15f, 34, 53, 73ff, 83; African hemiola style, 15ff, 72ff, 83, 100, 102; divisive (symmetric), 15ff, 34, 53, 66, 72ff, 78, 83; European hemiola, 15f, 66; free, 66, 72, 83, 100ff; isorhythm, 76; polyrhythm, 16, 77ff; syncopation, 16f, 34, 53, 73f; work, 34; also see hemiola style
rhythmic *Gestalt*, 79
rhythmic line, dominant, 79
riddle song, 171ff
rondo, 91
Rouget, Gilbert, 5
Ruanda-Urundi: ceremonial, 22, 29ff; culture area, 3f, 35; in general, 35; language, 5f; music, 59, 66, 68, 70, 72, 77, 79f, 83, 88f, 91f; musical ethnology, 38, 46; race, 6f; territory, 3; tribes, 260; and *passim*
Sachs, Curt, 7, 9, 13ff, 17, 21f, 27ff, 35, 37f, 41, 44ff, 47ff, 54f, 58f, 65f, 70, 72f, 76, 83f
sacrifice: bull, 7, 29; human, 24
salendro, 6, 71f
sanza (*mbira*, *lukembe*) (African thumb-plucked idiophone), 28, 31f, 62, 67f, 72, 81, 83ff, 87, 89, 176, 202, 235; cent-frequency chart, 251, 253, 256
scale: chasmatonic, 18, 70ff, 100; diatonic, 17, 70, 100; expressed in melody types, 51ff; isotonic, 17, 71f; microtonic, 17; pentatonic, 17f, 70ff; span, 57ff, 70, 100; tempered and non-tempered, 17, 70ff; and *passim*
Schaeffner, André, 25
Schebesta, Paul, 4f, 42, 45
Schmidt, P. Wilhelm, 6
Schneider, Marius, 9
Scotch-snap, 98f
sculpture, 43, 102f
second: melodic, 53ff, 59f, 62f, 65, 98; size of, 70ff; vertical, 87ff, 90; also see one- or two-step melody
secret society (secret cult), 3f, 21ff, 28f, 45f
sequence, 92
seriation, 55, 92, 100, 102
seventh, vertical, 88f; also see minor seventh melody
shaman, 21ff, 31, 34f, 37, 45, 53, 69, 102, 193
shouting, 98, 102
singing style, 58, 66, 72, 86f, 93ff, 100ff; men's, 96ff, 100; women's, 95, 97f, 100; also see register (vocal), resonance, gutturalness, hoarseness
singing, syllabic, 99f
sixth, parallel, 86; also see hexachord
slit drum, 40, 48ff, 166
solo, 89, 91f, and *passim*
Sons of Sô (N'Gundi secret society), 28, 176
South Africa, 5
speech melody, 47ff, 166
Spellig, Fritz, 22f, 33, 46
Sprechstimme, 99
Stanley, Douglas, 94, 96ff
stress, see accent
Sudanic: language, 5f, 47f; music, see Mangbetu

and Baya; territory, 5; tribes, 5, 7, 260
Sullivan, Louis R., 4
Sumeria, 6, 29f, 35, 37
sumponiāh, 83
symmetry, 64, 67f, 74, 83, 101f
syncopation, see rhythm
taboo, 21, 26, 30, 43
tāla, 76
talking drum, see drum telegraphy
Tanganyika: ceremonial, 22ff, 29; culture area, 3f; language, 5f, 47; music, 23, 31. 57, 62f, 69f, 75f, 77, 81ff, 84ff, 90ff; musical ethnology, 22ff, 29, 31, 36, 72; race, 6; territory, 3; tribes, 260; and *passim*
tangishi (Tuchiokwe circumcision dancer-drummer), 25
taqsîm, 66, 83
telegraphy, see drum telegraphy; vocal, 48f
temperament, see tuning; equal, 70
tempo, 44, 82f, 100
tenor, 96f
Tervueren: Musée du Congo Belge, 36, 42
tetrachord: descending, 57ff, 66, 247; diatonic, 17, 58f, 66; disjunct, 87f; chasmatonic, 17f, 58ff, 68, 71f
theatre, 43f, 102
theory (system), musical, 14, 35, 37, 71, 84
third (interval of): "consonance" and chronology of, 14, 84; importance in functional harmony, 13f, 84ff; ladder of thirds, 13, 69f, 84, 248; nuclear third, 51ff, 60f, 65; parallel thirds, 13, 67f, 84ff; size of, 70ff; vertical, 87, 89, 100; zigzag thirds, 13, 67f, 84, 248; also see one- or two-step melody
thomo (Basuto one-stringed instrument), 18
thorax muscles, 98
thoum (Uganda lyre), 18
thyroid muscles, 94ff
tie, see syncopation
timbre, 74, 79, 93ff
time signature, 73ff
tonemes (pitch levels), see language
tongue flutter, 98
totem, 26, 28, 43, 45; also see religion
Toynbee, Arnold, 11
Tracey, Hugh, 18, 107
tradition, 33, 93f, and *passim*
transcriptions: 111ff; index of, 257ff; preface to, 107ff; special signs used in, 108
tremolo, 98
triad, dovetailed, 67f; also see pentachord and third (ladder of)
tribe, see tribal index, 260, and also individual name of tribe
Trilles, R. P., 31, 41
tritone ("augmented fourth") melody, 63ff, 70, 72, 248
Trowell, Margaret, 18, 38, 71
trumpet, 36
Tshwa Pygmies, 4
Tuchiokwe, 25
tundanji (Tuchiokwe circumcision subjects), 25
tuning, 17, 70ff, 100, 202; just, 70; method of, 71; also see scale

tuning fork, 107
Turkey, 66, 83
Turnbull, Colin M., 21, 24
Uganda: ceremonial, 23f, 30, 32; culture area, 3f, 35; in general, 35; language, 5f; music, 32, 53f, 60, 63, 72, 83, 91; musical ethnology, 23, 30, 32, 37, 42, 71; race, 6f; territory, 3; tribes, 260; and *passim*
umerego (Watutsi hummed introduction), 38, 66
unison, 86
upbeat (offbeat), 52f, 73f, 78f; also see syncopation
Vancoillie, G., 48, 50
variation, 56, 63, 87, 89f, 92, 102
Verwilghen, Leo A., 38f, 107
vibrato, 98
vocal cords, 94f, 97
vocal music, *passim;* also see choral style, singing style
voice production, see singing style
Wabende, 36, 38
Wachaga: culture area, see agricultural area; language (Kichaga), 260; music, 63, 70, 90, 98, *238ff;* territory, 260
Wachsmann, K. P., 18, 38, 71
Wagner, 52
Wahehe: ceremonial, 24, 32; culture area, see cattle area; language (Kihehe), 260; music, 65, 69, 84f, *243ff;* musical ethnology, 32, 96; territory, 260
Wameru: culture area, see cattle area; language, 260; music, 16, 18, 23, 57, 77, 81, 88, 99, *241f;* territory, 260
Wanger, B. W., 6
Wanyamwezi: ceremonial, 22f, 28f, 31, 45; culture area, see cattle area; language (Kinyamwezi), 260; music, 29, 31, 61, 67, 69, 82f, 87, 91f, 101, *229ff,* 256; musical ethnology, 22, 29, 31, 33, 45, 72, 99; territory, 260
war song, 66, 162f
Wasukuma: ceremonial, 31; culture area, see cattle area; language (Kisukuma), 260; music, 16, 31, 75f, 86f, 101, *225ff;* musical ethnology, 31; territory, 260
Waswezi (Wanyamwezi secret healing-cult), 22f, 28
Waterman, Richard A., 59, 96
Watutsi: ceremonial, 21f, 29f; culture area, 3, 7, 35, 43; language (Kyniaruanda), 7; music, 10, 16, 48, 66, 72, 77, 79f, 83, 92, 99ff, *152ff;* musical ethnology, 38f, 42, 46, 72, 99ff; race, 6f; territory, 6, 260
wedding song, 75f, 86f, 225, 235
West Africa, 25, 50, 96
Westermann, D., 4ff, 47
whistle: instrument, 27, 36, 48; vocal, 29, 99
work song, 32ff, 67, 83, 87, 91, 101, 199f
xylophone, 6, 32, 36, 54, 57, 60, 80, 83, 91, 102, 133f, 221; calabash-resonated, 71f, 187, 252; cent-frequency chart, 249, 252f, 255; fixed-log, 71; loose-log, 71f, 208, 249, 253, 255
Yaswa, 57, 71, 80, *187ff,* 252
yodel, 87, 93, 96, 99, 181ff
zither: cent-frequency chart, 251; idiochordic, 84f, 171, 251; Madagascar, 84; stick, 48; trough, 18
Zulu, 47